To: Sandy

"Enjoy The Book"
Rick + Dick
Hoyt

11/16/13

ONE
LETTER
at a TIME

Dick and Rick Hoyt
with Todd Civin

Todd Civin
2 Robbins Road
Winchendon, MA 01475.

Library of Congress Control Number: 2012945252

ISBN-10: 1620861119
ISBN-13: 9781620861110
CPSIA Code: PRB0812A

Book design by Joshua Taggert

Printed in the United States

www.mascotbooks.com

Dedication

by Rick Hoyt

I would like to thank my brother, Rob, for always being there for me and for having me as your best man. Thank you for always making me laugh. I would like to thank Russell for being there for me too, and for figuring out, with my help, how to develop our letter-speaking method that I use every day to communicate with others. I would like to thank my dad for helping me to compete. Running together is the best feeling in the world. I do not feel like I am handicapped when I am out there with you. I would like to thank my mom. She struggled heroically to ensure I would get the best education there was and that I would be included in everyday events. Without her, I wouldn't have the education and college degree I hold today. I would like to thank Todd Civin. Hey, man, thanks for the journey. At times I had my doubts as to whether or not this would ever be written and finished, but "Yes, We Can!" I love you, man. Thanks for everything. To Jessica Gauthier, thanks for taking over and helping me finish my writing. This was a long journey—and a very good one—completed one letter at a time. Thanks for being a pain in my bottom. Thanks for the encouragement you have shown to me. I would also like to thank all of the doctors, teachers, and professors who have helped me and who have encouraged me along the way to never give up and to continually make the effort.

Finally, I'd like to thank the many Personal Care Attendants (PCAs) who have helped me live the independent life I always wanted.

~ Thank you!

Dedication

by Todd Civin

I would like to dedicate this book to the same loving family that I also dedicate every moment, every breath, every victory, and every challenge. Without my loving parents, wife, sister, brother, children and grandchild, things may have had a drastically different ending. Without your love and support, little in my life would have been possible. Special thanks to you, my children, Corey, Erika, Julia, Kate, and Dakota. You are my heartbeat, my soul, and my reason for taking each breath. I'd like to underline and bold face that thank you to my wife, Katie, who put up with many a long night while I sat with my computer in my lap, ignoring her while trying to turn this book into a reality.

I'd like to thank Dick Hoyt, Rick Hoyt, and Kathy Sullivan Boyer for allowing me into your lives. The bad news is I have no immediate plans to leave.

I would also like to thank the many friends-turned-authors who contributed their time, love and incredible talents to Rick in order to participate in his book. That is the true testament of an incredible person, to have his friends and loved ones tripping over themselves to participate in his project.

Lastly, to the Team Hoyt Boston Marathon Team, Years 2011 and 2012: thank you for including me in your accomplishments. It is through your spirit that I gain strength.

Table of Contents

Foreword

by Todd Civin

Forever etched in my mind is the memory of sitting in the backseat of our 1966 Dodge station wagon, pea green with the wood-paneled sides, as my family drove to our destination du jour. We seemed to travel nearly every weekend, taking day trips to a variety of multi-colored pinheads stuck into Dad's mental road map. Many times, we set off on random journeys into the unknown, without a pre-determined destination. The goal was simply to get in the car, drive and spend several hours of "quality family time" together.

With the heat blasting into the backseat and the atmosphere inside the wagon filled with a thick, white cloud of Lucky Strike smoke from Dad's endless parade of filter-less smokes, big sis, Melanie, younger bro, Keith, and I, in the middle, jockeyed for position in the oversized leatherette backseat of the family-mobile. While Dad played the monotonous "tunes" of talk radio (which I now know was left of center, liberal banter) from one of the five pre-set buttons on the AM dial, the three Civin offspring elbowed each other incessantly as we began fighting for personal space by the time we reached the bottom of High Street hill.

As another billow of second-hand smoke and a stream of wind-blown embers made their way into the backseat—and the numbers on the odometer flipped in rapid succession—Mom knew it was time to break out her virtual catalogue of old-time melodies to entertain and pre-occupy her increasingly restless troops. Classics including "She'll Be Coming Round the Mountain," "Oh, Susanna," "There's a Hole in the Bucket," and "I've Been Working on the Railroad" were part of every mid-1960 mother's personal juke box, each sung in rounds so that by the end of each stanza her three offspring were utterly confused, yet totally entertained. Most times, even Dad surrendered, lowered the sound of Jerry William's liberal politics, and sang the part of the oft out-of-tune baritone. Stanza upon stanza, ditty after ditty, our voices mingled until the concert came to a rousing conclusion and ended with an encore of the songs "Found a Peanut" and "On Top of Spaghetti." By that time, the kids were duly entertained, though likely carsick and asphyxiated while Dad and Mom settled into a short-lived session of "adult" conversation.

As hour number one ticked off the clock and the family was halfway to their then-decided destination, Keith was crumpled in the corner fast asleep. Melanie and I leaned forward, unbelted, with our chins resting on the front bench seat, hoping to participate in every conversation that Mom and Dad attempted. Any time the rating of the talk went from G to PG, Mother and Father, and to my utter frustration, Melanie, instantly translated the chat from English to Pig Latin so my tender ears wouldn't become jaded. "Todd will never understand what we are saying" became foreign to me, and me alone, as it magically transformed to "Odd-tay, ill-way, ever-nay, understand-ay (okay, I got that one), ut-way, e-way, are-ay, aying-say." Though I listened intently and made out a word here and there, I was unable to break the code necessary to participate in their subversive conversations.

Discussion after discussion, mile upon mile, words were spoken in a tongue that prevented me from contributing my thoughts, ideas and suggestions to the conversation that took place in front of me. I sat frustrated, alienated, and stigmatized. No matter how I tried, I had lost the attention of those around me because I was unable to converse in a way they would understand. I dejectedly settled into the backseat with my sleeping baby brother, knowing I was unable to communicate with the world around me.

And such was the life of Rick Hoyt for the first decade of his life. Unable to communicate or even to make the world aware that he understood, Rick sat in the backseat of life and simply watched as the world of communication took place without his input or interaction. Though seemingly aware of what was taking place, Rick's eyes would follow his family members around the room as they discussed the topics of the day. Trapped in his wheel-chair, inside a body that didn't function upon his command, Rick sat and listened and thought. But he didn't possess the mechanism that would allow him to join the world of conversation.

Like me in my youth, struggling to decode the intricacies of Pig Latin, Rick didn't have the ability to verbally interact, so he was relegated to being only a spectator as years of conversation passed him by.

Discussion after discussion, mile upon mile, words were spoken in a tongue that prevented Rick from contributing his thoughts, ideas and suggestions to the conversation that took place in front of him. He, too, sat frustrated, alienated, and stigmatized. No matter how he tried, he couldn't capture the attention of those around him because he was unable to converse in a way that they would understand.

Though likely more frustrating for Rick than for his family members, it was also extremely challenging for his parents, Dick and Judy, and his brothers, Rob and Russell, to be unable to hear Rick speak. A spastic wave of his arms, a nod of his head, or a glance in a specific direction were amongst the very limited weapons that Rick had in his communications arsenal.

Rick explains his use of the unspoken gesture in the following matter-of-fact manner: "Another way I communicate is by looking at what I want. When I am in my apartment, if I look towards the bathroom, this means I have to go to the bathroom. If I turn my head to look at the chair I am sitting in, that means I need to sit up."

He continually exhibits an appreciation of life that truly exemplifies who Rick is. "It seems obvious to some, but I often remember there are some disabled people who would love to be able to use my method of nods and head shakes to express what they want. It is all in what you are used to and why I never stop forgetting how lucky I really am."

So one can imagine how incredibly liberating it was when Rick's occupational therapist at the time, Fay Kimball, attended a seminar held by a group of engineers at Tufts University, where they discussed the use of computers to enhance communication. Following the seminar, Dick and Judy met with Dr. William Crochetiere, the chairman of the engineering department at Tufts University, and were told they would need to raise $5,000 to fund development of such a speaking device. Months ensued as the family worked diligently to raise the sum before Rick Foulds and a team of other Tufts' grad students created the Tufts Interactive Communication Device (TIC).

The Hoyt family fondly nicknamed the computer the "Hope Machine," as it gave Rick hope to be able to enter the world as a communicator. As the story goes, the family waited with exuberance when the machine was unveiled and Rick was about to utter his first words through the use of the computer's synthesized voice. Judy put out the friendly wager that Rick's first words would be "Hi, Mom," while Dick raised the stakes and bet on "Hi, Dad." Well, the year was 1972 and the Boston Bruins were in the Stanley Cup playoffs. Rick was a die-hard Bruins fan. To this day, Rick believes that if he hadn't been disabled, he would've played for the Bruins. Much to the mixed emotions of Dick and Judy, Rick's first words were not a tribute to either of his parents, but instead were "Go, Bruins."

Rick's younger brother, Russell, further helped his big bro communicate when he developed what has since become known as the "Russell Method." The family, which was frustrated by the relatively slow speed of TIC, had felt it was necessary to create a more "user-friendly" means of conversing.

Rick explains the Russell Method using, of course, the method that carries its name. "It requires a person to spell with me, one letter at a time. This involves someone saying the vowels from the alphabet one letter at a time. Is it an A? Is it an E? Is it an I? An O? A U? I shake my head yes or no until I select the vowel which contains the letter I want to begin with. When I nod my head yes, they ask if it's that vowel specifically or the group, which contains all the consonants between that vowel and the next. Once we get a few letters, the speller usually helps by trying to guess the word. With me being spelling-challenged, this can be a bit trying at times."

Letter by letter, failed guess after failed guess, Rick "speaks" to those who have taken the time and expended the effort to learn his primitive, often pain-staking method of speech.

Admittedly much more challenging than the Pig Latin of my youth, the Russell Method allowed Rick to climb out of the backseat and take the wheel after many years of being left on the sidewalk while the world of conversation drove by.

Rick's life had changed for the better with the creation of the Hope Machine and was forever enhanced after convincing Dick to enter their first road race in 1977, but it is through Rick's entry into the world of communication that Rick truly became less disabled.

And so, Rick, I hope you understand when I tell you, "Es-Yay, Ou-Yay, An-Cay."

The Meeting

by Todd Civin

> *"If you go looking for a friend, you're going to find they're very scarce. If you go out to be a friend, you'll find them everywhere."*
>
> —Zig Ziglar

I've always been a sucker for a good story; not only to write one, which happens on occasion, but to read one, or even more exhilarating, to become part of one. To become inspired, motivated, and pushed to my own personal limits after not only reading it, but upon ingesting it into my very fiber.

If you don't live, you don't grow. Being pushed to the ground and having the strength to get back up, brush yourself off, pick the little specks of road dirt from the palms of your bleeding hands, and continuing on, defines the very essence of strength.

If one has never faced adversity and witnessed what down-in-the-dumps actually smells like, how can the scent of a rose ever be truly appreciated? Sometimes through our own misfortune—and often times through the battles of another—we learn that the little pebble in the bottom of our penny loafers is just that and nothing compared to the boulders that are thrust upon the shoulders of others.

I believe that our own difficult life experiences, as well as the challenges of others that we may be blessed enough to witness, are placed before us so that we may learn, grow, flourish, become better human beings, and raise our own personal bars. This belief makes the "whys" in life seem a little less arbitrary, a lot more easily explained, and perhaps even accepted.

"Why did this have to happen?" is somewhat more easily understood if answered by "Because it serves a greater purpose."

Being a spiritual person, I patiently live each day and wait, hoping for a peek into the secrets of life at the end of the day. It would be incredibly fulfilling to learn once and for all that the misfortune we face throughout life is explained simply as a lesson to be used, taught and passed on in order to make another's experience a touch easier.

I often think of the poem, "The Bridge Builder," by Will Allen Dromgoole, which I memorized thirty years ago while pledging Tau Epsilon Phi fraternity at Syracuse University. I recite this poem when I attempt to make sense of the enormous mountain that some are forced to ascend during points in their lives. It helps me to understand why some are saddled with seemingly insurmountable difficulties.

> An old man, going a lone highway,
> Came, at the evening, cold and gray,
> To a chasm, vast, and deep, and wide,
> Through which was flowing a sullen tide.
>
> The old man crossed in the twilight dim;
> The sullen stream had no fear for him;
> But he turned, when safe on the other side,
> And built a bridge to span the tide.

"Old man," said a fellow pilgrim, near,

"You are wasting strength with building here;

Your journey will end with the ending day;

You never again will pass this way;

You've crossed the chasm, deep and wide-

Why build you this bridge at the evening tide?"

The builder lifted his old gray head:

"Good friend, in the path I have come," he said,

"There followeth after me today,

A youth, whose feet must pass this way.

This chasm, that has been naught to me,

To that fair-haired youth may a pitfall, be.

He, too, must cross in the twilight dim;

Good friend, I am building this bridge for him."

I've been blessed to have become friends with Dick and Rick Hoyt over the past several years. For those who are not paying attention to the good in the world that may be taking place outside their very window, Dick and Rick are the father and son marathon and triathlon team who have spent the last three decades teaching all of us "less fortunate" folk the phrase "Yes, You Can" through their every action.

The Hoyts have competed in nearly 1100 racing competitions, despite the fact that Rick is a fifty-year-old spastic quadriplegic relegated to spending life in a wheelchair, and Dick is his seventy-two-year-old father who has pushed, carried, towed, and pedaled Rick "to victory" over the past 33 years and have taught anyone who knows their story the meaning of love, dedication, and perseverance.

Dick is the muscle and the physical strength of the world-renowned team, while Rick is the heart, the soul, and the emotional spirit. If you ask Rick about this, he will jokingly add that he is "the brains" of the team as well.

In addition to being known as tremendous athletes and competitors, the Hoyt family is also widely recognized for the way they have included Rick in every facet of their everyday lives over the past half a century and taught other families facing similar challenges the meaning of love, acceptance and indomitable spirit. Many of the doors the Hoyt family has knocked on, knocked down, charged through, and ultimately opened, remain ajar so that those who follow will find a welcome mat outside to greet them.

My friendship with both Dick and Rick began about three years ago, when I was fortunate enough to have the opportunity to write a story about them as part of a series for a website called *The Bleacher Report*. Dissatisfied by rants highlighting the negative in sports, I began searching for the heart and soul of sports; the stories where we witness the overcoming of obstacles and tales that fulfill us. How much more inspiring it is to read about an autistic high school athlete hitting for twenty points in four minutes or a wrestler void of limbs winning the state wrestling championship, then it is to read of steroids, escalating salaries, and highly paid athletes who don't hustle to first base?

I knew of the Hoyts, having watched them compete in the Boston Marathon every Patriot's Day for as long as I can remember. Whether witnessing their endeavors on TV or while standing as one of hundreds of thousands lining the streets of Route 9 somewhere between Hopkinton and Copley Square in Boston, I, like most New Englanders, knew of the Hoyts. Even those who don't know them by name are quickly reminded when told of "that father who pushes his son in a wheelchair in the Boston Marathon." Rarely, if ever, is that phrase not met with a retort of "Oh, yes. I've seen them. They are amazing."

Growing up somewhat local to the Hoyts, I emailed them and

requested an interview. Though I cannot claim to be a household name in the world of sports journalism, I hoped that being from a neighboring town would get me in their front door and allow me to experience my shining moment as a sports blogger.

In the email, I shared a bit about myself and the type of stories I enjoy writing. Within hours, I heard the ping of an AOL email and read the response to my request. Team Hoyt Office Manager Kathy Boyer, who doubles as Dick's girlfriend, responded, "We are only able to grant a handful of face-to-face interviews a year due to Dick's busy schedule." I expected the worst, but read on. Her letter continued, "But Dick is willing to spend a couple hours with you this Saturday."

I began to quiver as I read her words and realized how fortunate I was to be granted such an opportunity. As Kathy, Dick, and Rick say to this day, "We let him into our house three years ago and haven't been able to get him out of our lives since."

Upon arriving at his home, which rests on the shores of beautiful Hamilton Reservoir in Holland, Massachusetts, I anticipated seeing Dick Hoyt burst out of a phone booth, wearing tights, a super hero's cape, and an "S" emblazoned across his chest. Much to my surprise (though not really), I found him dressed in a Team Hoyt T-shirt, running shorts and sneakers, sweeping grass clippings off his driveway.

My thought was that if any man is truly faster than a speeding bullet, more powerful than a locomotive, or able to leap tall buildings in a single bound, it's Dick Hoyt. Now that I've come to know him as well as I have, however, it really wouldn't surprise me at all if he is indeed able to accomplish any one of these feats. I've never, however, witnessed him wearing tights or the cape for those of you who wondered.

Dick escorted me into his home, where I was introduced to Kathy, the holder of the golden key that unlocked time on Dick's calendar, thus granting me access into his and Rick's lives. I was amazed as I scoured the walls of the quaint, wood-paneled kitchen. Nearly covering the walls, yet extremely tastefully displayed, were dozens of framed photos, certificates, poems and other mementos acknowledging the team's decades of accomplishments. One that immediately caught my eye was a photograph of former President Ronald Reagan greeting a younger Dick and Rick during an invite to his office in California. I have to admit that even a die-hard democrat like me got a kick out of seeing the Hoyt's with The Gipper.

Dick and Kathy gave me some time to myself while I examined the walls of their home. I felt as if I had entered a museum as I made note of incredible race times, medals, and framed awards of achievement that had been bestowed upon them over the years. I began reading a framed letter that hung proudly in the center of the shrine, much like a child's grade school art work would hang on the middle of the fridge.

Rick had written the letter to Dick on Father's Day, and it was published in the June 2007 edition of *Men's Health Magazine*. It was entitled "What My Father Means to Me" by Richard E. Hoyt, Jr. Since I hadn't yet met Rick, this was my first glance into the mind and heart of the inspirational man I would come to meet, befriend, and admire.

"What My Father Means to Me" by Richard E. Hoyt, Jr.

My name is Richard E. Hoyt Jr. and I have cerebral palsy. I cannot speak or walk. To write this story, I'm using a computer with special software. When I move my head slightly, the cursor moves across an alphabet. When it gets to the letter I want, I press a switch at the side of my head.

I am half of Team Hoyt. We are a father-and-son team and we compete in marathons and triathlons around the world. Our goal is to educate people about how the disabled can lead normal lives. We started racing in 1979. My high school was having a road race to raise money for a lacrosse player who was paralyzed in an accident.

I wanted to show this athlete that life can go on, so I asked my dad if he would push me. My wheelchair was not built for racing, but Dad managed to push me the entire five miles. We came in next to last, but in the photos of us crossing the finish line, I was smiling from ear to ear!

When we got home, I used my computer to tell Dad, "When I'm running, I feel like my disability disappears!" So we joined a running club, had a special running chair built, and entered our first official race. Many of the athletes didn't want us to participate, but the executive director of the event gave us permission.

Soon we were running three races a weekend, and we even did our first double event—a three-mile run and a half-mile swim. Dad held me by the back of the neck and did the sidestroke for the entire swim. We wanted to run in the Boston Marathon, but we were not allowed to enter because we had not done a qualifying run. So in late 1980, we competed in the Marine Corps Marathon in Washington, DC, finishing in 2 hours, 45 minutes. That qualified us for Boston!

A few years later, after a road race in Falmouth, Massachusetts, a man came up to my dad and said, "You are quite an athlete. You should consider a triathlon." Dad said, "Sure, as long as I can do it with Rick." The man just walked away. The next year, the same man said the same thing. Again, Dad said he'd do it, but only with me. This time the man said, "Okay, let's figure out what special equipment you'll need."

So on Father's Day in 1985, we competed in our first triathlon. It included a 10-mile run, during which Dad pushed me; a 1-mile swim, during which Dad pulled me in a life raft with a rope tied around his chest; and a 50-mile bike ride, during which he towed me in a cart behind him.

We finished next to last, but we both loved it. Soon after, we did our first Ironman Triathlon. We've now competed in more than 950 races, including 25 Boston Marathons and six Ironmans. During every event, I feel like my disability has disappeared.

People often ask me, "What would you do if you were not disabled?" When I was first asked, I said I'd probably play baseball or hockey. But when I thought about it some more, I realized that I'd tell my father to sit down in my wheelchair so I could push him.

If it weren't for him, I'd probably be living in a home for people with disabilities. He is not just my arms and legs. He's my inspiration, the *person who allows me to live my life to the fullest and inspire others to do the same."*

While reading Rick's letter, a lump formed in my throat and a tear formed at the corner of my eye before traveling down my cheek and dropping onto Dick and Kathy's sparkling kitchen floor. I couldn't help but wish that at some point during my life I had taken the time on Father's Day to have written a similar letter to my dad. Now that I have gotten to know Rick, I fail miserably when stacked up next to him. But, as he does with many who know him, he inspires us to improve.

I looked over at Dick, who also wiped a tear from his eye as he watched me do the same. Despite the fact he had read the letter from his oldest son hundreds of times, I sensed that he overflowed each time he re-read it. Feeling a bit overwhelmed and slightly embarrassed, the two of us continued into the living area and took a seat on adjoining couches as we began the formal part of our interview. I knew, however, before either of us had uttered our next word, that my life had been infinitely enhanced and would never again be the same.

We sat for the next two hours, the exact amount of time that Kathy had granted me in her email, talking about their amazing life. Dick told me about his life as a boy growing up in North Reading, Massachusetts, and explained how life as the sixth in a line of ten children helped to instill the ideals of love, hard work, and commitment, which helped to make him the person he has become. He shared stories about his life with his former wife, Rick's mother, Judy, who transformed from high school sweetheart to loving young bride to mother of a severely disabled child all in the duration of a year, and the decisions that the two of them were faced with in determining the fate of Rick's life.

I learned about Rick's younger brothers, Rob and Russ, tremendously gifted athletes in their own rights, and the sacrifices they made while helping to assimilate Rick into a world that was less "disabled friendly" than it is today. Dick told me how Judy fought tirelessly to get Rick accepted into public schools, and through her efforts doors were opened so that disabled children that followed Rick are allowed in the classroom today.

Dick continued with stories about doors being slammed when they tried to enter the Boston Marathon and numerous other races over the course of the thousand plus racing events they have participated in, and of the negative whispers they encountered as they tried to dip their toes into the racing circuit. No one wanted them because they were different and were viewed as more of a circus sideshow than as the inspirational athletes they have since become.

Dick swelled with pride and again overflowed with emotion as he told me of Rick's accomplishments, including acceptance into public schools, graduation from not only high school, but from Boston University with a degree in special education, and how he has lived on his own independently for his entire adult life. Though any parent would exhibit similar emotions when recapping the achievements of their children, Dick's chest seemed to puff up just a bit more. He knew what tremendous effort each and every one of these accomplishments had required on the part of not only Rick, but on the part of the entire Hoyt brood.

As we completed our interview, I tried to grasp all the information I had just learned about Dick and Rick and wondered how I would ever be able to do justice to their story; how would I be able to make their story, my story?

Dick shook my hand, and he and Kathy told me that if I needed anything else, I should feel free to give them a call. How special I felt having the phone number of a sports legend on my speed dial. As I left, I thanked them for their time and asked them if they had ever considered using Facebook to share their story. As incredible as it seems with the popularity of Facebook today, it was just increasing in popularity and the Hoyts hadn't yet taken full advantage of the widespread impact it could have in spreading their story and their message of inclusion. That, and the fact that Kathy is a one-person office who answers each and every one of several hundred emails they receive daily while planning the team's racing and public speaking itinerary, made Facebook growth simply an item on her wish list. I offered to take the task on to assist them and to help fill the hours in my day, since I was in the midst of a period of under-employment. Little did any of us know that I would still hold that position today and wear the title proudly as Team Hoyt's Social Media Director.

At this point, I published the story of Dick and Rick Hoyt, having never had the pleasure of actually meeting the other half of the team. I assumed that I would go through life knowing a few of the inspirational anecdotes about Rick, but perhaps never having the opportunity to meet him in the flesh. After all, the life of an internet blogger rarely includes inviting oneself to dinner and never leaving. Like bubblegum stuck to the sole of his sneaker, I often tease Rick.

About a week later, after my story went to press and gained an extremely positive response, I received a call from Kathy, who rather sheepishly asked me if my wife, Katie, and I would be interested in attending a black-tie affair at an elegant restaurant in Foxboro, Massachusetts, as guests of Dick, Rick, and Kathy. The event was known as the Legend's Ball, and it was held annually to raise funds for the Hockomock YMCA. Dick had purchased a table, and at the last moment, one of his brothers and his brother's wife could not attend. Kathy apologized for the late notice and wasn't sure if I would be interested. Apparently, she hadn't had the opportunity to get to know me very well, as hanging out with New England Sports' biggest legends while eating and drinking for free is my definition of Nirvana. "Apology accepted," I told Kathy.

Katie and I arrived at Christina's Restaurant that evening and felt like absolute royalty. I equate the experience to that of a little boy opening up his sports card collection and realizing that all the cards inside have shed the rubber bands that held them together and have suddenly come to life. Throughout the expansive ballroom, I witnessed legends who hadn't stepped on the field for several decades shaking hands with players who caught touchdowns just last weekend.

I quickly realized, however, that I wasn't there to break bread with the likes of the Orrs or the Yastrzemskis that evening, but instead to hang with my own personal legends, Dick and Rick Hoyt, who would be sitting across the table from us for the next several hours.

As we entered the ballroom, I spotted Rick at the table sipping from a drink with the help of his Personal Care Attendant (PCA), Mike Adams. Rick finished his sip, and Mike wiped his mouth with the maroon-colored towel that Rick wore around his neck so he wouldn't spill on his finely pressed, black tuxedo. Rick looked stunning; had he not been sitting in a wheelchair with a terrycloth hand towel around his neck, I may not have realized that he was the same disabled figure that I had seen race by me during so many Boston Marathons.

I felt completely at ease with Rick from the moment I met him, despite the fact I would have expected a reasonable amount of tension upon meeting a sports icon for the first time. That, coupled with the fact that Rick was unable to shake my hand or verbally respond to my greeting, could make for an uncomfortable initial introduction.

I lifted Rick's right hand and shook it as I would anyone's and immediately acknowledged the strength of Rick's grip. Though he couldn't lift his arm on his own and certainly couldn't shake my hand without assistance, he was able to squeeze my hand firmly. I've since learned that this is more of an uncontrolled spasm or reflexive action, but for that moment it served as a suitable handshake.

I joked with Rick how soft his hands were and teased that he has never done a hard day's work in his life. Dick had told me about Rick's incredible sense of humor, and I figured he better get used to mine, which falls somewhere between dry and Sahara Desert on the humor scale. Rick shook his head side to side and spasmed uncontrollably. Over the subsequent years, I have learned that Rick not only takes, but hands out, a pretty brutal ribbing at any opportunity. He sees this as his way to connect instantly with the world of verbal communicators, which he strives valiantly to be a part of.

Rick looked up at me from his wheelchair and smiled with his huge recognizable grin. His eyes had an amazing way of communicating his every thought, as if to make up for his inability to communicate verbally.

The wait staff pedaled tray upon tray of tantalizing hors d'oeuvres and the bar was open throughout the cocktail hour, but I was far more interested in eating up the amazing blessing which had been bestowed upon me.

Rick seemed to motion to Dick with his head, indicating that he wanted to say something. I watched with intrigue as Dick pulled a small yellow note pad out of Rick's pack and began their intricate method of uncovering what Rick was attempting to say. The two worked tirelessly as Rick communicated his thoughts. Their method, which I later learned was called the Russell Method, since it was devised by Rick's younger brother Russell, was Rick's effective, yet relatively slow way of communicating with the handful of people who had the patience to assist Rick in sharing his thoughts with the world around him.

"Is it an A? An E? An I? An O?" Dick asked, trying to corral the first letter of the word that Rick was hoping to convey. Once they agreed on a vowel through a gentle nod of Rick's head, they would then try to hone in on the actual letter.

"Is it O by itself? Is it P? Q? R? S? T?

"It's a T," Dick confirmed as Rick nodded slightly.

With the first letter in the word scribbled down on Dick's scratch pad, he proceeded to take on letter number two. He ultimately added an H as the second letter, after eliminating F and G, which followed the vowel E.

"It's an H," Dick said. "Is it The? Is it This? Is it Thank you?" he inquired, trying to expedite the process by randomly stabbing at Rick's intention.

Dick had correctly read Rick's thoughts on guess number three and reduced the time needed to translate Rick's entire sentence. Clearly, they'd done this often enough over the years that they'd gotten pretty adept at Rick's personal game of twenty questions.

"You want to say, Thank you for coming, Todd?"

Rick nodded again.

I swallowed hard and held back the first of many tears that would tumble down my cheek over the course of the night.

I quickly realized that though the running side of their life is truly amazing, merely finding the strength and courage to communicate, eat, laugh, and live each day may be more of a feat than many of us would choose to take on.

Over the next several hours, I bonded with Rick while trying to divide my time evenly between Kate, Dick, Kathy, and Kirk Joslin, the President of Easter Seals Massachusetts and his wife, Sheila, who were also residing at table number 30.

Our table was made complete by Rick's PCA, Mike, who was on the clock that night feeding Rick. He also gave him frequent sips of Rick's beverage of choice that evening, "Sex on the Beach," which had been poured into the plastic water bottle that Rick drank from to avoid wearing it on his cummerbund. Though Mike was a hired employee, it was clear that he enjoyed spending the evening with the Legends almost as much as Rick and I did. I later learned that Rick employs several PCAs who he interviews, hires, and manages just as any employer would. I did notice however that Rick may have allowed his employee enjoy a Dirty Martini or two over the course of this special evening.

Though I couldn't help but scour the room to find out what other sports icons were in attendance, it was Rick who grabbed the lion's share of my attention as we joked about finding ourselves a couple of hot blondes to complete our perfect night. "Boys will be boys," Katie muttered, shaking her head at the two over-aged college boys.

There were several magic moments over the course of the evening that made my heart grow exponentially. The first occurred when I managed to accompany Dick and Rick to the VIP room as they signed posters alongside the other Legends. I had no business being there, as it was well guarded and for VIP's only, but I convinced the guard at the door that I needed to be there. I wasn't really lying, as I had convinced myself that I really needed to be there. The pile of posters to be autographed was about forty to fifty deep, with one to be given to each Legend as a memento of his participation in the event.

Dick placed a Sharpie into Rick's permanently contorted hand and guided it as the two of them combined to sign Rick's autograph. Perhaps it would have been easier for Dick to write Rick's name or to simply sign as Team Hoyt, but the two wouldn't even consider this. It would have been out of line with what they stand for and the "Yes, You Can" message they promote.

At that moment, New England Patriots stars Matt Light, Stephen Neal, Joe Andruzzi, and Troy Brown entered the room, and I, once again, began to perspire profusely. Never had I been in the presence of one, let alone six, sports legends.

The quartet entered the room, laughing and joking, and seemed to be mildly impressed by their own notoriety. Four larger-than-life football greats wearing blinders that prevented them from seeing what was going on around them, as if left sightless by the fame that the game had bestowed upon them.

And then they noticed the Hoyts.

Each of the four went immediately silent and stopped dead in their tracks. Their eyes widened and their jaws dropped slightly as they realized who they were in the presence of. While goose bumps formed on my forearms, these football giants seemed to shrink in size. Matt Light was especially awestruck and told Dick and Rick how honored he was to meet them. The father and son legends had spontaneously humanized the other legends—brought them back to earth as they realized that as great as they may be on the gridiron each Sunday afternoon, they were miniatures next to these two "true giants."

The trio joined Light in his acknowledgment. Andruzzi, who himself has overcome amazing challenges after battling and conquering non-Hodgkin lymphoma, agreed to let Rick try on his Super Bowl ring.

Rick had expressed a personal wish earlier in the evening to wear a Super Bowl ring, and Andruzzi graciously obliged when told of Rick's request. However, before he dislodged it from his enormous hand, the Legends were called away to be introduced to the anxiously awaiting crowd.

About three hundred guests looked on as each of the Legends was escorted to his respective table by special needs young adults from the Hockomock Y. The escorts likely had their own inspiring life story, as many had Down syndrome or some other obvious disability. Several of the legends high-fived their escorts playfully, to the thrill and jubilation of both their escort and the adoring crowd.

The Legends received warm ovations from the crowd as each was announced. Tim Fox, Jon Williams, John Smith, and Patrick Sullivan of Patriots' days gone by; Joe Morgan, Ted Lepcio, and Bobby Doerr of the Sox; and Rick Middleton of the Bruins were presented one by one by Master of Ceremonies Butch Stearns of Fox Channel 25 News fame.

When it was time for my guys to be announced, the crowd stood and cheered wildly in a rousing and well-deserved applause. As Dick wheeled Rick in, the crowd honored them with the most overwhelming ovation of the event. Seconds turned to minutes as the crowd stood and cheered. Rick waved his arms frantically and smiled his well-recognized, nearly toothless grin in much the same way that the world had often witnessed as he rolled down Boylston Street nearing the finish line of another Boston Marathon. Again, that all-too-familiar lump took residence in my throat.

Throughout the evening, dozens of adoring fans shook the Hoyts' hands, posed for photos, and thanked them for being inspirations to so many throughout the world. My two, extremely humble friends took it all in stride and thanked their fans for thanking them.

As our evening ended, I again whispered to Kate, "It doesn't get any better than this."

And then, of course, it did.

As Rick was being wheeled out of the banquet hall as the evening came to a close, Andruzzi hustled over and reminded Rick of the promise to model his Super Bowl ring.

Rick wore that ear-to-ear grin as Andruzzi slipped the ring onto his soft little hand. Andruzzi's enormous ring could have laid claim to two of Rick's fingers, as the trio of sports giants posed for another Kodak moment. It became amazingly clear to me that heroes come in all shapes and sizes.

As the evening ended, I accompanied Rick to his van, which was parked in the handicapped spot near the door. Perhaps feeling a little too comfortable with my new friend, I fast forwarded the relationship a bit and asked Rick if he would consider writing a book together. I wanted the opportunity to become the voice of Rick Hoyt similar to how his father had become his legs, while giving Rick the opportunity to share his story with the world. He motioned for Dick to come over again and Dick of course obliged.

"Is it an A? An E? An I? O? U?"

Rick nodded slightly at U.

"U by itself? V? X? Y?"

Rick nodded at Y.

As the clock ticked and with tomorrow's work day peeking just over the horizon, Rick continued to tap out his thoughts with Dick's assistance.

Y became Y-E, which became Y-E-S. New word became Y followed by O and joined at the end by letter U.

New word again was spelled C-A-N.

"Yes, You Can," Dick advised. These three words that would become the most widely used words in my newly established vocabulary, and the three words that defined the very essence of Dick and Rick Hoyt.

Welcome to My World

by Rick Hoyt with Todd Civin

> *"Fate is like a strange, unpopular restaurant filled with odd little waiters who bring you things you never asked for and don't always like."*
>
> —Lemony Snicket

My name is Rick Hoyt, and I am known throughout the world as a marathon runner and triathlete. There are many people around the globe who have gained fame by being world class runners and championship level triathletes, but my story is unique because of my disability. I am a spastic quadriplegic with cerebral palsy. I was born with my umbilical cord tangled around my neck. Though doctors untangled it as quickly as they could, my brain was deprived oxygen for a short period of time, and this deprivation resulted in severe brain damage. This condition is known as CP or cerebral palsy; a condition that has left me unable to walk, run, speak, or control the majority of my muscles.

You may be asking yourself, how I can be classified as a world class athlete despite the fact that I can neither run nor walk? It doesn't seem like I would get very far, does it? I run with the help of my father, Dick Hoyt, who serves as my strength and my legs during these athletic events. He pushes me in a specially designed running chair for each and every step of the 26.2 miles that make up a marathon. I consider myself to be the heart and soul of the team, but that does not mean that my father is lacking either heart or soul. In fact, I can't think of a person who has more of either. If you asked anyone who knows me, it also doesn't mean that I am lacking in strength. Much of what I do on a daily basis requires a tremendous amount of strength. But this is the life that I know and love, just like you know and love your own life.

I am writing this book about my life because I want people to know that despite my disabilities, I am very much like most people on the inside. I live a normal life and think, love, and laugh just like anyone else. We don't use the word "normal" in our family because normal is simply what you know; so my life is normal. This is all I have ever known, so I have nothing to compare it to. Though my life may be very different than your own, it does not make me abnormal; it simply makes me different.

Just as my dad helps me to compete in athletic events because I couldn't do it as well without him, Todd is helping me to write this book. What you will be reading are my thoughts and words, simply dressed up a bit by Todd, because just as I couldn't be a world-class triathlete without using my dad's legs, I also wouldn't be a world-class writer without Todd's ability to take my words and polish them up a bit.

Though I am able to communicate using my computer, I am using it very little to share my story with you. When we came up with the idea of writing a book, I needed to be able to communicate my thoughts and feelings without having Todd sit in my apartment with me for days on end. As you can imagine, communicating one letter at a time is not the quickest method in the world, but it is what works best for me, so this is how I communicate my thoughts. Todd sends me a list of questions on many different topics and events that have occurred throughout my life—memories from grade school and Christmas at the Hoyt house; places I've been and people I've met; questions about how I was accepted into public schools and my graduation from Boston University. Over the past several months, these questions have allowed me to relive my life as I've thought about many topics I hadn't thought about in years. It's sort of like me reading a book about my own life as you, the reader, are also reading a book about me.

Once I get the questions, one of my PCAs, Jessica, reads them to me and then waits while I think about the answer. So I am not only writing a book, but I am *thinking* a book as well. Jessica then begins retrieving my answer from me, one letter at a time, which is how I communicate. Jessica runs through the series of vowels A, E, I, O, U until she can pinpoint the group of letters that contains the first letter of the word I am spelling out. The method is known in our family as the *Russell Method*, because it was invented by my younger brother Russell, who was frustrated by the slow and laborious way I communicate using my computer. As slow as the Russell Method seems, it is still faster than trying to use my computer to converse. Once Jessica and I pinpoint the group of letters that contains the letter I am trying to say, we hone in on the actual letter. So, if you understand what I am trying to convey, the book is indeed being written *One Letter at a Time*.

I am thankful to Todd for not only writing this with me, but also thankful to Jessica for taking the time to help me to put my thoughts on paper.

Todd said that writing this book with me reminds him a bit of the book *Tuesdays With Morrie* by Mitch Albom, in which Mitch visits with Morrie every Tuesday to document his life as his health deteriorates. Though my health is not failing at all, Todd, Jessica, and I meet several times a week to capture my thoughts about a variety of topics and eventually will be able to share my story with those who care to learn more about me and the obstacles I've overcome.

I also thought it would be interesting to tell you my story through the eyes and memories of those who have gotten to know me over the first fifty years of my life. Sometimes you may see your own life in a certain way, but it may be interesting to hear your own story the way others have seen it. So not only will you read chapters written by me, but also chapters by many family members and friends who have been a part of my life either throughout or during various parts of my life. I know I have found it very interesting to relive various chapters of my own life while reading the chapters that have been written about me and I hope you find these equally interesting.

I hope as you learn my story and get to know a little bit more about me, you will grow as a human being and open your heart and your mind a bit more the next time you see someone with a disability. Don't feel bad for them; feel good about them. Go up and talk to them and get to know them and treat them as you would want to be treated yourself. Behind their eyes and inside their body that may not work the same way yours does is a living, breathing, loving person who wants to get to know you.

How It All Began

by Rick Hoyt with Todd Civin

> *"We, the ones who are challenged, need to be heard. To be seen not as a disability, but as a person who has and who will continue to bloom. To be seen not only as a handicap, but as an intact human being."*
>
> —Robert M. Hensel

I have cerebral palsy. Though many people think that it isn't proper to define myself by my disability, it's how I choose to do it. Not because of the way my disability limits me, but because of the way I have been able to overcome it. Being unable to move or speak doesn't make me any less of a human being. I have the same feelings as anyone else does. I feel sadness, happiness, joy, anger, hunger, love, compassion, and even pain. Though my body doesn't work the way it was intended to, everything in my heart and soul functions the way it is supposed to. I think, I feel, I laugh, and I cry. I am able to experience joy, love, and heartache. My inner self is not disabled, but because my body doesn't function the way it is supposed to, perhaps my inner self makes up for my other limitations and operates even better than designed. Through my actions, I believe that I am able to love more strongly, to live more happily, and to experience more thoroughly.

I was born on January 10, 1962, and even though I don't remember much of my life from before the age of four or five, I've heard the story enough times that I know it by heart.

My parents did everything right prior to my birth. Even in the minutes leading up to my birth, everything was perfectly fine. My mother carried me for a couple weeks beyond her due date, which was really the only issue during a very normal pregnancy. I was born in Winchester Hospital, the same place my dad and later, my brothers, Rob and Russell, were born. I think that they chose to return to Winchester Hospital for the births of my brothers is a good indicator that my parents believe that nothing could have been done differently by the doctors to have prevented my disability.

In those days, fathers weren't welcome in the delivery room, so my dad was at work when doctors decided it was time for Mom to give birth to me. Dad had dropped Mom off in the middle of the night and went off to work as he did every day. It was mid-morning when Dad got a call from the hospital to give Dad the good news-bad news type message. The good news was that Dad was the father of a son, which he says to this day was exactly what he was hoping for. The bad news, however, was that there were complications, and though my mom was doing quite well, I was in distress.

I was a very active baby while I was being born and apparently got turned around somehow just minutes before birth. These were the days before monitors and C-sections. If the doctors had known the position I had worked myself into, they would have likely been able to prevent the damage done to my brain. My umbilical cord was wrapped around my neck, and I technically strangled myself. Even though the doctors tried desperately to untangle the cord as quickly as they could, the deprivation of oxygen to my brain caused irreparable damage.

Though my mom was anxious to hold me—as any mother would be—it was obvious in the delivery room that something was wrong. Doctors and nurses were scurrying around and speaking in alarmed voices. When the doctors finally delivered me, I did not cry and did not make sounds like other babies did. Mom knew something was very wrong.

Dad arrived at the hospital. He said the hour-long trip from his work to the hospital seemed like it lasted forever. Doctors spoke to him in a way that sounded optimistic, but could not guarantee him that everything would be okay. They finally brought Dad up to the Labor and Delivery section of the hospital, where he could get his first peek at his bouncing baby boy. Only rather than bouncing, I was lying on my stomach and doing what looked like pushups. Dad says that he was amazed at how strong I was and started to do what every new father does—he envisioned himself playing baseball and football with his new young boy. He later found out that I wasn't doing pushups at all but was having muscles spasms. My muscles were very tight and would spasm because the brain wasn't sending the proper message to the muscles.

Cerebral palsy actually means brain paralysis, and during the time when oxygen was deprived to my brain, the section that controls muscles and motor activity was damaged. I still have spasms to this day, because once the brain is damaged there is nothing that can be done to reverse it. As much as Dad wanted his son to be doing pushups, he would soon learn that I would never be able to do them.

Mom and Dad later met with the doctors, who told them the severity of my birth defect. They weren't even sure at the time that I would survive; if I did, I would live my life with disabilities. At the time, of course, they did not know exactly what my disabilities would be, but it was obvious that I was not going to be the son who played football, baseball, and hockey like my dad had envisioned.

Though Mom never came right out and said it, Dad often wondered if she wished that I wouldn't survive and that God would spare not only me, but them, of the pain they were sure to endure. They were young parents, in their early twenties, and life can be difficult enough without having to care for a newborn with major disabilities.

Mom and Dad had decided before my birth to name me Richard, after my dad, and Mom even questioned him, after finding out that I was disabled, if he still wanted me to carry his name. She thought that maybe Dad would want to put the name on hold and save it for a son who would enter the world in better shape than I did. As you can tell, if you know the rest of our story, he decided to name me after him, and the story of Richard Eugene Hoyt, Jr., officially began.

The doctors actually wanted me to stay at the hospital for a while after my Mom was released, as they thought it would be better for me to be cared for in the hospital than at home. This would have been very frustrating to my mom, because every mother wants to bring her baby home and show him off to the world. Not only would she not be able to bring me home, but she couldn't hold me or hug me or feed me. I was extremely quiet and didn't even cry or coo like most babies. If you think about it, it was sort of surprising that most mothers wouldn't want to have a baby just like me. No crying, no noise, and I'd stay in my crib all day doing pushups. Sounds like the perfect child.

Finally after some long discussions with the medical staff, it was decided that I could go home with my new parents. So off I went to the Hoyt family homestead in North Reading, Massachusetts.

I also have a condition which is known as a reverse tongue, which means that rather than helping to push my food down my throat, it actually works in reverse and pushes everything back up. As a baby, this was especially frustrating to Mom, because I was very difficult to feed and was not getting proper nourishment. Part of a mother's joy is to feed her newborn child, and my reverse tongue wasn't making this very pleasurable for her. I still obviously have this condition, which is why I have to wear a chuck around my neck so I don't get food all over whatever I am wearing. I also gag, cough, and choke quite easily, which at times leaves my brothers and my nephews ducking for cover while I'm eating. Though it may be funny to some now, it certainly wasn't entertaining to Mom when I was an infant.

Mom and Dad wanted to believe that I would eventually get better, and though maybe deep down inside they knew that I would never be perfect, they at least hoped for improvement. At that point, they did not have an official diagnosis of cerebral palsy, so they just went about each day hoping they would wake up and everything would be okay. Day by day, they looked for the slightest sign that things would change, but day after day they would be disappointed. I would sleep for hours on end. I didn't cry or eat well. I didn't roll off my stomach, and I certainly didn't sit or crawl. Mom didn't even like to take me out in public because she would have to answer questions about me and would have to compare her baby to the active and outgoing babies of the other mothers.

After nearly eight months of hope and prayer and disappointment, Mom and Dad met with doctors, who finally gave them the official diagnosis of cerebral palsy. Mom and Dad had never heard of it before. They greeted the news with disbelief as the doctors explained their options to them. They told them that if I were to have brain surgery, the odds were only 50/50 that I would even survive, and there was no assurance that it would do anything to improve my condition.

The doctors went on to say that the best thing my parents could do was to put me in an institution and go on with their lives as if I never existed. They said I would never be anything more than a vegetable. Dad and I often joke about this now and try to figure out which vegetable I am. The doctor encouraged Mom and Dad to have other children because the odds are in no way inflated that their future children will have CP. It is not hereditary or a genetic birth defect—it's just caused by an unfortunate set of circumstances. Dad and Mom did not know anyone who was institutionalized, but they had heard terrible stories about these places in which people are sent to and basically forgotten about. They are subjected to less than human conditions where they are left in front of television sets, wearing soiled clothing, with little or nothing that resembles mental or physical stimulation of the brain or muscles. They are basically left there to grow old and die.

Mom and Dad didn't even have to think about it. They looked at each other and didn't even discuss it. Their answer was "no." They were going to take me home and try to bring me up like they would any child. It wouldn't be easy, but they never second guessed that decision.

Now that they knew what my condition was called and that it was not going to improve over time, Mom and Dad made the commitment to deal with it the best way they could. The first eight months of my life had been met with anger, denial, and confusion, but now that they had some answers, they could approach their infant son a bit differently. They met with their pastor, as well as with Dr. Robert Fitzgerald, a psychologist at Children's Hospital Boston. Dr. Fitzgerald was afflicted with polio and had spent his life since childhood in a wheelchair. He worked as a family counselor, and since he knew what living life with a disability was like, Mom and Dad felt he would offer them solid advice. Dr. Fitzgerald did exactly that. He advised Mom and Dad to treat me as they would any able-bodied child and to enrich my life with the same experiences they would if I didn't have a disability. As you hear more about me throughout the pages of this book, it will be clear that Mom and Dad took the doctor's advice to heart.

Dr. Fitzgerald also gave my parents some bad advice. He said it would be perfectly okay to have another child; the odds of giving birth to another child with cerebral palsy were very unlikely. I was about eighteen months old at the time, and a little more than nine months later, my parents gave birth to my younger brother, Rob. You think I was a handful—well, you haven't met Rob.

I joke that having Rob was bad advice, but that is just typical of the relationship Rob and my other brother Russ and I have with one another to this day. That is how I know they love me and hopefully, how they know I love them. It would have been easy for them to resent me growing up, and I know at times they did. I demanded an awful lot of attention, more than the average child, and with only one set of parents to go around, Rob and Russ were forced to take a backseat at times.

They were also a big part of my day care team, and without their support, I would have struggled mightily. I probably don't say it as often as I should, but I can't imagine what my life would have been like if they weren't a part of it. However, for the point of this story, I'm going to stick with the thought that having Rob was bad advice from Dr. Fitzgerald.

When I was five and Rob was about two and a half, Mom gave birth to Russell. Dad had always wanted enough children for a football team, as he came from a family of ten children. Maybe he and Mom would've gone for that if I hadn't been such a challenge to lead off. Our family of five was complete, and Dad would have to recruit kids from the neighborhood if he really wanted a football team.

True to their commitment, Mom and Dad, along with Rob and Russell, treated me like any other kid and included me in all kinds of activities. We went camping and hiking, boating, and swimming. Dad even used to take me to work with him sometimes and would bring me up on the roof during masonry jobs. I'm sure the neighbors thought we were a little bit crazy.

If I hadn't been born with a disability, I dreamed that I would've probably played professional hockey for the Boston Bruins. I guess it's hard to argue with that. Most people who love hockey aren't fortunate or talented enough to make it to the pros—but who is to argue with me? Dad was very athletic and loved to play hockey, and Russ, Rob and I played a lot of hockey as kids. Many of the most exciting events in my life surround the Bruins, so I've always felt the odds were good that I would have played for the Bruins. As a kid, Rob, and Russ would tie a goalie stick and a pillow to my wheelchair and stand behind me to maneuver my chair. I was a part of most neighborhood street hockey games and made a damn good goalkeeper, if I do say so myself.

As we grew up, we were mischievous little kids, and while Dad was at work each day, Mom would spend hours pulling her hair out. The stories that I could tell are endless, and though Mom and Dad didn't think most of them were funny at the time, I think they learned to laugh at the humor their three boys brought to the household.

As a child, I could make little movements with my legs like a baby can. When Rob was sitting in front of the TV and not paying attention to me, I would slowly crawl over to him by moving both my arms and legs in a rhythmic, circular motion. This would cause my body to spasm. A spasm is an involuntary tightening of my muscles, usually over my entire body. They tighten up so much that it's very painful. When my body would spasm like this, it would make me move farther and faster. If you can think of the movement as sort of like an inch worm, I would spasm, expand, spasm, expand as I made my way across the living room floor.

Though I only moved across the floor at a rate of what seemed like an inch every few minutes, I would finally get to my somewhat oblivious brother. When I finally got over to Rob, I made a kicking motion at him, striking him wherever my foot happened to land. I didn't sneak up on him every time, but I succeeded once in a while. Rob was not very far away from me, but it was well worth my effort. It felt like it took me about a half hour to go thirty feet but after the long struggle I was able to get my point across. Unfortunately, it took me so long, that by the time I got to him, I probably had forgotten what that point was.

When I was younger, I had to fight in my own way to defend myself. As many people know, I've made my reputation as a lover, not a fighter, but Rob didn't think twice about taking advantage of me. I had to use whatever I could to remind him who the older brother was, the boss of the Hoyt family. I'm not really equipped to fight in the conventional way, so I had to develop my own methods of defense. If I couldn't beat him with brawn, I had to beat him with my intelligence.

My recollection of the battles between my brothers and me is that I usually came out victorious, but as you read their personal chapters in this book, I think you will find that they have a differing viewpoint. All in all, though, our family adapted and learned to get along pretty well despite the challenges that we faced.

Boys Will Be Boys

by Robert Hoyt

Rick's Brother

> *"The opportunity for doing mischief is found a hundred times a day, and of doing good once in a year."*
>
> —*Voltaire*

I am one of the many whose life was not only changed, but has been immeasurably enhanced by knowing and experiencing Rick's existence. Watching and being part of doors opening, walls being breached, and dreams coming true was, and is still, an amazing thing to behold.

Sometimes I wonder how anybody can complain about life's inequities or insurmountable challenges after witnessing first-hand what Rick endures on a daily basis. I often think, "Wow, try on his pants for a day, week or a month. My Lord, toughen up." As you can imagine, it was difficult for me to complain about life's quirks when Rick is forced to deal with so much more than most of us could ever envision. I cannot begin to fathom my life without Rick; it's silly to try to imagine him being any different than he is. I simply know him as my big bro.

I think back often with fond memories of our yearly vacations as a family. True to our parents' ideals and beliefs, we raised Rick just like anyone else. We traveled across the country towing a camper and camping all the way. And since once is never enough with the Hoyts, we did it twice! Seeing America first-hand was really eye-opening. It was a learning experience for three young boys growing up together.

Looking back now, my parents were slightly nuts. Wherever we went and whatever we did, Rick did it too. We went mountain climbing and on Disney World rides, Grand Canyon mule riding and horseback riding with Pueblo Indians. We experienced bullfights in Mexico and actually handed out beads in The Big Easy, New Orleans. Rick and the rest of us rode the rapids in Colorado and went cross-country skiing, inner tubing, and tobogganing in the snow. That's right, my brother, the spastic quadriplegic who was supposed to be left in a home as part of a three-bean salad has ridden snowmobiles, been ice-fishing, gone down waterslides, went horseback riding, climbed mountains, and been ocean fishing.

The reaction of people seeing Dad with Rick slung over his shoulder going up a mountain trail was special. One time, while cross-country skiing on a down slope, Dad towed Rick in a red sled. He sped up and went through Dad's legs, taking them both to the bottom with Dad on top of him and Rick laughing all the way. That's the thing that is most memorable about Rick and all of our experiences with him—that smile; that ever-present, toothless smile.

It was Mom and Dad's will to have Rick included and raised the same as everyone else. That desire to be treated as an equal not only resonated in Rick, but became a huge part of how Russ and I lived, played and grew together.

Our second home in Westfield, Massachusetts, was on Shadow Lane in a neighborhood called Glenwood Heights. We had a nice wooded back yard, as well as a large grass yard where we built our own little Fenway Park to play whiffle ball. Rick acted as the umpire.

As kids do, we spent our fair share of time playing in the woods.

One day we decided to build a tree fort out in the woods, so we dragged wood, nails, and about every tool from Dad's toolbox—along with Rick in his wheelchair—out into the middle of our mini forest.

The project went well in the beginning. We found a good spot in the middle of a pack of trees, cleared the roots and flattened the floor. Slowly the walls began to take shape with scrap wood and whatever other materials we could scavenge. It looked a little like The He-Man Woman Haters Club from the show *Little Rascals*.

Now I'm not saying that Russ and I can't be mistaken for Tim "The Tool Man" Allen, but at our young ages we began to run out of steam once we were knee deep into the project. Our attention span had been played out for fort building, and Russ and I were ready for something else to do.

Rick, on the other hand, had not had enough, and our fort was not completed to the foremen's liking. Boy, did he let us know by having a fit, complete with flailing arms, kicking legs, and frothing at the mouth. The dude was mad—and truthfully, when Rick gets in this state, there is not much we can do.

So we left him right there, smack dab in the middle of the woods, next to that half-ass fort, and went inside, had a snack, and watched a little TV. It's a little fuzzy for me now, this many years later, to remember how Rick came home, but I think a neighbor called the police and our parents were summoned to bring his whiny little butt home. Perhaps Rick should have run the Big Dig in Boston!

Our parents are, and always have been, very, very generous, spoiling us from day one. Rick was a lot more mobile when he was younger. Who wasn't? One Christmas morning, Rick was on his creeper and somehow sucked up a piece of tinsel from the tree. My mom freaked out, screaming that it would wrap around his intestines and he'd die. Well, Rick took off creeping as fast as he could go, laughing hysterically until we caught him and pulled the tinsel out of his throat.

It was also fun on Christmas morning, when we were younger, as we had to help Rick open his presents as well as ours. There were so many gifts that Russ and I could help ourselves to any presents we wanted to and Rick couldn't say a thing.

Now that we're older, Rick has evolved into a new role. He seems to select one family member to pick on or seek revenge against for something that happened or was said earlier that year. One Christmas, my new wife, who was not known as being a gourmet chef, received a carefully selected and contrived gift from Rick—he bought her a huge plastic kitchen set, oven and all. The thing must have cost over a hundred dollars. No expense was too much for my big brother, as long as he got the joke across.

Dad and I once built a railroad tie ramp from our front door to Shadow Lane in our cul-de-sac in Glenwood Heights. The house was set down from the road rather steeply, and this ramp would serve as a bridge from the yard into the house. Well, one day Rick got ticked off at Mom for some reason and ran away. Yup, he ran away; took his electric wheelchair and smashed through the screen door, across the ramp to Shadow Lane, and right on down the road. It was a warm spring day and rain began to splatter down. Rick drove his chair onto a neighbor's lawn and under a tree for protection. He got bogged down in the spring mud, and there he sat until Dad got home from work. Rick got home soaking wet and covered in mud. Rick sure made his point! To no one's surprise, Rick never ran away again.

The Wonder Years

by Rick Hoyt with Todd Civin

> "Growing up is never easy. You hold on to things that were. You wonder what's to come. But that night, I think we knew it was time to let go of what had been, and look ahead to what would be. Other days. New days. Days to come. The thing is, we didn't have to hate each other for getting older. We just had to forgive ourselves... for growing up."
>
> —*The Wonder Years* TV Show

In a way, Rob, Russ and I were typical boys. Like all boys, we got into our fair share of trouble. I think we often caused some neighbors to have panic attacks. We were sort of a cross between *Leave It to Beaver* and the *Three Stooges* with maybe a little bit of *Dennis the Menace* sprinkled in. We picked on each other endlessly, and to this day, we still do. In a lot of ways, I think it was my brothers' way of making me feel accepted and equal to them. Who do you pick on most, but the one you love?

Around the time we were kids, the movie *Animal House* was popular. Dad once took the three of us to the Officers' Club at Hanscom Air Force Base in Bedford, Massachusetts. I had a guest come along, and somehow the food fight scene from the movie got reenacted, much to Dad's displeasure.

When we lived in Falmouth, Massachusetts, on a finger lake, which led to the ocean, Rob and Russ would take me out in a canoe and purposely tip it over. Mom got a few phone calls from neighbors saying, "Do you know what your two sons are doing to your disabled son?" She would tell them she knew exactly what they are doing. It was not only boys being boys, but I found it fun and it taught all of us some very important lessons. It taught me to swim and how to survive if I was in trouble. It taught Russ and Rob that no matter how hard they tried to get rid of me, I was here to stay.

When we lived in North Reading, Rob and Russ would bring me out into the woods to build tree forts. When other kids came along, both Rob and Russ would go off to play and leave me out in the woods. When they were done playing, they would come and get me and tell Mom that we had spent the whole afternoon building the tree fort. So if you wonder why to this day I still tease Rob and Russ when I have the opportunity, you only have to think back to the days they would drown me or leave me out to be eaten by wild animals.

I'd be lying if I didn't admit that I would wish I could have played along with Russ and Rob. Sometimes I would cry, but I also accepted the fact that I was not able to play with them and other children. It wouldn't be healthy if I spent my whole life sitting at the window watching and wishing that I could play like everyone else. Maybe I would have felt that way if I had been at one time able-bodied and it was taken away from me, but this is all I've ever known. As I said earlier, Russ once asked Mom if all families have someone in a wheelchair. If this is all someone knows, it isn't as difficult to adjust to. I did get used to watching them play, and they tried to involve me as much as they could. When they played baseball, I was the umpire. This was a pretty good role for me and was much safer than when Rob would tell me I could be second base.

When they played hockey, Dad would strap a pillow to my chest and a stick to my wheelchair and I would make believe I was Gerry

Cheevers, who was the Bruins goalie during the early 1970s. Someone would maneuver my wheelchair from behind so I was a lot like the goalie in a game of table top hockey. Plus with my toothless grin, I think I looked like one of the Bruins players from the early seventies.

Though I couldn't participate in Little League or high school sports, I loved watching my brothers play. I would sit there and wave my arms like crazy, which was my way of cheering them on. Once again, I wasn't loud, but I was enthusiastic. They knew I would go to every game they played. I became their biggest fan!

I was thinking the other day of a funny story that happened when I was about seventeen. One day Russ picked me up from school after his wrestling practice. He pulled into McDonald's to get some food and left me and the car keys inside. When he came outside with a bag full of burgers and fries, he couldn't get into the car. He tried to get me to unlock the door, but quickly realized this wasn't going to happen. Finally Russ decided to call the police. I was laughing at first, but as time went by I got scared at the thought of the police coming. The police unlocked the door with one of those special tools in a matter of seconds. I laughed so hard again, but Russ was not happy that he had to call the police.

Rob was often jealous of all the attention that Mom and Dad would give me. He couldn't understand why Mom and Dad had to take me to my therapist or doctor's appointments or anywhere else they regularly had to take me. In Rob's young mind, I think he felt a bit cheated out of Mom and Dad's love. I understand it, as I guess it happens in many families and I required a lot more attention than most.

There was a time in our younger years that Rob would actually use me to help him make friends. Sort of like bringing a puppy to the park to meet girls, Rob would take me places and used my charm as an ice breaker to meet kids. Once Rob made a connection and his "new" friend asked Rob to go off somewhere to play with him, I got left behind. This hurt my feelings and made me cry.

Both Rob and Russ loved to tease me and took turns ticking me off by changing the television channel during a show that I wanted to watch or by drinking a Coke in front of me and not letting me have any. I loved Coke and they knew it. They would come home from school and immediately go to the refrigerator. Each of them would take out a can and drink it. The whole time they would be talking about how good and cold and how refreshing it was. Then when they were done, they would put the empty cans on the counter right out of my reach and walk away. That would agitate me to no end.

Rob would take care of me after school when he was about fifteen. He was okay as a babysitter, except when he wanted to watch something different than I wanted to on TV. At that time, we had two yellow chairs in the living room that tipped over easily. He would tease me to the point where I would have a fit; I would tip over and fall off the chair. He would then punish me like I was a child and put me in my bedroom so he got to watch what he wanted.

I remember one time, though, when I got the last laugh. I had a motorized wheelchair and I managed to maneuver it between the bathroom and the basement. Rob was in a rush to go to work at some chicken place and went down into the basement to get something. I kept on backing up the wheelchair with all my might and trapped him in the basement. Pay back, huh, Rob?

When I was fifteen, I became friends with Mary. I began public school in the same class. She would come over to the house and we would spend time and just hang out. Mary and I went sledding quite a few times during the winter. She was younger than me, so I guess she liked me because I was not only extremely handsome, but I was also an older man. We hung out at her house and just watched television together. Mary lived near my friend Jeffrey. There were always a few of us who would hang out together. When it was just the boys, we would watch television and sports and sometimes play with our matchbox cars. If I remember correctly, Mary wasn't much into matchboxes.

In high school, Mary would also feed me when I needed to eat.

Sometimes feeding me isn't the greatest job in the world, so I consider her a true friend for that alone. Anyone who feeds me and doesn't get paid for doing it is a true friend for life.

Mary had an interest in Rob, but at the time Rob had a girlfriend. One night, Rob was at a bar and Mary just happened to be there too. Legend has it that they may have had a bit too much to drink and they started to make out. That night started their relationship. They eventually married, and I was the best man at the wedding. A short time later they divorced. For a while, I felt like sort of a match-maker, having introduced Rob to the woman he would ultimately marry. After things didn't work out so well, I tried hard not to remind Rob that I was the guy who brought them together. It's funny how things change like that.

Rob chose me to be the best man at his wedding, but he had to prepare for the worst in the event that my technology failed. He had two best men at his wedding just in case this happened. It didn't, and I gave the toast at the reception. I got a rousing ovation with the last line of the toast, which was, "Let's party!"

I had several girlfriends throughout elementary school. A cute little girl named Patty was my first official date. She was very good looking but extremely quiet; a lot like me, if you think about it; devilish good looks, but a man of very few words. I took Patty to a dance in Westfield when we were in fifth grade and, though I was in my wheelchair and Patty was light on her feet, I held my own on the dance floor. I could really move my arms to the rhythm of the music. I probably wasn't going to win any dance contests, but people got a big kick by watching me do the Twist or Hang Ten to the Beach Boys.

I have been kissed by women, but not passionately. I have sent flowers to girls and not just on Valentine's Day. I liked a girl in high school by the name of Pam. She knew I liked her. I took her to the prom and we danced. I had a girlfriend in college by the name of Joy. She was my PCA. We never kissed, but since there weren't many women I felt that way about, I still considered her my girlfriend.

Though no one has ever had the nerve to ask me directly, I know many people have wondered if I experience sexual feelings and fantasies, and, for that matter, if I have ever had a sexual encounter. It may surprise many to know that I do think of things like that and fantasize just like an able-bodied person may. Though I don't feel that my book should be the type of tell-all tabloid that you find at the grocery store check-out lines, the answer is yes. I am hoping with this admission, though, the Paparazzi don't start lining up outside my apartment door.

Rick's Not So Greatest Moments

by Russell Hoyt

Rick's Brother

> *"My father used to play with my brother and me in the yard. Mother would come out and say, 'You're tearing up the grass.' 'We're not raising grass,' Dad would reply. 'We're raising boys.'"*
>
> — *Harmon Killebrew*

I can't help but laugh as I think back on my big brother Rick's life. Most people think his life has been filled with nothing but shining moments as his face has graced newspapers and magazines, websites and TV sets around the globe. Of course, I'm proud of my brother for shuffling a deck that was heavily stacked against him.

But as his little brother, I've also had the grave and sometimes humorous pleasure of witnessing the many times that life has kicked him in the proverbial groin and left him on the ground writhing in comedic pain.

Among the many stories—and trust me, there have been many— three tales of humor and misfortune immediately come to mind. I can't help but laugh as I recount them and feel like we were plucked into a real-life episode of *The Three Stooges* with Rick, unfortunately, playing all three roles as Curly, Larry, and Moe.

When Rick, Rob and I were young, about fourteen, twelve, and nine respectively, our parents would leave us at home during school vacation weeks while they were working. One time, Rick (and it was, of course, all his idea) decided we should dress him up in one of my Mom's dresses. Rob and I, being the caring and obedient brothers we were, decided to honor Rick's request. We got fresh oranges—or maybe even grapefruits— and placed them on Rick's chest, supported by our mother's bra. We then put Mom's dress on Rick and put him in his wheelchair looking "oh, so fine" right in front of the door so that when Mom arrived home, he would be the first thing she would see.

Rob and I decided to play catch in the front yard while waiting so we could be close by to hear her reaction and yet still be outside so we could run away and hide to avoid any immediate repercussions. Well, before Mom got home, our neighbor stopped by to leave something for her, so we said, "Go ahead in." Well, she screamed and ran back out, told us how awful we were, and that she would be calling our mother. As she stormed back to her house, our mother arrived home with groceries in the car. We offered to carry them in for her so she could go right inside. Mom entered the house, screamed, said some profanity and flew back outside to find all the groceries unloaded from the car and left on the top stair of the porch. Neither Rob nor I were to be found anywhere. When we finally came home several hours later, Mom said that what upset her most was that he looked better in her dress than she did.

When we were all finally of legal drinking age, we often had fun at the local drinking establishments. We were in Boston, and Rick had this huge, very difficult to steer electric wheelchair that he could maneuver through the use of a head switch. After a few beers and rum and cokes, we decided it was time to head home. Well, Rick went flying out the door of the bar and bumped into a parked car with this monstrous wheelchair. I looked it over and there was no major damage—just a small mark on the side of the car. I said, "You're okay. Nothing you'll get arrested for." Well, Rick started laughing his "you didn't just say what I think you said" laugh and his evil body started shaking. He then backed the chair up and careened forward, smashing into the car with enough force to make a small dent. He was now laughing even harder. I said, "That was stupid, Rick. Are you trying to get arrested?" He nodded and started laughing so hard that I thought he was going to pee his pants. He then jerked the chair back, flew toward another car, hit the side of it, and dragged the chair along the edge, scraping the paint. At this point a police car pulled up and a young cop got out and yelled at me, "What the hell is going on here?" I said, "He just hit two cars." The cop said, "Are you trying to get arrested?" I said, "No, he is." Rick started laughing so loud it startled the cop. Now an older cop got out and said to the young cop, "Do you know who that is? It's Ricky Hoyt. He owns this town." He looked at me and said, "If you don't get him home, we're taking you in." So I released Rick's drive belt and started pushing his three-hundred pound wheelchair away from the scene of his crime.

One time, Rick and I had been asked by United Cerebral Palsy (UCP) to speak at their national conference. We were flown to San Diego and put up in a fancy hotel. The night before our presentation, we had a nice dinner and a few drinks and decided to see how much fun we could have in the hallway of the hotel. I helped Rick out of his chair and into the middle of the hall just where I could see him through the room's peephole. A couple of minutes after I shut the door, the elevator doors opened and a man who had had a few too many drinks stepped out. Rick began his familiar laugh where he starts shaking before any sound even comes out. The drunk from the elevator stumbled over to Rick and asked him if he was okay. Rick just snorted and continued shaking. The drunk said, "I think you've had a few too many, pal. I better help you up."

He tried to stand Rick up, who of course fell over into a lump. He now was laughing out loud and shaking even more. The drunk said, "Buddy, you need to walk this off," and tried to stand him up again. Rick fell over and roared with laughter. The drunk guy said, "I better get you some help. I'll be right back." He stumbled into his room. I ran out, grabbed Rick, and dragged him quickly into our room. The drunk came back out, scratched his head and looked around for a minute. Then hotel security arrived and the drunk waved his arms in the air and told a very animated tale about a man who was so drunk he couldn't stand up or walk or even talk! Rick and I laughed so hard it took us twenty minutes before I could compose myself enough to lift him back into his wheelchair and call it a night.

She Was the Wind Beneath My Wings

by Rick Hoyt with Todd Civin

> "A mother is a person who seeing there are only four pieces of pie for five people, promptly announces she never did care for pie."
>
> —Tenneva Jordan

My mom was my caregiver. She fought tirelessly to get me into public school and refused to take no for an answer. Mom did everything for me and even taught swimming lessons as a tradeoff for my physical therapy, speech therapy, and occupational therapy. Mom taught life-saving techniques to Rob and to our cousins. She taught them how to save someone who was drowning, and poor Rob had to practice by saving our cousins who were much older and stronger than he was.

When my grandpa on my mothers' side lived on Cape Cod, he had a good-sized motor boat. He would take Mom, Aunt Nancy, and me to a beach where the only access to shore was by swimming. Both my mom and Nancy would take turns on each visit to the beach—the first one in the water would catch me, while the other one threw me in. The catcher would put me in the cross-chest carry and swim to shore with me. The other one jumped off after and swam in with the food. The distance was about fifteen hundred yards, or almost a mile. By the time we got there, I think they were probably happier that the food made it to shore dry than they were that I made it there somewhat safe.

Both Aunt Nancy and Mom prepared lunch before we left the house and took the greatest care to be sure everything was prepared well and safely wrapped so it didn't get wet. In those days, I think they wrapped everything in wax paper, which was not the most waterproof wrapping. These were the days before clingy plastic wrap, as amazing as that may seem to younger people. The lunch would usually be peanut butter and jelly or ham and cheese sandwiches. They would also pack Ring Dings (my favorite snack at the time), grapes, and a drink. They would then pack everything in a backpack. Once I was in the safety of Aunt Nancy's arms, Mom would slip on the backpack of food and jump in. She would use the breast stroke so lunch would not get too wet. Despite their careful preparation, lunch always got wet.

I remember a story where Mom and a couple of counselors at camp were out in a canoe. Mom was scared of frogs, so I encouraged the counselors to put frogs in the canoe. She saw them and seemed to eject automatically from the canoe and into the cold water. I knew she would react, but never expected her to jump into the water. I can't remember if that dose of mischief was greeted with laughter or a spanking, but somehow I think I recall a spanking.

On another occasion, Mom had an idea to have a race. Rather than have the counselors run and push a camper's wheelchair, they would have to hop. This didn't make a lot of sense to me, but who was I to argue with Mom? I'm a man of very few words, and Mom had more of them than she needed. As luck would have it, one of the counselors' ties got wrapped around my wheelchair bar and he tumbled "ass over teakettle." I went face first onto the dusty ground and my front teeth got knocked out.

Instead of wearing a gold medal around my neck following the race,

I wore a temporary tinsel tooth cap for several years. I was, of course, known as "tinsel tooth." The temporary cap remained a part of my gorgeous appearance until a girl named Marilyn was carrying me during a camp floor hockey game several years later. We scored a goal, and in all the excitement, she dropped me on my face and knocked out my tinsel tooth permanently. Sometimes playing sports can be hazardous to my health.

At one point in my life, Mom envisioned a camp where every kid would be welcomed and accepted. She founded Kamp for Kids on the grounds of Western Mass Hospital. The camp allowed children from age three to twenty-one, both disabled and able-bodied. Unfortunately for me, as Rob and Russ rose in the staff, I was sort of left behind. There were many mornings I didn't want to go to camp. I felt like just a regular camper instead of the son of the founder, and nobody would listen to me. One day I was having a temper-tantrum. Russ was so fed up with my childish behavior that he fed me lunch in only three bites and nearly choked me.

Mom was really good at talking people into whatever she wanted. Kamp for Kids was a day camp, but for two summers in a row she talked my PCAs from BU into turning it into a two-week overnight camp. I had an "unpaid" job, which was to watch the interaction between the staff and the kids, and to give my advice as to how to make the interaction better. I was sort of a spy, a sociologist, and an advice columnist all rolled into one unpaid little package.

One of my jobs at the Kamp was built around one of the skills I have developed as a result of my disability. Being the son of the founder, I got to train people on how to feed and how to toilet a person with a disability. I developed a dislike of applesauce, because year after year I ate applesauce for around fifty new counselors. If you think about it, that probably helped with the toileting aspect of my job requirements, too.

As I stated earlier, I was not happy about just being a camper, so I spent most of my time in the executive office and became good friends with the assistant bookkeeper named Bob. He spoke with me using the Russell Method and helped make camp a little more tolerable for me.

When Mom died in September of 2010, I was crushed. Even though I didn't see her as often in recent years as in the past, she remained a huge part of my life and my thoughts. Her obituary read as follows: *Mrs. Hoyt was a resident of North Reading, Westfield and Holland, where she raised her family. Judy was a Master of Education and a pioneer in changing the field of education. Her efforts on behalf of her eldest son, Rick, allowed countless individuals with disabilities to be educated in public schools alongside their non-disabled siblings, friends and peers. Judy founded ASHS, Association for the Support of Human Services, a human service agency that created Kamp for Kids, the first ever summer camp for children with and without disabilities. In her later years, Judy worked as a secretary for the Town of Thompson, CT, H&R Block, Last Green Valley and Beltane Farm, marketing organic goat cheeses.*

As we were preparing for Mom's funeral, I felt it would be important for me to say a few words to not only remember her, but also to try to use my sense of humor to help the friends and family leave with a good feeling in their hearts. Mom was, of course, known for everything she did for me and for other people with disabilities, but as my mother the memories were much more personal. I tried to share a couple silly little memories that probably meant more to me than they did to anyone else. As difficult as it was for me to try to hold back my own tears, I shared the following eulogy in honor of Mom.

Hello, my name is Rick. I would like to share memories of my mother, who is known by many names. I called her "Mom." Some of you called her "A.J." Some of you called her "Judy" and some of you called her just "E." Mom fought for the rights of me and thousands of others to enter public school. She pushed ahead even if it meant calling senators from different states to make sure her point was heard.

Mom always included me in everything, both good and bad, as you will soon hear. One of my best memories has to do with my grandfather's motorboat. *Mom and her sister would drive the boat out into breakwater to have lunch at an ocean-side beach. Mom would take me with them even though she would have to wrap both me and the lunch around the upper part of her arm. My aunt would jump into the water and Mom would hand me to my aunt. Mom would then jump in, take me and the lunch from my aunt, and swim to shore. Although the lunch got a little wet, we had a great time together. It was important to Mom that I be fully included.*

On the other hand, a not-so-great memory of Mom, fully including me and focused on punishment. Mom used to use a hairbrush on my and my brothers' butts. Once when we lived in Texas, I was being a very bad boy while we were visiting a friend. Mom asked if she could borrow her hairbrush. Oh boy, did Mom let me have it. Much later, Mom found out that her friend's brush was a metal brush. My butt hurt for a week!

In recent years, she was really into goats. Mom worked on a farm that raised goats. She milked them; she cooked with goat cheese; she sold goat soap; and from this comes another great memory—Mom's famous goat cheese lasagna. Goodbye, Mom. Fly high. I love you.

I will never forget my Mom for as long as I live. She was my inspiration. She never gave up on me. She never gave up on other people with disabilities, either. She believed in everyone. If it wasn't for her, I wouldn't have had the education that I have today. At her funeral, the organist and singer played the song, "You Are the Wind Beneath My Wings." I can't think of a more fitting tribute to an amazing woman. As I write this part, I am crying and need to call it a day before I continue writing any more. I love you, Mom.

Team Hoyt
and Easter Seals

by Kirk Joslin
President of Easter Seals Massachusetts

///

> *"Everything is possible. The impossible just takes a little longer."*
>
> —*Unknown*

Long before Rick Hoyt became part of the world-famous Team Hoyt, he was famous to me.

In the mid-1970s, the disability rights movement was coming into its own. People with disabilities were demanding the right to live independently, go into public places without facing architectural barriers, and to have equal access to education. They were demanding equal opportunities and independence. They did not want to live in institutions.

At the time, I was working for Easter Seals as an education advocate for kids with disabilities. The laws were changing rapidly. For the first time, kids with disabilities had the right to attend their local public schools with their siblings and friends. Before these changes, their options were few and often only included special schools where they would live away from their families during the week and come home on weekends.

To those of us working to make the promise of these new laws a reality for every child with a disability, Rick Hoyt's story was legendary. He was a boy with cerebral palsy who could not control the movement of any part of his body but his head. He also had no speech.

Rick's successful inclusion in school was a real, visible demonstration of the promise of the new laws and our society's commitment to equal opportunities for people with disabilities. It also was a testament to his parents' perseverance and persistence—especially to his mother Judy, a fierce and fearless advocate for her son.

Judy was the first member of the Hoyt family I got to know. We met when I came to Easter Seals in 1976. Like me, she was a community advocate for the organization. Judy was covering Western Massachusetts and I covered Boston. We organized disability awareness programs, advocacy groups around architectural barrier removal, parent workshops, and a host of recreation programs for people with disabilities.

It was this kind of work that brought me to Easter Seals, and it was Judy's work that helped define much of its substance and direction. Her work was informed by her years of experience, making it possible for Rick to participate in every aspect of life. Her energy and passion left a legacy that is still part of Easter Seals today.

Meeting Rick

The next summer I met Rick. He was part of a unique overnight summer camp program sponsored by Easter Seals and Northeastern University. The camp was located in Ashland, Massachusetts—only a mile or so from the Boston Marathon route Rick would go on to conquer so many times.

What made the camp unique was that it included kids with and without disabilities. There was only one other program like it in the country. The camp director was a Northeastern professor named Frank

Robinson. Known as "Coach" to the campers, he created an environment where everyone, regardless of his or her ability, could participate in all activities. His focus was on what campers could do, not what they couldn't.

It was exactly the right place for Rick, whose family brought him up the same as his brothers without disabilities.

What I loved about Rick was his great sense of humor. He loved participating in camp pranks. He liked being the instigator, but he also never minded being the butt of a joke played by others. Whether it was pie-in-the-face clowning around or hiding out in the girls' cabin, Rick was a part of all the fun.

Many years later, at Rick's fiftieth birthday party, Coach Robinson and I were among Rick's "roasters," sharing stories of those early days at Easter Seals camp.

Thanks to Rick, I Got the Girl

Rick's entrance into the public school system demonstrated what was possible for kids with disabilities. It was a breakthrough in the cause of equal access to education. I didn't know at the time that it also would be a personal breakthrough for me.

Rick's presence in a regular classroom necessitated the hiring of classroom aides. One of them, Sheila Donovan, was the woman I would eventually marry—even though I didn't meet her until three years later.

Judy and Sheila became friends, and Judy recruited Sheila into Easter Seals. The two of them ran Easter Seals' swim and recreational programs, disability awareness workshops, and a summer day camp. When I came to Easter Seals, I met Sheila. Rick was at our wedding two years later. He didn't give the bride away, but if it hadn't been for him, I would've never met my wife of thirty-three years.

Thank you, Rick. Your breakthrough into the public schools was what brought Sheila and me together. I can't help but rub it in that I got the girl.

Reuniting the Hoyts and Easter Seals

By the time Sheila and I were married, Rick and his dad had already run their first race out in Westfield. None of us knew then that this would be the start of an incredible phenomenon that would touch people all over the world, changing the way they see the possibilities for people with disabilities—and for themselves.

As the years went on, Rick and Dick became Team Hoyt. Their fame in the Boston area began to spread nationwide and worldwide. What started as a one-time 5K run, turned Rick and Dick into the most prolific race team in the world. The number of road races and marathons they competed in multiplied nationally and even internationally. No feat was more inspiring and effective in raising the cause of disability awareness than their cross-country trek from Santa Monica to Boston in 1992. That 45-day, 3,770 mile trip brought the Hoyts' message of "Yes, You Can" to cities and towns across America.

In 2001, Easter Seals reached out to Team Hoyt for help. We had a team of runners in the Boston Marathon committed to raising $25,000 to help send kids to our summer camp—the same type of program Rick attended as a child. I knew Rick and Dick could get our runners pumped up for the challenge. I also recognized that they were now celebrities with many obligations.

No surprise to anyone who knows them, they didn't hesitate in saying "yes" to Easter Seals. On one of the busiest weekends of their year—just before the Boston Marathon—Team Hoyt spoke to our Easter Seals' runners.

Using his computer, Rick spoke about attending Easter Seals' camp. He said, "It gave me my first taste of independence." That experience helped when he went off to Boston University, where he earned his degree in special education. He also spoke about the special feeling he got during the Boston Marathon as he and Dick ran through Ashland, the location of the camp he attended.

Several years later, Easter Seals decided to recognize Rick and Dick for all they had done to break down barriers for people with disabilities. I sat down for lunch with Dick to tell him how we planned to honor Team Hoyt. Before I could start, he said, "Rick and I have a great idea. This coming year is our twenty-fifth anniversary Boston Marathon and we would like to dedicate it to Easter Seals."

That year, 2007, Easter Seals and Team Hoyt launched a fundraising campaign that raised more than $350,000 to support Easter Seals' services for children and adults with disabilities. In their honor, Easter Seals created the Team Hoyt Award to recognize individuals and organizations that break down barriers facing people with disabilities. In a reception held days before their historic marathon run, Rick and Dick became the first recipients of the award.

Team Hoyt and Easter Seals share a common vision—that people with disabilities should be empowered to reach their full potential. Team Hoyt's mission says this simply: Yes You Can! It is about unleashing the spirit inside of you to overcome barriers and do what you really want to do.

Easter Seals' mission focuses on ensuring equal opportunities to live, learn, work and play. It's about providing the supports and services necessary to enable people with disabilities to empower themselves so they can reach their potential and be able to say, "Yes I Can!"

Branches on My Family Tree

by Rick Hoyt with Todd Civin

> "The family. We were a strange little band of characters drudging through life sharing diseases and toothpaste, coveting one another's desserts, hiding shampoo, borrowing money, locking each other out of our rooms … and trying to figure out the common thread that bound us all together."
>
> —Erma Bombeck

I am incredibly blessed to have a wonderful family who supports me in almost everything that I do. Without the support and encouragement that I received throughout life from my dad and mom and from Rob, Russ, and their families, I wouldn't have been able to accomplish nearly as much as I have. Like marathon running or bike racing, without a good support team and people who believe in you and share your vision, things would be much more difficult.

In addition to the family members you've already met, I'd like to introduce you to the other members of my family—the family that makes up the branches on our family tree.

As you may have heard, Dad was one of ten children. Dad was number six in line and all the children slept in two rooms. The girls slept in one room and the boys slept in another. They only had one toilet and had to eat in shifts because there wasn't enough room at the kitchen table for everyone. Dad always told me they were known as the cleanest and healthiest kids in the school and they rarely if ever had any disagreements.

There are so many of them, I always have difficulty rattling off all of the names. I have Aunt Arline, Uncle Al, Aunt Barbara, Aunt Alice, Aunt Kathy, Uncle Jason, Uncle Herbie, Aunt Ruth, and Uncle Phil.

I was very fond of my Uncle Dave, who has since passed away. He was married to Aunt Arline. They had four kids named Sharon, Tom, Dave Jr., and Kim. Uncle Dave was so much fun to be around. He loved to goof around and really took a special interest in me. He responded to me and treated me like he was my second dad. He would not think twice when Mom and Dad would ask him to look after me when they had to go to a meeting about my education. When I was about five years old, Uncle Dave would spoil me by giving me a little bit of his mixed drink. It was only a sip, and I'm not much of a tattletale, so the secret remained with us until Uncle Dave died. I remember sitting around one night watching the movie *The Towering Inferno* with him. For some reason, it is one of my fondest memories. It's funny the little things you remember about someone you love. Maybe it was nothing more than the quality time that Uncle Dave and I spent together or the fact that he treated me in a way that not everyone did. Unfortunately, Uncle Dave was taken from us far too early, as he died from lung cancer.

Aunt Mary is married to Dad's younger brother, Herbie. I remember one time when we were at their house visiting, Aunt Mary made an angel food cake. She asked me if I would like a piece, and, of course, I nodded my head yes. I ate every morsel, and ever since that day, Aunt Mary really likes me and thinks I am an angel. She didn't try to smother me with affection. She has a brother with Down syndrome, which may have helped teach her how to treat others with disabilities.

If you ever have the pleasure to come to a Hoyt family reunion, you'll see that all Dad's brothers and sisters look pretty much like Dad.

Many people especially confuse Uncle Herbie for my dad.

I don't see my relatives as often as I would like to, but I do get to see them mostly around holidays. Uncle Al has Alzheimer's disease and is in a nursing home in North Andover, Massachusetts, so we rarely get to see him anymore. Uncle Philip lives in Florida with his wife, Pat. Uncle Herbie lives in Foxboro, Massachusetts, with his wife, Mary. Uncle Jason lives in Stoneham, Massachusetts, with his dogs. Aunt Arline and her husband, Chuck, live in North Reading, Massachusetts, where the family grew up and became quite well-known throughout the town. I lived in North Reading when I was a young boy. Aunt Ruth lives in North Andover, Massachusetts. Aunt Kathy lives with her husband, Ted, and their son, Trevor, in Florida, and Aunt Alice recently moved to Oklahoma to live with her son.

Aunt Barbara is Dad's older sister. She also lives in North Reading. Barbara was a school bus driver. One summer, she drove the family in a school bus to Dad's house for a family get-together. I guess that is one of the perks of being a bus driver. She treated me like she did the rest of my cousins. I enjoyed going to her softball games. She made the best chocolate cake, which to this day is one of my weaknesses. Be it breakfast, lunch or dinner, I can never get enough chocolate cake. Unfortunately for Dad, it has made me a bit less aero-dynamic when it comes to race day.

Mom just had two sisters and no brothers. Her sisters are Aunt Nancy and Aunt Susan, both of whom I have always been close to and remain very close to this day. Mom was the oldest of the three, followed by Nancy and Susan.

Aunt Nancy is one of the kindest people in the world. She lives in Colorado. She and Mom took lifesaving classes together to learn how to save my brothers and me in case we were ever in trouble swimming. As part of their lifesaving training, they had to practice getting out of a full body lock. A full body lock is when a person is going under water and a lifeguard swims out to the person to try to rescue him. However, when he gets there, the person panics and wraps his whole body around the lifeguard. This is very dangerous to both the victim and the lifeguard, of course. In their training, they practiced the technique using Dad as the victim. Dad locked his body around Mom and Aunt Nancy. Unfortunately, Dad was too strong for them and almost took them both under. Thankfully, they never had to use the technique in a real-life situation.

When Aunt Nancy married Uncle David, the wedding reception was held at our house. It was one heck of an event and lasted through the night and into the morning. The reception turned into a large party with a lot of drinking games. One game that I remember took place under a bed sheet. When people have a lot to drink their logical reasoning is impaired. The guests would throw a sheet over two drunks' heads and scream, "Take off whatever you don't need" while the rest of the people yelled, "No, not that. Take off something else." It confused the drunks under the sheet and they would take off items of clothing instead of just taking off the sheet. I remember watching this game for what seemed like most of the night and laughed my head off. This was one game I didn't mind being excluded from. It was more fun just being an innocent bystander.

Aunt Nancy really loves me, but is a bit of a worry wart. Every time I had the slightest cough she would insist that Mom take me to the doctor. Even to this day, at fifty years old, she still worries about my feeding tube.

Aunt Susan is my mother's youngest sister. When she got married for the first time, I was about nine years old. I was so honored because she asked me to be the ring bearer. She always treats me and speaks to me as if I am an able-bodied person, and she invited me to her New Year's Eve party this year. At one time my Mom asked Sue to be my guardian, and though I'm sure she would've been a great guardian, I'm glad I didn't have to take her up on it.

Though Mom's family understood my disability and treated me like one of the gang, Dad's mom didn't cope or accept me very well. She always talked to me like I was a baby, which irritated me to no end. Mom's mom, who I called Granny, was more understanding and treated me like the little brat I really was. I have a story which illustrates my bratty behavior quite well.

Granny lived on Cape Cod, where it's really hard to grow anything because of the soil and the saltwater and salt air. One day, Dad and Mom had to go out, and Granny babysat for us. She had miraculously grown quite a few tomatoes in her little garden and was so proud of herself. She asked if I wanted to try a bite of her "prize winning" tomato. I was sitting in a rocking chair with towels down on the floor. She walked over and popped a piece of tomato into my mouth. I immediately spit it out; it rolled down the towels and onto her shoes. Granny got upset and yelled that it took her four months to grow that tomato. To be truthful, it didn't taste that bad, but I was a brat and this was my way of reminding her who was in charge.

A Pebble in Her Shoe

by Nancy Stackhouse
Ricky's Aunt

> *"I don't believe an accident of birth makes people sisters or brothers. It makes them siblings, gives them mutuality of parentage. Sisterhood and brotherhood is a condition people have to work at."*
>
> —*Maya Angelou*

I was a young girl of only sixteen when Ricky was born. Here I was a junior in high school, trying to figure out what my own life was about. It was quite an event to have the beginning of a new generation being born into our family. To say we were all very excited was an understatement. We found out rather quickly that not all had gone well with the birth of my new nephew and that there might be complications. Judy and Richie (what many members of the family still call Dick to this day) were very young, just a little over twenty. They were practically kids themselves, and now they were faced with the challenge of raising a child with multiple disabilities. Despite a deck that life had stacked against them, they decided that no matter what, Ricky was coming home with them.

They had a small home in North Reading near to where they both had grown up and married as high school sweethearts. As soon as he was strong enough, Ricky came home from the hospital and joined them in their little home. There was certainly plenty of family around to help out, as Judy's parents and two sisters, as well as Richie's parents and nine sisters and brothers were all in the area. Both Judy and Richie decided this special child would have as normal a life as was possible, and that he certainly did.

Richie worked two jobs so Judy could stay home and bring up her new family. Richie and Judy made the decision to have another child, and Robbie was born two years later in 1964, and Russell came along in 1967. Judy was absolutely amazing as a mom. She included Ricky in every activity—and there were lots of them. When the other boys took swimming lessons, so did Ricky. When the neighborhood kids were all out in the street playing hockey, so was Ricky. He just went along with everything that was going on in the world around him—camping trips, vacations, hiking, biking—and he smiled every moment.

I remember one summer when Ricky was eighteen; the family came out to California to visit us for two weeks. We did all the usual tourist things. We went camping and hiking in Yosemite, then up to Tahoe for more camping and sightseeing. We even went sailing on Tomales Bay. Ricky went along on all of our excursions just like everyone else. His only disappointment on the entire trip was when Richie took him down to the casinos in South Lake Tahoe and they wouldn't let him gamble. This, of course, had nothing to do with his disability but only because he was under twenty-one.

Judy made sure he started school when he was supposed to and that he attended regular classes with an aide helping him. He graduated from high school, went on to Boston University, and graduated with his degree in special education. The family couldn't have been more proud. Ricky lived in Boston by himself with the help of attendants and worked at both BU and the Children's Museum of Science.

I credit my sister, Judy, who worked tirelessly to make all of this happen. She not only brought up a handicapped child along with two other sons, but also ran a summer camp for kids with and without disabilities called Kamp for Kids. Her goal was to make sure that disabled kids were included in activities alongside kids with no disabilities. It was a magical place. My family was living in California during this period, and my kids and I had to come east one summer just to see what the camp was all about. What an incredible time we all had. The kids took part in many activities where everyone had to solve problems together.

Judy was very much a champion for inclusion of handicapped people into regular life and was instrumental in the passage of Chapter 766 in 1972. Fighting for the rights of the disabled is what she spent her entire adult life doing. Even when she was in her last few years of life, Judy still worked for and helped out handicapped people.

I don't think anyone could ever be prepared to face the challenges that life presented to my sister, but somehow it seemed as if she was trained in advance for the challenges that life would present to her. While many face challenges as if they are trying to move mountains, my sister Judy approached things as if this were just a pebble in her shoe.

Memories from My Childhood

by Rick Hoyt with Todd Civin

> "In childhood, we press our nose to the pane, looking out. In memories of childhood, we press our nose to the pane, looking in."
>
> —Robert Brault

My actual memories of life begin about the age of four when the family was still living in North Reading. Rob was about two at the time and Russell hadn't yet been born. I've heard about the details of my birth and of the early years so many times, I feel like I have actual memories of both, but like most people, I really don't have much recollection of the first few years of my life.

My earliest memories seem to be primarily about Mom and Dad working diligently to prove that I was capable of learning. Mom spent the first four years of my life trying to educate me by cutting out the alphabet from sheets of sandpaper to teach me my ABCs by sound and feel. Mom also put labels on everything in the house that didn't move so I would learn the name and spelling of it. After four years of trying to educate me on their own, Mom and Dad decided it was time to get me into school. Being disabled and still a bit too young to enter public school, Mom took me to a church-run kindergarten taught by a woman named Miss Ham. Mom got volunteers to help me with the classwork throughout the day.

I was a little scared, since it was my first time going to school, but as the day progressed, I became more relaxed and was very happy to be attending a real school. I spent two years in kindergarten and enjoyed every single day of it. The kids really accepted me, and that helped ease my nerves. I stayed in that class until Miss Ham told Mom that I had learned all they had to teach.

About the time I was attending kindergarten at the church, Mom and Dad took me to the United Cerebral Palsy Center in Lawrence, Massachusetts. I went each day Monday through Friday and met with my occupational therapist, Fay Kimball. Fay was a very influential person in my life and loved both me and Mom. She knew that I was intelligent and said she could tell by the looks in my eyes that there was something going on in there. I always knew there was, but it was difficult for me to express myself and that caused many people to think I wasn't intelligent. Fay could tell by the way I laughed and followed what was going on around the room. She called me "Mr. Ricky." As I will tell you later in more detail, it was Fay who took me to Tufts University to meet Rick Foulds, who was instrumental in building my first computer. Without Fay and Rick, I may have never been able to communicate.

Mom fought with the school department so they would allow me to attend regular classes in public schools. She tried to convince school officials that just because I couldn't communicate didn't mean I was unable to learn, understand, grow, socialize, and become educated. Every obstacle that the school tried to throw in front of Mom, she leaped over with a rebuttal to offset their objection. She explained that I was able to understand, was toilet trained, and would have a person with me at all times to assist with my medical needs, feeding, and trips to the bathroom. Still, the school refused to allow me to enter regular classes. As frustrated as I was, Mom and Dad were equally angry and agitated.

For a while, Mom taught me at home using work the school sent her. This was difficult for both of us. Mom wasn't really a teacher, even though she tried her best, and I still wasn't getting to meet and hang with kids my age. Part of the idea of mainstreaming is the socialization that goes hand-in-hand with being in a classroom of your peers—and sitting at home learning with Mom didn't allow for that. Mom would be very frustrated by the end of the day and would tell Dad that she didn't know if she could continue.

For a while, Mom and Dad put me in a school for the disabled, but this was not something they wanted to do long term. Unfortunately, it was more of a day care with a small bit of learning taking place than it was a real classroom. The kids in there were either physically or mentally disabled or both. There wasn't much learning that went on because the place would get loud and unruly. There were only two classrooms in the entire school; one was for disabled kids ages four to eight and the other was for ages nine and up. There was only one teacher for every twelve kids, and then each class had a helper or two. Mom taught swimming there to help pay for my education, but she didn't participate in my actual classroom. Though I did learn some things there, Mom and Dad knew I wasn't getting the same quality education I would in a regular classroom with children of able minds and bodies. I thought this school was better than being taught at home because there were kids my own age, but I also knew that public school was where I wanted to be. I would come home angry every day. Mom and Dad would ask me if I liked it there and I would shake my head.

For about six months, we lived in El Paso, Texas, while Dad went to military school. We returned to North Reading, and Mom and my second teacher from the cerebral palsy center, Miss Johnson, got my class moved to a public school in North Reading. This was still not mainstreaming as we know it. It was simply a classroom for special needs kids within the public school. Miss Johnson talked to a third grade teacher, who actually allowed me to join the class for math. My granny would come into class each day to help me with my math problems. Granny couldn't understand what the math teacher was teaching, but we still managed to get some of the answers right.

My math skills are pretty good now, and I like to think it was because of the foundation that I got in this class with Granny's help. I can add and subtract. I did have to learn some algebra to receive my Special Ed degree at BU, but like anyone, I'm not sure if I really understand it to this day. Like any kid, I've always asked the question, "When am I going to use this in my everyday life?" As long as Dad knows to stop once we hit 26.2 miles, that's pretty much all the math I will ever need.

For my eighth birthday, Mom let me invite a few friends over from the math class for my party. Mom forgot to put baking soda in the cake, and it was a solid brick. Not a highlight for either Mom or I. It was difficult enough for me to make friends and get them to come over without Mom producing an epic fail with the birthday cake.

When I was in school, we used to have the Spring Music Festival where all of the kids in the school would perform the songs that we learned in music class. I'd try to sing, but nothing would come out. I would wave my hand in joy and would try to sing by moving my mouth. I didn't want people in the audience to look at me and think I wasn't even trying.

I was also in music therapy with Easter Seals and I played the tambourine. I wanted to play the drums, but I wasn't very good at holding the sticks or even being in tune when hitting the drum. It looked easy enough watching other people do it, but I guess there is more to it than I thought. I was able to hold the tambourine pretty well, and when the teacher would point to me, I would raise my hand to move the tambourine enough to make music. I didn't learn how to read sheet music, but I felt like I was a part of something and that made me feel good on the inside.

I didn't really have a lot of kids I would call friends until we moved to Westfield, Massachusetts. I began fifth grade there and met a boy named Jeffrey Rogers. He lived on the other side of town. Sometimes after school Mom would drive me over to his house. Jeffrey had severe diabetes, which limited him, so in a many ways we had a lot in common. Though he wasn't disabled like I was, he was still looked at as sort of an outcast in the classroom. Like me, he was different, and as we see, especially with all the bullying that goes on today, different isn't really the best thing to be. Jeffrey would have to eat different foods than the rest of the class and didn't participate very much in the outside activities, sort of like me. That's why we ended up being such good friends.

We took turns sleeping over at each other's house. At that time period, most parents were scared to let children ask me to come over, so I'm very grateful that Jeffrey and his parents were open-minded enough to let us be friends. It was nice to finally be able to stay over at a friend's house and have sleepovers like other children. We would play matchbox cars and watch TV together and stay up too late and probably eat a bit too much. From what I hear, we had a pretty typical sleepover.

When I wasn't in school or playing with the neighborhood children, Mom, Dad, and I would try to attend every one of Rob and Russ' Little League games. I knew my body was not going to allow me to participate in their games, so I made a conscious decision to become their biggest fan. Sometimes you need to accept your limitations and strive to really excel at the things you can do. I may not be able to hit a home run, but I can sure show my enthusiasm when my brothers succeed. Though I couldn't cheer like some of the other fans, they couldn't wave their arms and show as much enthusiasm as I could.

A neighbor at the beginning of our street in North Reading ran a 4H train club in his basement. The basement was huge and the track took up a quarter of the basement. The parents would help carry me down to the basement, where there were about twelve neighborhood boys playing. We used to play with the trains for hours. My part was to choose the colors of the railroad cars. One of the boys would point to each color and I would shake my head to choose the color for that car.

Christmas morning at the Hoyt house was always a load of fun. When I was about seven years old, we moved back to North Reading. On Christmas morning, I would get out of bed and crawl over to Rob and Russ' bed to wake them up. This took me probably a good hour to crawl about twenty feet across our bedroom. I think both of them were probably awake, but they knew by the time I made my way across the bedroom they could catch another twenty minutes sleep.

Rob would carry me and Russ would follow us into Mom and Dad's room. Mom and Dad gave us our socks filled with stocking stuffers to keep us busy until breakfast. When Mom's parents came over after breakfast, we finally got to open our presents. We'd sit around the living room and open presents in order; first went Russ, then Rob, then me, and then Mom and Dad. One of my favorite Christmas presents ever was the 1967 Red Sox record *The Impossible Dream*. The record had a song about Red Sox left fielder Carl Yastrzemski. I would listen to the song over and over again. The song was very contagious, and even though I couldn't sing out loud, I would sing it over and over in my head. It went, "CAAARL Yastrzemski…CAAARL Yastrzemski…CAAARL Yastrzemski…The man we call Yaz. We Love 'Em!" They also had bread they called Yaz Special Fitness Bread. I'm not sure if it really made you any more fit, but the commercials said it did. Maybe the Sox of today should try to find Yaz Bread to help them win a few more games.

When I was younger, I went out with my parents to pick out what I wanted to give my family for Christmas. I still buy every year for my family members and for my nephews. Dad and Kathy send me a list of suggestions through email so I know what to get everyone.

Back then, after we opened our presents, most of Dad's family would join us at Dad's parents' house, which was about six miles from our house. Dad's father gave McDonald's gift certificates to all of us grandchildren each year. For about five years in a row, some of Dad's family went up to North Conway, New Hampshire, over Christmas break. One year all of us stayed in a condo together. I was about ten years old at the time, and Uncle Dave and his son, Tom, took me for a ride. They were smoking weed in the car and I remember feeling very relaxed. Maybe this was another reason that Dave was my favorite uncle.

At that young age, I would become very frustrated because I was not able-bodied. I can't explain how aggravating it was for me to watch neighborhood children play while I wasn't able to. I really wanted to somehow find a way to get out of my body because it didn't move the way I wanted it to. I remember when I was about four years old, just lying on the floor in the living room. I could hear all the kids playing outside while I sat in the window. I watched for about a half hour before I started crying. Mom didn't really feel like being very understanding on that day and put me in my bedroom because she didn't want to hear me crying anymore. I'm sure that much of this wasn't very easy on her either, and though my disability was in no way my parents fault, I think Mom felt guilty at times.

It made me feel both sad and disappointed to be excluded from events. I think the kids my age knew me as an interesting and funny guy and wanted me to come over to their house and have a good time with them. It was disappointing though, because often times it was the parents who didn't understand that I was just like anyone else. I'd think the person who has lived more of life and knew that I have a working, functioning heart, soul, and mind would be more understanding and compassionate. The only part of me that doesn't work like their child is my body. Everything else between my ears and in my heart is the same or maybe even better than most people because of the way I have been able to experience life. In many ways, I think the adults were being lazy because I would need some help if I came over and that would add a strain to their life.

There are parts of me now that wonder if I should've had emotional therapy as a child, but in those days they didn't have therapy for children like they do today. The emotional therapy was more for my Mom, but not me. It was basically just a counselor for her who taught her how to remain strong and to cope with the personal sacrifices that it takes to raise a child with disabilities. As I said earlier, lucky for me it was the therapist that encouraged my Mom to have Rob.

He Molded the Clay

by Annie Mason

Rick's Art Teacher

Fort Meadow Elementary, 1972

> *"The dream begins, most of the time, with a teacher who believes in you, who tugs and pushes and leads you on to the next plateau, sometimes poking you with a sharp stick called truth."*
>
> —Dan Rather

During the fall of 1972, I graduated from Westfield (Mass) State College with a degree in Fine Arts and a minor in Education. After a short temp-job, I started my "real" job as an elementary art teacher in the local school system. The first few years I was nervous but enthusiastic, and I loved these kids. Art was a pretty exciting subject at the kindergarten through fifth grade level. The usual format of the art instructors was to go from room to room each day within several different schools per week. We would have between 800 and 900 students a week.

One of my schools was Fort Meadow Elementary. The classroom teacher in one of the fourth grades told me one day there would be a new "special-needs" student who was being mainstreamed into her room. He came into the classroom accompanied by the para-educator who served him. I had all the usual feelings: What were his issues? What could he do? What would I have to do? I was filled with some fear and some apprehension.

Rick Hoyt was wheeled in and brought to the back of the room. Over time, I slowly got to know him. My recollection is that the classroom teacher at one point explained that his wheelchair was "state of the art." It had some sort of computer that allowed him to "tap out his answers" that would be translated by his teachers. I remember this teacher telling me that some of the other students were eventually able to figure out the "codes" and that they used Ricky as their "cheat sheet" on math problems. I was blown away by this technology. Remember, this was the mid-1970s, well before a computer had been introduced to most classrooms.

My typical art curriculum involved drawing, painting, crayons, chalk, cut and paste, and other two-dimensional projects. Every so often I would throw in more unique lessons. On this day we were going to make "pinch pots" with clay—real clay, not Playdoh. The process involves giving each student a hand-sized clump of clay. They would then roll it into a smooth ball, poke in their thumbs and begin to form out a little pot. They would initial the bottom, and these would be taken to another one of my schools that had a kiln.

I start giving out the clay, and the classroom became alive with excitement. I demonstrated the technique and began to pass out the clay chunks. Ricky was one of the last students I approached as he waited patiently with his para. I took Ricky's hands and plopped the clay into them. He immediately screeched at a level that could probably be heard two classrooms down the hall.

I was horrified and concerned that I had upset him. Then, I got closer to him and looked at his face. It was bright with enthusiasm and he was grinning ear to ear. I couldn't believe it. I had made a connection with Rick that I previously had not made. For the first time—and probably the last—I left the rest of my students on their own and spent this time working with Rick's hands and forming this little pot that would be his treasure.

I moved on to another school system in Maine, where I wrote the art curriculum for the Farmington school district. After fourteen years, I went back to get my Master's degree in Art History, and subsequently worked at the Yale Center for British Art in New Haven, Connecticut. I met my husband, Doug, and I now live in Virginia.

After we had our daughter, I opted to work as a consultant for Creative Memories, an in-home business selling scrapbooking supplies. Typical of home sales, they have a convention, this one in Minneapolis where the albums are made. The conventions are rowdy and raucous, but they have their touching and motivational moments. The jumbo screens began overhead and the lights dimmed. Suddenly I was listening to the narrative of a man and his son—the legend of Rick Hoyt and his dad, Dick. I was stunned. This little boy that I had known briefly back in Westfield was moving this audience to tears. It's a story of triumph, courage and attitude.

It's a story that I have encountered once again in my own family. Our daughter was diagnosed with hydrocephalus in 2005. This condition is not well-known, but affects millions of all ages. It's an abnormal accumulation of cerebral spinal fluid in the ventricles of the brain. So our family has had to face the world of hospitals, doctors, IVs, MRIs, and the myriad of doings while living with a medical circumstance.

In this modern age, social media brings together those with similar issues. I have watched how Team Hoyt and everyone involved continue to embrace those who have physical challenges and inspire them to stretch themselves. Our daughter has been through two brain surgeries and several complications, yet she was accepted by a prestigious college and is doing very well. That's what Rick and his father have done their whole life. Yes, push yourself, but with a mission. That's what Ricky did: he molded the clay.

Fleeting Thoughts from Auntie Susan

by Susan Grillo
Ricky's Aunt

> *"But kids don't stay with you if you do it right. It's the one job where, the better you are, the more surely you won't be needed in the long run."*
>
> —*Barbara Kingsolver, Pigs In Heaven*

When "Ricky" was born on January 10, 1962, I was only nine and a half years old—still a child and too young to realize what had just happened. I only knew that my big sister had a baby. I was so excited to be an auntie and couldn't wait to hold my first nephew. I remember watching Judy and Dick (who we called Richie) in tears as they talked to my mom when they came home from the hospital without Rick. I thought this was odd that not only did they come home without my new nephew, but that they would be crying instead of being filled with joy. I learned that something was wrong as they talked about things I couldn't even begin to understand; words like brain damage, breach birth, no hope, and institutionalize. I was scared and just wanted to hold the baby. When I look back now, at an age of almost sixty, I remember that my sister was only twenty at the time and I realize how scary this must have been for her. Yet she was so brave.

A few days later, Rick came home. I was so excited, because now I was sure that everything was going to be okay. From the moment I saw him, I knew Rick was special. He was the most beautiful baby I'd ever seen and he never cried or fussed in the least. He was so tiny. I couldn't wait to hold him in my arms. Little did I know just how special Rick really was. As an infant, there was no visible sign that he was different than other babies, yet there was something unique about him.

As Rick grew, it became clear that he was not developing physically as other kids did. He didn't roll over or crawl and couldn't sit up unless we helped him. My mom and I learned to prop him up so we could take pictures where he looked the same as other babies. Judy taught us how to do his physical therapy exercises to stretch, strengthen, and relax his tight muscles every day. Going into Boston Children's Hospital with Judy and Rick was always an adventure, and I felt important and eager to be helpful with my special nephew. Back then, there were no toddler car seats or seat belts, and I remember sitting in the backseat with Rick next to me in a baby basket as Judy drove carefully in the Boston city traffic. Suddenly she jammed on the brakes and Rick went flying off the seat. I was instantly petrified, but nothing seemed to faze Rick, who smiled through it all. It's almost as if he knew then that such a tumble was nothing compared to some of the bumps and bruises he was going to experience throughout his life.

A few years after Rick was born, his brother, Rob, came into the world, and then Russ. My mom suddenly became known as "Granny," and now I was a really busy auntie. I was always at my sister's house in North Reading after school and sports, babysitting, and helping with the kids—changing diapers—lots of diapers—giving bottles, reading stories, and playing games with them. They were all such a huge part of my life as a teenager, and I loved being with them. Granny and I would babysit on occasion for an entire weekend to give Judy and Dick a break. When they came home, we were always exhausted and happy to go home to recover from the two days of chaos. I don't know how Judy and Dick did it every day, but they made taking care of three busy boys look so easy.

Rick always had a sparkle in his eyes, and it was clear that he fully understood what was going on around him. From my perspective, Rick was just like all the other children, only he couldn't do things by himself—*at least yet, I thought*—so he needed help. We just brought him along everywhere and helped him do all the fun things that other kids would do. I never really believed that anything was wrong—just different, and that was okay. Judy was an amazing pillar of strength and confidence, with boundless amounts of energy. She taught me to accept the challenges life presents and just make the best of things.

Some of my fondest memories with Rick are the adventures we took the boys on with Judy's best friend, Meri, and her four boys. We thought nothing of traveling into Lechmere Station in Cambridge, getting on the subway, and heading into Boston to take the kids to see Santa, the Enchanted Village at Jordan Marsh, and the Christmas lights on the Common. We just hauled Rick in his wheelchair on and off the train, up the bumpy sidewalks, over the curbs, and through over-sized doors not designed at all for handicapped access, let alone for three women with a gaggle of silly kids. During the summer, we would go up to Meri's mother's camp in New Hampshire to hike and swim and play. I remember a few times when Judy and Meri would sit on the porch drinking wine while I had all the kids lined up on a bench playing "Who can be silent the longest?"—a silly game that always ended in laughter, usually with Rick being the one to break the silence with a howl. I always loved our excursions to Plum Island, Cranes, and Wingarsheek Beaches, plopping our entire herd down on blankets that quickly were covered with sand as the boys ran around. I think Rick probably ate more than his share of sand back then, and he couldn't get enough of the water. Those were fun times that I will never forget. Little did I know I was going to own a beach house on Plum Island one day, where I still live today.

Although Rick wasn't able talk or walk, it was clear he was intelligent and understood what the other kids were learning. We made sure Rick was learning too, practicing letters and numbers with him through touch and feel methods that Judy invented and doing his exercises every day. It was amazing to watch Rick interact with his brothers as they rough and tumbled with him. Often times, Rick's way of participating was more by observing and enjoying the frenzy of activity, but he loved being in the thick of it—just as he does today with all his athletic and social activities.

Judy insisted and persisted that Rick be integrated into the public school system and be educated along with his peers. As Rick became accepted in the classroom, everyone whose life he touched learned from him and became comfortable with his limitations—some were even fascinated by him. Rick's upbeat personality came across and he captured people's hearts, just as he continues to do today at the age of fifty—and many thought he would never live so long. Without my sister's determination and his father's strength and ambition, along with his family's love, Rick would not be who or where he is today. Many people know Rick as the Team Hoyt runner. Dick has given Rick the physical power to do some incredible things, but looking back, I believe it was Judy who gave them both the courage to enter their first race over thirty years ago.

Knowing Rick and being part of his life has truly been a privilege for me. I am continually amazed at his accomplishments and his ability to just get up every day and inspire people. I am so proud of you, Rick. I don't know where you get the strength and ambition to get through every day with all your challenges—never mind to complete the Boston Marathon year after year in the cold, rainy, or hot and humid weather.

And now with technology advancements and the Internet exposure, Rick is changing people's lives around the globe and giving others the hope and courage to overcome their challenges and change their lives. How lucky am I to be a part of his life? Very!

Pioneering the Impossible

by Jessica Gauthier
Rick's PCA

> *"So many of our dreams at first seem impossible, then they seem improbable, and then, when we summon the will, they soon become inevitable."*
>
> —Christopher Reeve

Meeting Rick for the first time was very awkward for me. I learned about the open position for a Personal Care Attendant through a good friend of mine who works at a bank I often go to. He asked me if I had ever done PCA work before. I had, but it was not something I was really interested in doing as a career. However, at the time I was at a turning point in my life and needed to make a vocational change, so I decided to at least go for the interview.

I knocked on the door of Rick's apartment and was welcomed in by one of his PCAs. I entered the apartment and found Rick sitting in his big over-stuffed blue chair. He greeted me with a kind and gentle smile. I didn't know what I was in for, but, of course, I politely smiled back. The interview consisted of a brief question and answer session conducted primarily by the PCA, Mike, and also entailed me lifting Rick from his bed to his chair. I was unsure if I could do it, but I did. I sat and wondered, however, if I could do this on an every-day basis.

During our brief interview, I looked around Rick's apartment and saw all of his medals, awards, and photos with famous people that hung proudly on the walls of his quaint three-room efficiency. As I glanced around, I couldn't help but spy his prized *Sports Illustrated* pin-up girls hanging on the wall. Mike asked Rick if he had any questions for me. He responded in the following manner: "A?" Nod. "B? C? D?" Nod. "D?"

Oh, my God, I thought. Why was he not talking to me? I knew going into the interview that he couldn't move from the neck down, but I wasn't aware he couldn't speak. When he finally got through spelling out his question, Mike translated the sentence: "Do you mind my girls?" I looked around the room, having long forgotten about the SI models who adorned his apartment wall. I laughed and responded that I didn't mind at all. The ice had been broken, and I now felt a lot more at ease asking questions. I asked if he could speak at all. Rick looked away and Mike told me that was his way of saying no.

Mike explained more about the job, which entailed waking Rick up, taking him to the bathroom, giving him a bath, shaving him, and feeding him breakfast. They only needed a backup person at the time. My interview was over in about fifteen minutes. I thanked him for his time and walked out of his apartment door.

As I walked away, a lot of things ran through my head. I was really apprehensive, as I wasn't even sure I could do the job. I am a talker and he couldn't converse back with me. Would I be able to carry him or shave him? I have never shaved anyone before. I was actually scared—unsure whether or not I could succeed. I also knew that once I committed to something, especially something like this, there was no turning back. Maybe it would be better to walk away and not commit.

I went home and opened up my laptop, deciding to learn more about who this man really was. I knew of him, but not about him, so of course I Googled him. By the end of the night, I was not only in tears, but more motivated than I had ever been. The Hoyt message, "Yes You

Can," spoke directly to me. I was convinced that I could do this and do it well, and hoped more than anything that I would get a call back.

I received the much-anticipated phone call several days later and went over to my new employer's house the following week to give him a bath. Boy, did that sentence sound odd to me. I arrived and was greeted by a different PCA, who told me exactly what I had to do. I did everything from carrying him into the bathroom, putting him on the toilet, and setting him down into the tub. Washing him up was easy compared to the nerve-racking part, which was the shave. I told him I had never shaved anyone in my life, except for myself, which elicited a long, stress-breaking laugh from Rick. When I saw his smile and the look in his eyes, I absolutely melted. I had never witnessed such a trusting look. As I shaved him, I told him he was my first. He again laughed so hard that his arms spasmed in the bathtub and he ended up splashing me and most of the bathroom floor. I looked at his clean-shaven face and was pretty damn proud of myself for not cutting him. Not bad for my first, I said, and again he laughed and splashed me. I was officially hired several weeks later as a backup PCA to be called in when needed. About two months later, I was hired for a regular shift.

As many months have now passed, I have come to enjoy being Rick's PCA. Despite his inability to verbally communicate, we talk about a lot of different things. Learning to communicate with Rick was a little hard initially. It took me about twenty minutes just to complete a sentence using his "One Letter at a Time" method. I kept apologizing to him, as it was me who seemed to slow down the process. Rick would just smile and tell me not to worry. So I didn't. I learned to go with the flow, sort of like Rick does.

Our conversations now flow quite freely, and although it still takes time to communicate, the subjects we cover are many. We talk about his family, and he tells me stories about all the amazing things he has experienced. I sit there and listen, as I say, even though I do ALL the talking. He just communicates his thoughts, one letter at a time, and nods when I happen to encounter the correct letter, word and sentence that he is trying to verbalize.

Rick asks me what I do with my kids and about what I did in college and what my dreams are. He once told me he will help me accomplish my dreams if it's what I really want. When I asked him why, he told me he saw the compassion in my eyes when I talk about my children, and compassion is what all parents with young children with disabilities need; someone to help them accomplish their goals and see all of their dreams to come true.

In a way, it seems as if we have sort of a Mr. Miyagi and Daniel-son relationship, as I often think he is teaching me a valuable life lesson as we chat. We don't often talk about the sport of running or his and his father's accomplishments. We speak more often of his childhood and the accomplishments of his mother, as I am a mom, after all. I often thirst to know more, as I have a child with a learning disability and another child with a mental and behavioral disability.

One day we spoke for nearly the entire day about nothing except my children and me. I told him about the Individualized Education Program (IEP), and how I had a fight coming up with the board of education to make sure everything is right for my kids. We talked about the struggles I was having as a mother. I sat back and wondered about the struggles his mother had just to put him into the public school system. I wondered about how he graduated college. Then it hit me, and I know it hit him, too. We had something more in common. I was a fighting mother who fought for my son to get the education he deserved, and he had a fighting mother who fought for him to get the best education possible too. He and his mother were the pioneers of special education. I instantly realized that not only had I been put into his life for a special reason, but he too had been put into mine.

After learning more about him and getting to know him even better while working on his book, I wondered how I would start or end this story. I look at him now in a different way than I did before delving so deep into his life. I see him not just as an athlete through the work of his father, but as a fighter through the work of his mother. After all, that is what I am—a mother and a fighter.

Everyone knows Rick and his father as the running duo. Everyone should also know about his mother, the woman behind the scenes. She helped to get him to where he is today. She has done so much to help those with disabilities to be included in the public school system. Besides running thousands of miles, Rick has also run through boundaries, as he has helped young disabled children everywhere be a part of the public school system. His mother was his advocate, his voice to put him in the school system and to be included. I was often told when my son was younger that, "You are the best voice for your child." I never knew what that meant until we entered a new school system in a new town. As I said previously, I have a child who has an IEP and a daughter who has ADHD/behavioral issues. I have to advocate for them every day. I know what it feels like to have to jump through hoops to get what is right for the education for my child. My baby was born with Torticollis and had to wear a helmet. Torticollis means "twisted neck," and when a child has this condition, the head will be tilted to one side while the chin is turned to the other side. While it may look painful, it usually isn't. When trying to find daycare, I learned that daycare centers did not have to accept her. Here we are living in the twenty-first century and family childcare can still choose to exclude children with disabilities. They are not supposed to, but they can exclude disabled children by claiming their slots are full or someone called ahead or some other concocted excuse.

As I sit in on IEP meetings for my child and learn more and more about the rights for disabled children, I never dreamed I would ever meet the child and the mother who single-handedly created Chapter 766 and influenced changes for disabled education throughout the state of Massachusetts, the United States, and a large portion of the industrialized world.

When we're not busy changing the world, we like to go for walks and go swimming together. During the winter, Rick trains me to get stronger so that in the late spring and summer I will be able to tow him around the lake. Because of his drive and determination—and the fact that he encourages me to be equally driven and determined—I will compete in my first 5k this year. I told him I would have never even considered it before we met. He smiled and told me that he knows I won't finish last, a mantra that his father and he have used during their thirty-year race career. So, our little inside joke is wondering which one of us will finish ahead of the other. We have an ice cream bet, with the last person to cross the finish line buying the ice cream.

Rick and I laugh a lot together. I think he talks way too much, even more than me. I tell him stories about things my six children do, and then he tells tales of things his brothers and he would do to his parents. Sometimes we even argue. He has told me that he considers me a friend. I feel very honored when he says this. I told him the way we argue and laugh together that he is like a big brother to me. I may have not grown up with him, but I think his entire family has accepted my family as well. It's a blessing to be a part of the Hoyt family and to be a part of history as it unfolds.

Now that I've become familiar with Rick's daily routine, it's sort of interesting to be privy to a day in the life of this world-renowned athlete. I feel a little like a reporter for a supermarket tabloid by sharing Rick's secrets with the world, but he gave me permission to do so, so I don't feel quite as slimy.

A day in the life of Rick—when he is not participating in races—is quite regimented and follows roughly the same schedule each and every day with very little variation. When I arrive in the morning, I enter Rick's bedroom to get him out of bed. Rick sleeps in the nude, so I have to prepare myself for a glimpse of his backside each morning. He sleeps on his belly with a pillow under his legs for comfort.

When I wake him up, I carry him to the bathroom. He will sit on the toilet and pee, and then I lift him up and place him in the tub. I've already run the water to a comfortable temperature, which I test before placing him in the tub for a bath, hair wash, and the now well-documented shave. He brushes his teeth in the morning and at night—with the help of one of his PCAs of course—using a spin brush.

When he's done bathing, I lift him out of tub and carry him to his bedroom. I choose his pants and he chooses a shirt. I give him two options, and he will look towards the shirt he wants to wear that day.

Rick's diet is a bit unique, especially for a world-renowned athlete. He eats chocolate cake and ice cream for breakfast every single morning, and eats popsicles throughout the day. Though Rick has recently had a feeding tube inserted into his belly area, he only takes liquid and his crushed up meds through the feeding tube. Any consumption of alcohol goes through his mouth, as it would be very dangerous to feed him alcohol directly into his stomach.

Rick has what is known as a reverse tongue, which means it tries to push food up and out of his mouth as opposed to down into his digestive track. This makes feeding him a challenging adventure for both Rick and anyone in the immediate vicinity. Rick wears what we call a chuck under his chin to prevent food from getting on his clothing, but he often coughs and chokes a bit while eating, so we tease him that we need to take cover if we see a cough coming.

He eats dinner at six each night, which is often something like poached fish and mashed potatoes, lasagna or Salisbury steak. All his food needs to go through the blender to puree it. Even when Rick and the family go to Legal Seafood, which they traditionally do on the eve of the Boston Marathon, and Rick orders a lobster, the kitchen is kind enough to puree it so that Rick can take it by spoon.

When Rick doesn't have an appointment to tend to outside of his apartment, he sits in his red recliner most of the day and watches TV. He and I will often leave the apartment to go to Friendly's or Howard's Drive-In in neighboring West Brookfield, Massachusetts. He also likes to do his own grocery shopping with his PCA.

I have frequently been advised that Rick doesn't know much about being "worldly." I didn't understand what that meant at first, so when I heard it again, I had to ask. I was told that he doesn't know anything about bills, money, finances, current events, and things like that. I discovered that this is because other people have always handled these things for him. So now, when the mail arrives, I open up his bills and show him what his payout is. I talk to him about things he asks people to buy, when many times he doesn't need the items. We talk about what is going on in the news. I read the paper to him just so he will know what is going on locally.

I was also told that Rick has "no control" of his body from the neck down. Boy, is that a lie. He knows exactly when he hits me, and though he claims he does it accidently, I know he absolutely does it on purpose. These are not spazzes, as he calls them; he knows when he hits me. He sometimes tries to aim his hits and has actually left scratches on me. When taking a picture with my little one, Rick was adorable. He moved his arm downward and tried to put his arm around her to pose as if he were holding her.

When I was initially asked to contribute to Rick's book, the first thing I thought was, "Oh, my goodness. Why?" I asked Rick if it was a mandatory part of my job as his PCA, as I wasn't sure if I would have the time needed to give the assignment it's just due. As I expected, he didn't let me off the hook. He said those often heard three words that dominate the Hoyt vocabulary. "Yes, You Can." All I could do was laugh and agree to make the time necessary to do this for Rick.

Writing this book with Rick has been an honor for me. He trusts me in everything he tells me. I was shocked by some responses, cried at others, and laughed at so many. Thank you, Rick, for sharing your thoughts and words and trusting in me to help you with this book. It was a long journey for the both of us and we both know it was told "one letter at a time."

Every Journey Begins with a Single Step

by Rick Hoyt with Todd Civin

"Fate, Chance, God's Will—we all try to account for our lives somehow. What are the chances that two raindrops, flung from the heavens, will merge on a windowpane? Gotta be fate."

—Robert Brault

Most of my middle school friends went to North Middle School for sixth grade, but because of the section of town I lived in, I went to South Middle. Even though I was disappointed that my friends went to a different school than I did, things sometimes have a way of working out. Earlier in this book, I wrote about the "what ifs" in life. What if I were born without a disability? What if my parents had decided to put me in a home? What if they had made the choice to shelter me and treat me like many disabled people are treated? As I said earlier, we can't spend our lives dwelling on the "what ifs." We have to accept life as it comes and simply hope that things happen as part of a grand scheme. With that being understood, one of the biggest "what ifs" I could ever imagine is, "What if I had attended North Middle instead of South Middle?" It was while attending South Middle that I met Mr. Sartori. He was the

Phys Ed teacher at the school and ultimately the man who changed the course of my own personal history.

Mr. Sartori was very tough on the outside and demanded the attention of those who participated in his gym class. On the inside, however, he was one of the nicest, kindest human beings I have ever met. He used his whistle throughout gym class, reminding me of the typical gym teacher like you'd see in the movies. He had a military background, which is where he learned his strict methods. We all had to show up on time, wearing our gym outfits, and every child had to take gym class. When the school bell sounded, "Coach" accepted no excuses from anyone for not taking the class.

When I saw Phys Ed on my schedule the first week of school, I thought that I'd be excused from attending class, since it was a physical class that required physical movement. I would have enjoyed going to PE, as I really liked playing and watching hockey, and I loved to go to all of my brother's games. I also loved to swim at cerebral palsy classes. But when it came time for gym class, I had my aide wheel me to the library to get caught up on my studies or to get a jump on my homework. That was, until Coach Sartori realized that this "Richard Hoyt, Jr." kid didn't attend his class. Coach called my mom and dad to let them know I had skipped his class. He had no idea I was disabled. Coach spoke to Mom on the phone, who advised him that I was disabled and lucky to have been admitted to school, let alone participate in his gym classes. Coach told Mom that she had two choices—either I participate in his classes or she would have to come and participate for me. Though in some ways I would have enjoyed seeing Mom do push-ups or play dodge ball with the rest of my class, Mom was thrilled that Mr. Sartori wanted to include me.

And once I started attending the class, he really made me work. He had me participate by doing exercises with my arms. While the rest of the class played basketball, dodgeball, and floor hockey, there I sat on the side lines doing exercises. It wasn't much, but at least I was participating. Coach also developed activities designed especially for me, and it really made me feel special. Dad says that I would come home from school, and all I wanted to talk about on my computer was gym class. Coach had really tapped into something that interested me, and after years of sitting on the sidelines, it was great to be involved in the games.

Mr. Sartori really seemed to like me, and though he made me work, he treated me like I was not only able-bodied, but like one of his friends. When I was about fifteen, Coach invited me to watch a college basketball game at Westfield State College. In addition to being our gym teacher at South Middle, he also coached men's hoop at Westfield State. Not that I would have let them tell me no, but I was so excited when Mom and Dad allowed me to go to the game. Dad joked that it was probably more to see the cheerleaders than to watch basketball, but I was excited to go to a game—and more importantly, to be included. As I said earlier, "what if" I had never attended that game?

I went to the game that night in Mr. Sartori's van and had a great time. I was introduced to some of the Westfield players, and even better, to some of the cheerleaders. I don't really remember who won, and as history will tell, that wasn't the most important part of the evening. What I do remember and will never forget is that at half time, one of the cheerleaders announced something about a charity road race that was being held to benefit a kid named Doogie, who had been paralyzed during a lacrosse game on May 7, 1970. Doogie, whose real name was Jimmy Banacos, was a star lacrosse player and track star at Westfield. The benefit was to raise funds for his medical bills. I went home that night and talked to my dad about this student and that I felt there was something I had to do. I wanted to show this person that life goes on and he could still lead a productive life despite finding himself disabled. That is why I turned to my dad and said that we have to run in this race. Dad agreed, and we ran in our first race.

We arrived at Westfield State that day and I was so excited. At that point, I had no idea that this would be the first of over one thousand races that Dad and I would do together. Up to this point, we were Dick and Rick Hoyt, but in a way this was the birth of Team Hoyt, as we have come to be known.

I wore a red sweat suit to the race that day with a matching red jacket and sweat pants, and had a blanket wrapped around me to stay warm on this fall New England day. My outfit was not nearly as stylish as the red, white, and blue Team Hoyt shirts that we run with today. Dad wore a white tank top and basketball sneakers, as he wasn't really a runner and didn't have a pair of running shoes in his closet. Coach Sartori used his clout to get us the number 00, which Dad taped to my wheelchair instead of pinning to his shirt, so that those watching the race would know we were a team.

These were the days before running chairs like you see so often today, so we were ready to race in my Mulholland wheelchair, which was more like a shopping cart with a seat. Though it was form-fitted and prescribed for my body shape, it was not the sleek racing chair that we run with these days. Dad has often said that if he had patented the running chair that would later be built for me, we would be wealthy men today, due to the popularity of running chairs and baby joggers.

The race was five miles long. My entire family was there to root us on. They didn't think that Dad and I would run the whole race, assuming we would make it to the corner and turn around. Apparently, they underestimated what Dad and I are able of doing when we put our minds to something. As we still say today, there is no word "can't" in the Hoyt vocabulary.

Well, as history goes, we didn't turn around at the corner and we did, in fact, finish the race, not last, but next to last. The chair didn't perform very well since it wasn't designed for running and kept pulling badly to the side. Dad had to keep straightening it out to keep us from going off the road. He said that he felt like he used muscles he didn't even know he had and actually had blood in his urine once the race ended and we got home. Dad said he was actually disabled himself for two weeks after that. I, however, loved it, and when I got home that night I typed on my computer the words, "Dad, when I'm running I feel like my disability disappears." I remember Dad crying as he read that. He asks the audience in his speeches these days to think what a powerful message that is to a parent of a disabled child. "When I'm running I feel like my disability disappears."

Now, thirty five years and almost 1100 races later, Dad and I have come a long way thanks to Coach Sartori and the fact that I attended South instead of North Middle School. "What if?"

When I run, it means I feel free from my disabilities. Running gives me the feeling of equality with all the other runners. My message to other people with disabilities is that you can do anything you want as long as you set your mind to it. Look at me, as an example. I am a high school graduate. I have a bachelor's degree in special education. I live independently in my own apartment. I have run a thousand races including thirty Boston Marathons, have been inducted into the Iron Man Hall of Fame, and have traveled to places around the world and met people of world acclaim. All because I put my mind to my goals and refuse to quit until they are achieved. Unlike marathon running, winning isn't determined by how long it takes to get to the finish. It is determined by your will to keep running. And though my message is a motivator to disabled people, it also holds true for anyone who questions their ability to succeed. We receive letters and emails on a daily basis from people facing all sorts of challenges thanking us for giving them the strength to press on. Simply by refusing to give up no matter how impossible the situation may seem. If I can do it, so can you.

Without racing, I am guessing I would have probably continued my education; maybe even gone as far as to earn my master's degree in special education. But racing has enhanced the quality of my life in many ways. Without it, I might have missed out on many of the experiences I've had, like going to many parts of the world like Hawaii,

Japan, Germany, and El Salvador, and seeing our country inch by inch in the "Trek Across America." But racing isn't what gives me my will to live. Meeting people in general is what gives me the will to live. I am a people person.

As I look back on the fact that Dad and I have competed in thirty Boston Marathons, the word that comes to mind to describe this is honored. To be mentioned in the same breath as the names Johnny Kelley, Uta Pippig, Joan Benoit Samuelson, and Bill Rodgers feels the same as when a baseball player is mentioned in the same breath as Babe Ruth and Cy Young. I think back and realize how honored I am, especially considering they didn't even want to allow us in to the race at the beginning. Dad had to fight to allow as to be included in our first several races, as people looked at us like we were freaks and thought Dad was exploiting me for his own fame and notoriety. We had to run the first couple Boston Marathons without numbers because they wouldn't let us enter as official entrants. Sometimes, runners jump into the race without either numbers or permission and they are known as bandits. Officials usually remove them from the course, since the BAA didn't approve of their involvement We were not bandits, however, as we ran with the blessing of the BAA. Dad and I did not have bib numbers the first three years, but we were given permission to line up behind the wheelchair runners, and therefore we weren't worried about getting pulled from the marathon. So, although we did not have bib numbers, we were not bandits in 1981, 1982 or 1983.

The BAA even kept track of us on their results listing and gave us these unofficial results as part of a presentation during our 25th Boston Marathon festivities. The results of our first five years are as follows:

1981: 3:18:00 (unofficial)

1982: 2:59:00 (unofficial)

1983: 2:58:00 (unofficial)

1984: 2:50:05

1985: 3:01:20

Now, thirty years later, we are still at it. We were named Centennial Heroes during the 100th running of the race in 1996; are having a bronze statue erected along the race route; just had a portrait painted of us to raise funds for Easter Seals and the Hoyt Foundation; and are recognized and cheered for during all 26.2 miles of the most famous marathon in the world.

I love running the Boston Marathon for several reasons. For one, it is the first marathon we ever competed in, and having fought so hard to be accepted and now to have reached such a high level of acclaim, makes it very satisfying. Also, our family was born and raised in the towns surrounding Boston, so there is something special in having people cheer and holler for us in the same Boston accents that we grew up listening to. Though I obviously don't speak with a Boston accent, I guess I hear with one, so it feels like home when I hear the sounds of Natick and Framingham and Hopkinton and "Southie" as we run the 26.2 mile course. Like no other race we participate in, we are treated like rock stars, and although Dad and I will always remain humble, there is something really amazing when hundreds of people come up and want to take their picture with us, and thousands of people are screaming our name or yelling "Yes, You Can" as we run by.

After running our thirtieth Boston Marathon this past Patriot's Day, I spent some time thinking about accomplishing such a feat and about my favorite parts of the Boston Marathon. I am grateful we have been able to compete in the event so many times and am so thankful for our principal sponsor, John Hancock, for treating us like royalty.

I wasn't sure if we would attain this milestone, since a few years ago Dad had a heart attack. I was concerned about his health and wondered if he would be able to continue. The fact that he was able to recover and wanted to keep running makes me enjoy each step and each event that much more.

These days we participate in the event with a team of runners from all over the country and other parts of the world, who not only run with us but raise hundreds of thousands of dollars for the Hoyt Foundation. These men and women range in age from early twenties to over sixty and are known as The Hoyt Foundation Boston Marathon Team. This past year, our thirtieth, we were given thirty bib numbers for the team, thanks to our primary sponsor, John Hancock. We also were joined by about a dozen qualified runners. Together, the team collected over $220,000 in donations for the Foundation in 2012. This money is used to help many charities that assist disabled people. We are coached each year by three-time Boston Marathon Woman's Champion, Uta Pippig, who not only helps train the runners via email tips, but also gives the team incredible advice and support through individual phone calls to the team's runners. Uta also joins us at our Saturday night Pasta Dinner and on the bus ride that we take from our hotel to the starting line on Marathon morning. Her participation is one of the highlights of the team's marathon weekend. The Pasta Dinner is a fun event because the runners on the team swap t-shirts with one another from previous races they have run. It is a great gesture that allows them to share their previous running experiences. They pass off the T-shirt and share a brief story about how they earned it and why it is special to them. Then in the spirit of giving, they pay it forward to someone else. There's always so much to do and so much going on during the dinner that I don't have time to eat while I am there, but in many ways the event is more about the team spirit and less about the pasta.

This past year was one of the highlights of our thirty-year running career. Though the event occurred in mid-April, the temperature hit nearly ninety degrees. All the runners were encouraged to take it more slowly than normal. Though Dad and I have slowed over the years as we've aged a bit, we took it even more slowly than normal and finished in just over seven hours. The highlight, however, occurred as we approached the finish line. Many of our runners forgot about their own personal times and slowed to run with Dad and me. We were all dressed in our red and white Team Hoyt shirts, with our motto "Yes, You Can" silk-screened on the back. The runners were there for one another and they encouraged and motivated each other to reach the finish line. All the runners seemed to work as an incredible team. The whole is greater than the sum of its parts.

Though one would think that my favorite part of the Boston Marathon is the finish line, I have to admit that I love running through Wellesley College. Wellesley College is an all-girls school located just after the twelve-mile mark of the race. The thing that is amazing is that you can hear the cheers from the Wellesley girls just after the eleven-mile mark. The girls line the streets with signs and balloons for about a quarter-mile and form what they call the scream tunnel. It is so loud, so ear-piercing, and so motivating that Dad runs through there so fast I don't think his feet touch the ground. You can see all the male runners puff out their chests and peacock a bit as they run through the scream tunnel. I sit and wave my arms and smile to see everyone cheering others on. I can't tell if they are cheering for Dad and me or for the other runners. I look around, take it all in and see the signs that are held up. Some say "Yes, You Can" while others say "Go, Team Hoyt."

Dad and I are also grateful and thankful for the support and friendship we've built over the years with Dave McGillivray, the race director of the Boston Marathon. Dave was instrumental in getting Dad and I interested in competing in triathlons from the start and over the years he has been one of our biggest supporters and fans.

We originally met Dave at the Falmouth Road Race, which is another one of our favorites. Falmouth is 7.1 miles long and is run each August. When we met Dave, he came up to Dad and asked if he had ever considered competing in triathlons. Dad didn't know how to swim at the time and hadn't been on a bike since he was six years old, but Dad is always up for adventure. Rather than declining the invitation due to the fact that he was deficient in two-thirds of the requirements, Dad said he would consider it, but only if he could compete with me. Dave took one look at me, turned, and walked away. I tend to think I intimidated him, being the chiseled specimen that I am. The next year at Falmouth, Dave approached Dad again and commented that he looked like he was in even better shape this year and had he given it any further thought? Dad responded the same way as the previous year—only if he could do it with me. This time Dave said, "Why don't you see what type of equipment you can get built?" That was all Dad needed to hear.

I had been after Dad the whole year after we first met Dave to do this, so I was spazzing with excitement once Dad agreed. I knew he couldn't swim or bike, but that was for him to figure out. Dad was in the process of being transferred from Westfield, Massachusetts, to Wellesley, so Mom and Dad were looking for a home halfway between, because Mom still had commitments in the western part of the state. So, as they searched for a new place to live, he and Mom decided on a house on Hamilton Reservoir in Holland, Massachusetts. Not only was the house great, but it had a built-in pool of sorts where Dad could learn to swim and train. Only my Dad goes to such extremes; he needed to learn to swim, so he bought a lake.

Following his first dive into Hamilton Reservoir—in which he sunk right to the bottom—Dad eventually learned to swim well enough to compete, though Russ and Rob still think he is more of an anchor than a propeller. The boat that Dad pulls me in and often accuses me of sleeping in is a nine-foot Boston Whaler—an inflatable dingy with a wooden bottom that provides me stability during the somewhat violent ocean swims. I sit in a beanbag chair, which molds nicely to the shape of my body and allows me to remain comfortable. Dad tows me using a parachute strapping with a tether that he got from the supply officer at the base. As I said, Dad accuses me of sleeping, but anyone who has seen how much he splashes when he kicks would understand that sleeping would not be humanly possible. I end up almost as wet as Dad does by the end of a swim.

After about nine months of training, we competed in the Bay State Triathlon, which is the event that Dave organizes. It was held on Spot

Pond in Medford, Massachusetts, on, appropriately enough, Father's Day in 1985. Dad had finally conquered the logistics associated with swimming while pulling his kid, of biking with me in tow, and, of course, of running while pushing me, as he always had. Since the Hoyts rarely do things the easy way, we had entered a competition as first time triathletes that consisted of a one-mile swim, a forty-mile bike ride, and a ten-mile run. Most first-timers choose to participate in a sprint triathlon, which is made up of lengths of about a third of a mile swim, a nine-to-twelve mile bike ride, and a 5k race. Need I say "Yes, You Can"? From that point on, Team Hoyt was hooked on Tri and we officially referred to ourselves as "Triathlon Freaks." We couldn't get enough.

We have competed in the Ironman in Kona eight times with mixed results. The first time we competed was in 1988. I had a mix of emotions throughout the day, ranging from sheer excitement to total fear. We didn't complete the race that year, since we had trouble during the swimming portion, so a year later it felt great to make the final turn down Ali'i Drive as we made our way to the finish line. At first the cheers seemed barely audible, but as we drew closer to the finish, the crowd was deafening; nothing ever sounded so sweet. When we crossed the finish line, I was blinded by the lights and truly overwhelmed and scared, but when I realized we had finished, I felt fantastic having achieved the goal of a lifetime.

When Dad and I ran the Iron Man in Kona in 1999, the brakes on our bike froze. I think somehow the foot rest of my chair pressed into the brakes, causing them to lock up. Despite this, we didn't quit. We finished; to me, finishing is so important. It is a representation of my life. Mom and Dad could have quit when I was born, but they didn't. They could have given up trying to help me learn to communicate or trying to get me into public school. They chose to continue, and because of that, I've had one heck of a ride. We never fail in our athletic competitions despite the fact that we have gotten lost during races and even finished with flat tires. We still continued and still finished the race.

Dad and I are not quitters.

It feels great to me when people tell Dad and me that we are inspirations, especially when we are struggling and they pat us on the back and say things like, "It is because of you two that I compete in triathlons" or "God bless the two of you." How can either of us even consider not completing a race or a triathlon or call a close to our career when we carry the hope and faith and motivation of other runners who look up to us as inspiration?

Competing in the Iron Man was an incredible experience. When I am competing, it feels like I am equal to any of my fellow competitors. I still swim the whole 2.4 miles, I still bike the entire 112 miles, and I still run every step of the 26.2 miles. By competing with my father, I send the message that everyone can set a goal and they can reach it, as long as they never give up.

In 2008, Dad and I were inducted into the Ironman Hall of Fame. I was inducted as the twenty-sixth member and Dad just behind me as the twenty-seventh, because, as you know, I always finish just ahead of Dad. Competing in the Ironman and ultimately being selected with my dad for induction into the Ironman Hall of Fame has given me several tremendous opportunities. First, as a man with disabilities, it has given me the chance to compete in one of the world's truly special sporting events. Second, allowing me to compete, led to the establishment of the physically challenged division. Third, it gave me the stage to show all types of different people that they can set, strive for and achieve their goals. And finally, I got to go to my favorite place on earth eight times.

Over the past few years, our times have slowed. We are no longer able to run Boston in under three hours or even four or five. We continue to do our best, though, and we are still not finishing last. Every year there seems to be something that may affect us, but that is life. We trained very well for this year's marathon. However, the heat got to us and many of the runners. Many runners finish with times that weren't their best.

But at this stage of our career, it is no longer about the fastest times. We have proven over the past thirty years that we have been capable of extraordinary times. With Dad's strength and endurance and my heart and enthusiasm, we have been able to accomplish amazing things, but now continuing to compete may be amazing enough. As I've said to Dad so many times, if we could only compete in one event per year it would be Boston.

I'm not ready to throw in the towel, and I pray to God every day that Dad is not ready either. I have never felt like I've had enough racing; stopping now is not an option. When we do stop, it will be a huge void because it will mean that maybe Dad passed away. It will be the saddest time of my life. I hate to think about that. I know it will happen, but I choose not to think about it. I could never replace my dad, but I would very much enjoy it if one of my nephews or even a friend pushed me in a race once in a while. It would be a way that the memory of Team Hoyt would be able to live on a bit longer.

I don't plan on ever having enough. First of all, competing makes me feel free from having a disability, and second, I love the spotlight. Birds are free to fly anywhere they want at any time, which is how I feel when we race. I do sometimes get scared because of Dad's health and wonder how much longer he can do this with me, but as long as we both want to continue and are able to do so, we will continue to compete in our favorite race. It takes us longer to finish than it once did, but that just gives me more time to wave to the fans as we run by.

I hope "Team Hoyt" will still be going strong in some way in the future. I know that after my father passes things may change. However, I would like to still be active in the Boston Marathon and in other races. If someone is willing to push, paddle, and pedal me, I'd like to compete in triathlons and Ironman for the next thirty years. How awesome would it be for me to finish a triathlon at the age of eighty? This would depend on who is willing and able to do the bike, swim, and run. And it isn't easy. My dad has often had people mention to him that they can do this when he is ready to hang it up. I just don't think they realize how hard it is to carry me and push me and swim with me. My dad makes it look easy. It's not, and I know this.

So to Coach Sartori—thanks for making me go to gym class. You launched one heck of a career for me.

She Saw It in His Eyes

by Todd Civin with Fay Kimball

> *"Courage is not the absence of fear, but rather the judgment that something else is more important than fear."*
>
> —Ambrose Redmoon

There are certain people we come across who cast an indelible print on life as we know it. Whether through their actions or their efforts and spirit, we exit our relationship with them knowing we are better off having met them. Those people may be few and far between, and oftentimes at the point of the interaction, we are not even conscious of the effect they are having on us.

A bit like a sculptor, they lightly press on a section of the clay that impacts the overall finished piece, but that slight impression helps to turn the lump of clay from an average piece of art into a masterpiece.

Amongst the thousands of questions that I asked Rick while working on his book, the one I asked him was, "Who, aside from your family, would you consider to be the most influential person in your life?" Without hesitation, Rick responded, "Fay Kimball."

At the time, I had never heard him mention Fay, so I was quite surprised she would leapfrog over more frequently mentioned motivators in Rick's life. After getting to know a bit more about this incredible woman, it became increasingly evident why he holds his former occupational therapist in such high regard.

"Fay was my occupational therapist in Lawrence, Massachusetts, at the Cerebral Palsy Clinic," explained Rick, who visited the clinic five days a week, Monday through Friday, while he lived in the neighboring town of North Reading. "Without her, I wouldn't be able to talk to other people by using a computer or probably have the degree I have from college. I eventually may have had a communication device, but without Fay's efforts that may have come much later in life and would have changed things incredibly."

Rick and Fay began working together in 1973, when Rick was about eleven years old. At that point, he was able to communicate only through nods of his head and gestures that those close to him may have recognized. Neither the Russell Method nor Rick's TIC computer had yet been created, so Rick was at the mercy of the outside world to help him convey his thoughts and ideas.

"I would look forward to going to the clinic every day to spend time with Fay," Rick said. "She would work with me to determine what part of my body may be most useful in helping me find a way to communicate or to perform other daily functions on my own. She tried to put my arm in a sling to see if I was able to feed myself. I could not accomplish that task. She also tried to get me to hit a switch to be able to stop a light on a sentence that I wanted to say or ask. She even allowed my mom to participate in our therapy, since Mom had as much to gain as I did if I was able to do things on my own.

"She really loved my Mom, and I know it is because Fay noticed that Mom was always sacrificing for me and trying to get me the best care possible. Fay recognized that and respected my Mom for it."

Rick described his friend in the following way: "She was short, about five feet, and was very, very funny. She always knew what to say to break the ice and put a smile on someone's face. She was also very talkative and friendly. She had two daughters, neither with a disability, but seemed like she had been around disabled people all of her life. She had a way about her."

Rick felt he stood out amongst many of the clients at the CP clinic because of his ability to understand and his level of intelligence. "There were many different people there, but the main disabilities represented were CP and Muscular Dystrophy. I think I was different from many of those there because I knew what people around me were saying and I laughed at jokes. One kid had a very mean personality and would not cooperate in anything they did or offered. He was always very rude. I liked to cooperate when I could and tried to volunteer as much as I could. Fay would see that and gave me special attention because of that."

During their six-year relationship, there was one event that stood out in Rick's mind that had the most profound and lasting impact on his life. Without this effort, Rick thinks that much of what he accomplished in life would have never occurred or at a minimum would have been greatly delayed.

"Fay went to a conference to learn about communication devices and met Rick Foulds while in attendance. Rick was a student in the engineering department at Tufts University and together with a group of other engineers is responsible for developing my first computer. Without the TIC (Tufts Interactive Communicator), I would not have learned to communicate. Without Fay, I wouldn't have met Rick Foulds."

Though I knew it may be quite a challenge, I hoped to uncover the whereabouts of Rick's inspirational friend in hopes of hearing about the friendship from her vantage point. My concern was that she was now about seventy-nine years old and having not worked with Rick for nearly thirty years; it may be a bit of a challenge to find her whereabouts. But molding myself in the light and spirit of Team Hoyt, I decided YES, I CAN!

To my surprise, but really not at all, I read about Fay Kimball in the Lawrence Eagle Tribune regarding her work with another inspiration, Kevin Wreghitt. Like Rick, Kevin has cerebral palsy and worked with Fay to reach a similar level of success and achievement.

I caught up with the affable Ms. Kimball, who resides in Merrimac, Massachusetts, not far from the CP Clinic where she worked with Rick. She was shocked to hear from a friend of Rick's after such a long time, but admitted to continually following his exploits on the marathon and triathlon circuit. To no surprise, Fay is a card carrying member of the unofficial Rick Hoyt Mutual Admiration Society.

"I became quite close with Ricky and also with his Mom, Judy. She was quite a lady, and I really got to know her pretty well. That woman never stopped pushing to get Ricky everything that life owed to him." Fay still works in the OT field even at her advanced age. "I was his occupational therapist at the time. Judy used to bring him in with Rick's two brothers, Rob and Russell, and we would all work together."

Fay admitted to working with people of many different levels of disability and immediately noticed that Ricky possessed a high degree of intelligence and seemed to stand out amongst many of the patients at the clinic.

"I'd often work with other therapists—speech therapists and physical therapists—and I'd always say to them, 'Look at this kid's eyes. There is definitely something going on in there.'

"We had some pretty severely disabled kids at the clinic. You'd watch them and be able to immediately pick out which kids had intelligence because they would look at every move you made. That was Mr. Ricky. You'd say something funny and he'd laugh hysterically and wave his arms. And I'd say, 'Oh boy, this kid knows what is going on.'

"I mainly tried to see what he was capable of doing and what usable parts he might have that would help him function most easily. We tried to use eye tracking and eye exams that the optometrist would do, and, of course, I realized that with Rick's spasticity, the hope of using his eyes to operate his computer wasn't really an option. I learned that his legs were the most usable."

Fay continued, remembering the story of her relationship with "Mr. Ricky" in much the same way that "Mr. Ricky" did. She shared an interesting anecdote about the steps that led to her discovery of Rick Foulds and the birth of the TIC.

"I knew him long before he had his computer, which he uses to speak. Western Electric was near where we used to work in North Andover, and some of the engineers seemed interested in the clinic. They would come over and do things for us. Well, they had the idea with Ricky in mind, that maybe if he had this communication device he could learn the alphabet and how to spell and vocalize. They built this thing and it was huge, believe me, and it had these lights that would sequence to different letters. Being his occupational therapist, I had to figure out what was his most controllable body part, as this would help him learn to operate the machine. This was way before they had the sophisticated devices they have now, like the eye switches and head switches.

"Well, Western Electric built this humongous wooden thing that had lights that would flash when we turned it on and were connected up to a switch. We thought Ricky might be able to activate the switch with his right knee. So a friend of mine who was a machinist, built a switch that we could attach to the tray of Ricky's wheelchair. We tried that, and sure enough, it worked.

"So we'd show Ricky the letter A with this series of cards, and before long Ricky learned the alphabet," she continued, all the while exhibiting the passion and enthusiasm in her voice that made Rick admire her to the degree that he does. "Well, a physical therapist who was there at the time, Marilyn Burns, worked with him. She and I heard about this meeting in Boston where a grad student, Rick Foulds from Tufts, who was a member of the engineering department, was working to develop a device that would help people communicate. Marilyn and I went to the meeting and spoke to him and his team and got them interested in

Ricky. They came out and worked with him and made this box, which was the size of today's computer screens and was much smaller than the big archaic wooden thing that Western Electric made. We were able to clamp it to the table in front of him, and they got into the more sophisticated head switches like the one I hear he still uses today.

"I can't say I was responsible for Mr. Ricky's communication", she concluded. "But I guess I gave the process a push. Sort of like his dad does."

Rick's Western Harem

by Margot (Boucher) Kawecki
Rick's Former Tenant

> *"Disability is a matter of perception. If you can do just one thing well, you're needed by someone."*
>
> —*Martina Navratilova*

My dear friend, Sara (Young) Donaruma, and I were the first official members of Rick Hoyt's Western Massachusetts' *harem*. The definition of the word harem is a group of women associated in any way with one man. Rick's Western Mass Harem, as it was affectionately called, started when Rick was only thirteen years old, and this is where our story begins.

Rick's family had been living on the north shore of Boston until September of 1975. It was at that time Rick's dad, Dick, was transferred to Barnes Air National Guard Base in Westfield, Massachusetts. Their new home was on Llewellyn Drive approximately one mile from Westfield State College.

The home was a simple, yet lovely, ranch located on a wooded lot at the end of a cul-de-sac. It had three bedrooms plus a cute, two-room in-law apartment attached to the living space in the upper level. Prior to moving into their new home, Dick and Judy decided to list the apartment for rent at the college's student housing office.

Sara was living in central Massachusetts at the time and was a transfer student entering her junior year at Westfield State College. I was living in South Jersey, though not a "typical" Jersey girl. I was also a transfer student entering my junior year. At the beginning of August, before the start of the school year, I went to the college in search of two important items—one, an apartment, and two, a roommate. The hunt began.

I looked in the newspaper and checked with local real estate agents, but had no success. A friend of mine from New Jersey who was attending Springfield College, came up with me to help me in my search. She suggested I check with the college's housing office. As luck would have it, when I went through their database—which consisted of a three-ring binder, since these were the days before computers—I found my answers. The Hoyts had not only just listed their apartment, but Sara had also recently filled out the "In Search of a Roommate" form. A phone call was made between the two future roommates—no emails or Facebook, just luck and blind faith—and it was decided that we would be roommates. We looked at the apartment once The Hoyt's arrived in Westfield, which was about a week after the fall semester began.

The first Saturday in September, Sara and I arrived at the Hoyt's house for a tour and to see if this was the apartment for us, even though we had pretty much decided that it was even before we had seen the place. Upon our arrival, Judy answered the door and invited us in. The first thing we saw was Ricky lying on the floor in the foyer behind Judy. She quickly called for her other sons, Robbie and Russell, introduced us, and instructed the boys to bring Ricky downstairs. Robbie picked Ricky up, threw him over his shoulder like a sack of potatoes and ventured down to the basement area. Sara and I looked at each other in amazement, at which point Judy casually stated that Ricky had CP. Sara and I had never met anyone with cerebral palsy. Little did we know he would be the first of many special needs children that we would work with in the years to follow.

We continued with the tour of the house and the apartment. The apartment was located at the end of a long hallway, about twenty-five feet from the front entry. We walked down the hallway and passed a study and the master bedroom. The apartment had a good-sized kitchen/living room area and one very large bedroom furnished with twin beds. It was perfect! Sara and I moved in a few days later.

We arrived at our new pad early in the afternoon. The Hoyt's were ready and the boys were excited to be having "the girls" move in. The first evening, Judy and Dick invited us to have the first of many family meals, which were shared at their dining room table. Burgers on the grill and Judy famous broccoli and cheese casserole were the Hoyt's two favorite foods. It was at this table that a special bond was formed. On countless occasions, we would sit for hours eating, laughing, drinking and even, sometimes, crying.

Robbie and Russell would quickly eat their meals and rush outside to play, usually street hockey or football or some other sport. Ricky also loved to play street hockey in his wheelchair, unless, of course, he had the option of sitting at the table with the girls. We quickly learned that, even though Ricky had very little motor control of his body, his brain was perfectly normal—he was a very normal thirteen-year-old boy. We learned that he was smart, very funny with a great sense of humor, and tenacious. These attributes became evident on the morning of our first Saturday in the apartment.

Sara and I were your typical college students, studying, hanging out with our friends, and attending campus events and late night parties. We were rarely in the apartment during the week, except to sleep. Our Saturday mornings were for sleeping in, especially if we had been out the night before. This is when we learned how tenacious Ricky was.

That first Saturday morning around ten, Sara and I were awakened by a very loud banging at our door. When Sara answered the door, there was Ricky, by himself, lying on the ground near the door, laughing hysterically. We later found out that Judy had removed Ricky from his wheelchair and placed him on the floor at the end of the twenty-five-foot hallway that led to our apartment around nine. Ricky was determined to wake us up. For about an hour, Rick wiggled and squirmed down the hallway until he reached our door. We could hardly believe that he had made that entire journey—and so began Ricky's weekly ritual. We had made an agreement that he could spend time with us, provided he didn't arrive until noon. We enjoyed our special visitor every Saturday morning. Little did Ricky know that we could hear him coming down the hall long before he knocked at our door. This was a wonderful way to start a weekend.

Ricky reveled in playing practical jokes on us through the years. One of my all-time favorites was during Christmas break, when Sara and I returned home to visit our families. The college decided to lengthen our break by a few weeks because the school wanted to save money on heating oil due to the oil crisis of the early 1970s. This meant that we would be away from the Hoyt family for about five weeks instead of the expected three. Earlier in the fall, Rick had received the famous "TIC" machine from MIT. This machine allowed Rick to communicate for the first time through a computer program. Using a special pad, Rick could type out words with his head. The words were printed on a thin piece of paper, similar to a ticker tape. While I was away visiting my family in New Jersey, I received an envelope in the mail from Ricky. In the envelope was a very long piece of ticker tape that said, "You must return soon or your rent will be $1,000,000,000,000,000.00." I laughed so hard.

When I gave him swimming lessons, Ricky was always a prankster. Judy had been running an integrated swimming program for children with special needs on the North Shore for years. When the Hoyts moved to western Massachusetts, Judy decided to start a similar program at the indoor heated pool at Westfield High School.

Judy was great at organizing, and all she needed were a few volunteers to help her teach the kids. During one of our many dinner conversations, Judy learned that my summer job in New Jersey was as a lifeguard and swimming instructor in my town's pool program. I had been teaching for about three years. Judy explained her plans for the new swimming program and asked me if I would help teach. At that point, Rick started thrashing in his chair as if begging me to do it. As it turned out, not only did he want me to help, but he also wanted me to teach him. Nervously, I agreed. Mind you, I had no experience teaching swimming to special needs children, which was a whole different challenge than teaching able-bodied children.

My first objective for Ricky was to have him attempt to float on his back solo. This was quite challenging because of the tightness and spasticity of his limbs. When Rick and I first started, we had the help of another volunteer. One of us would support his head, while the other would complete range of motion exercises with his arms and legs, which would allow the muscles in his limbs to relax. As weeks went by, I was able to work with Rick one-on-one. I remember one lesson when Rick was extremely relaxed and we decided that he was ready. He would attempt to float alone without me supporting his head.

As I removed my hand, which was supporting his neck, I let him go. He floated! He was so excited that he started to thrash and, you guessed it, he sank, all the while with a huge smile on his face. Of course, he'd swallowed some water, so when I brought him to the surface, he coughed. This happened often, and then one evening he decided to play a trick on me. When it was his turn to float, he intentionally caused himself to sink. He opened his mouth wider than normal and swallowed a large amount of water. I quickly brought him to the surface and he coughed and coughed. Ricky made me extremely nervous. When I asked him why he did that, he just laughed. Then someone said, "Maybe he wants you to do mouth-to-mouth resuscitation on him." It was at that moment Ricky really laughed, and I realized that was his plan all along. My slightly angry, slightly amused response was "Nice try, Ricky, but please do not do that again."

Life with the Hoyt's was a very special gift for both Sara and me—one we will treasure for a lifetime. As time went by, our bond with the family became stronger. Our circle of friends at the college also grew, and so did Ricky's harem. Two friends of ours who became close with the Hoyts were Sue (Nyzio) Van Sweden, who now lives in California, and Laurie (Hansen) Ambrose, who lives in New Hampshire. Both of these ladies were quickly recruited, drafted and volunteered for many events. Both of them would work with Ricky as a tutor after school. Sue recently shared a story with me about her experience when she tutored Ricky after the Hoyt's move from their house on Llewellyn Drive to the Shaker Heights section of Westfield. Sue would arrive at the Hoyt's house in time to meet Ricky's bus. Before Sue and Ricky started to hit the books, Ricky insisted on two things—to watch the sitcom *MASH* on TV and to have a snack. His favorite snack was Ring Dings. Ricky refused to do any work until both of his requests were met.

The four of us were also involved in "The Special Olympics," which Judy organized. We also worked at Kamp for Kids, an integrated summer program for children with special needs and "typical" children. This was also the brainchild of Judy.

Sara recently recalled a funny story about the first Special Olympics, which were held in Holyoke, Massachusetts. At that time there was a wonderfully funny sitcom called *Happy Days*, which starred Henry Winkler as "The Fonz." Ricky's favorite character was The Fonz because he was so cool. Rick thought it would be great if Henry Winkler could make a guest appearance at the Holyoke Special Olympics, so, using his TIC machine, he decided to write a letter to The Fonz inviting him to the event. It must have been an amazing letter, because Henry Winkler agreed to come. Ricky taught us again that anything is possible. You just have to try.

The Special Olympics took place on a very rainy Saturday. Because of the typhoon-like weather, the events were moved indoors to the Holyoke High School gym. It had been arranged that Sara and Laurie would meet "The Fonz" on Route 91 in Holyoke and escort him to the event. Sara and Laurie borrowed Dick and Judy's car and drove to the predetermined location, the shoulder of the road prior to Exit 16 of Route 91 southbound. It was pouring rain while they sat on the side of the road. As a precautionary measure, Laurie had the flashers going, plus the wipers, but not the engine. The ladies sat there waiting for quite a long time, until his large black limousine pulled up behind them. Once the limo stopped, the girls jumped out of their car, ran over to the limo and forcefully opened the passenger side door hitting the guardrail. They were very excited to be meeting The Fonz. The girls instructed the driver to follow them. When they returned to their car, they attempted to start it, but the car battery had died. The girls then ran back to the limo and explained what had occurred. The Fonz, being the cool guy he was, invited them to join him in the limo and drive with him to the high school. The girls, who were dripping wet, took their place in the limo. Sara and Laurie were so embarrassed, yet so excited. Not only were they with Henry Winkler, but also they were riding in a limo for the very first time. The limo finally arrived at the event. The athletes and spectators were overjoyed to meet The Fonz, especially Ricky. Sara and Laurie shared the car fiasco with the Hoyts, and everyone roared with laughter.

Life with the Hoyts was always an adventure. We graduated from Westfield State in 1977 and worked that summer as counselors at Kamp for Kids. Once summer was over, we entered the real world, while Sue and Laurie were still finishing up their senior year. As time passed, the Hoyt family eventually moved from Westfield to Holland, Massachusetts.

The Hoyts bought a house on a lake so Dick and Rick could train for triathlons. We were amazed by their determination. When we first met the Hoyts, Dick was not a runner. It was not long after Dick and Ricky's first race in Westfield, which was a fundraiser held for an injured athlete, that Ricky declared that one day he wanted to participate in the Boston Marathon. Never say that the Hoyts are not determined. They have now run in the famous marathon thirty times. I remember a story they shared with us after one of their earlier Boston marathons. During the marathon, Ricky's wheelchair got a flat tire. Did that stop them? No, they continued. Ricky with his sense of humor, decided to make the best of it. As Bill Rodgers, the famous runner from Boston ran by them, Ricky put out his thumb as if he was hitch-hiking. This made Dick laugh and gave him the strength to continue and finish.

With each race, Dick and Ricky and the Hoyts became more famous, yet they did not let their fame interfere with their humility and love for friends and family. One very special memory I will keep in my heart forever is the day of my wedding over twenty-six years ago. Not only did I marry my best friend, but we also shared that day with our family and special friends. Of course, the entire Hoyt family was invited because they too were family. My husband, Paul, and I were married in the small town of Peterborough, New Hampshire. My parents had moved there after twenty-five years in New Jersey. The wedding took place in September of 1985. During the portion of the ceremony where it was customary to shake hands with your neighbors, Paul and I also shook the hands of our bridal party and our parents. The Hoyts were sitting in the pew behind my family, and Ricky's wheelchair was in the aisle. As I went to kiss Ricky on the cheek, I was shocked at what I saw. His cheeks and forehead had major scrapes and were bleeding, yet he was still smiling. After the ceremony, we had learned that Ricky was so excited to be at the wedding that when Dick opened the van door, Ricky fell, face first, onto the blacktop of the parking lot. People suggested that he be taken to the hospital to get checked out. Not Ricky. He was not going to miss this. Even after the church ceremony, Ricky would not go see a doctor. He went to the reception and partied into the evening. The funniest part of this story is that Dick and Ricky had their first of many major network interviews with Jim McKay on the *Wide World of Sports* in Boston the following day. Another testament to tenacity and determination at its finest.

The lives of Sara, Sue, and me, Ricky's original harem, have all taken different paths, but the common thread that we have woven throughout our life's blanket is a thread made of purest gold. That thread is the Hoyts. We know that no matter how long it has been or where we live, when we see the Hoyt family, it feels like going home again. We want to thank all the Hoyts for the wonderful memories. May God continue to allow you to touch the lives of others for many, many more years. We love you all!

Extraordinary People

by Barry Nolan
Multi-Emmy Award-Winning Broadcast Journalist

> *"It is a waste of time to be angry about my disability. One has to get on with life and I haven't done badly. People won't have time for you if you are always angry or complaining."*
>
> —Stephen Hawking

It was the year 1981, back before the 500-channel TV universe of today, and *Evening Magazine* was a part of many people's daily lives. The show was a warm-hearted, good-natured, family-oriented magazine show with a little bit of something in it for everyone, from adventurous outings to cooking and health tips, to just plain interesting people. People watched it over dinner together, which sure sounds old-fashioned nowadays. I co-hosted the show along with Sara Edwards.

That winter, to give the show a little ratings boost, the station ran a contest called "Extraordinary People." Anyone and everyone in the audience were invited to let us know about extraordinary people they knew about in their communities. We would pick some of the most interesting and produce short profile stories. Then the audience would vote for a winner. We would then do a whole special about all the

"Extraordinary People" winners. It was sort of an early version of American Idol, only it wasn't about singing, it was about being. All the nominees were terrific people. One of our winners, for instance, started a program to bring Tibetan Sherpas to America to give them EMT training on the theory they could then go back home to Tibet and save lives both in their village and on the slopes of Everest. They were all good people. But Dick and Rick Hoyt really stood out, before we even met them.

I wish I could remember the name of the person who told us about the Hoyts. I would like to tell them how much I appreciate what they did. The audience overwhelmingly picked them as the winners, and I was sent, along with my producer, Janet Krause, and a crew to Albany, New York, where we would tape them running in an eighteen-mile race they hoped would help them gain entry into the Boston Marathon.

Of everything I remember about that long ago race, two things really stood out, for some reason. One was Ricky's sense of humor. Here's this guy who is about as disabled as you can be, and he has this wicked sense of humor. He loves to kid and be kidded back. The other thing was one of those small but telling encounters that for some reason just stays with you. There was this young kid who came up to Ricky and his mom after the race. He was curious about Ricky, who was still excited about finishing the race in good time—with a TV crew there to capture it all. Standing there by the side of Ricky's wheelchair, the kid looked at Ricky, who was laughing and drooling a bit. He looked at the racing chair and at the TV camera, and then he looked right past Ricky, almost as if he wasn't there, and made eye contact with Judy. The kid began asking questions about Rick. "Can he talk?" "No, but he can communicate with some help. You just have to be patient." "Can he get out of that chair?" "No, not by himself." "Did he understand what was going on?" "Oh, yes, really, he's just as smart as you or me. You can ask him questions if you want."

The kid gave a brief, curious, but slightly uncomfortable look as

Rick grinned wildly and tried his best to nod his head yes, his arms flailing. Rick made a slightly strangled sounding noise that was his way of saying, "Ready to talk. Fire away." The kid looked confused for a second, and then turned and left without saying a thing.

I asked Judy about what had just happened. "Does it bother you when someone like that, however well-meaning they may be, comes up and sort of treats Ricky like he's not here or he's just a vegetable?" Judy smiled and just shook it off. She said, "No, because you see, that's their handicap, the fact that they can't see who Ricky really is. And we are here, in part, to get people to accept others as they are—so . . . ." She went on to explain that this is all a part of what they do. They get Ricky out in the world—not just to enrich Ricky's experience and change him, but to enrich the world's experience and change it as well.

And even writing this now, I look up above and notice . . . that I asked Judy first about this. I should have asked Ricky. I realize that now. Maybe I am even slower than that kid. But, this is how the Hoyts would change the world over the years. Slowly, softly, relentlessly, with one kind and courageous encounter at a time. I would see it happen again and again stretching out over thirty years. The cumulative effect that is hard to measure, but I believe it is enormous.

After the race, we went to their home to do interviews with the family and one of Ricky's friends. Over the next couple of days, we would go to school with Rick, look at old photos and go on family outings.

To tell you the truth, I have a pretty bad memory for some things; names, for instance. I'm awful. But I know I will never forget what I learned about the Hoyt family in those few days. There just wasn't an ounce of "quit" in them. When they were told, "There is no way you can take care of such a severely handicapped child at home," they basically just ignored that easy out. When they were told, "There is no way he could be mainstreamed into public education," they simply overcame all the resistance. When someone said, "If he gets his own electric wheelchair, he'll just have an accident with it and kill himself," they just laughed at it and, of course, got him an electric wheelchair. That was thirty years ago. This kid that doctors had said should just be warehoused like a can of vegetables has had a pretty remarkable life instead—and has left his mark on the world.

After a couple days with the family, we went back to Boston. Janet Kraus did all the hard work of writing an edit plan and working with an editor to put the story together for our "Extraordinary People" special. They also put together a "drop-in" story to use in our coverage of the Boston Marathon. Despite the fact that Dick and Ricky finished the Albany race with a good enough time for Dick to get an official number in the Boston Marathon, the Race Committee turned down their request for two official numbers. There were categories for people in wheelchairs and for able-bodied runners, but there wasn't a category for an able-bodied runner who pushes a guy in a wheelchair. So the Hoyts decided they would just have to be in a category of one and they were going to run anyway, as thousands do every year, as unofficial runners at the back of the pack.

This was before they had non-stop, wire to wire coverage of marathons with the help of motorcycle mounted cameras and microwave dishes linked up to a helicopter like they do now. Back then, there were long patches when you really didn't have any shots of the race leaders, just lots of unknown people running by in shorts. Without a few good "drop in" stories, it was a bit like watching traffic after a while.

I was stationed with my co-host, Sara Edwards, on the edge of the park in the center of Natick to cover the race. Natick is a town about ten miles from Hopkinton where the race starts. There was a huge cheer when the leaders come through, and it was all very exciting. Back then, in those no-live motorcycle shot days, it was just guys you didn't know, running by you on a road for a long time. But then, here come the Hoyts. The crowd didn't quite know what to make of them. It simply wasn't something they'd ever seen before. We were, after all, at the ten-mile mark in the race. Uncertain cheering started. And then it got big. And then it got wild.

After a breathless "live" intro about this "amazing father-son team," the edited drop-in piece aired. People at home were beginning to get misty. And then, back on the street, the Hoyts hit Wellesley, and the coeds, who line the streets, started to smile and point and cheer madly for this boy who's smiling like a crazy man, I think because he realized that at this moment, for the first time in his life, he was absolutely the hottest man in town. And he was waving his arms wildly in the wheelchair and his dad was pushing him down the main street through Wellesley.

Then twenty miles in to the twenty-six-mile race, they turned the corner past the Newton firehouse and faced the infamous challenge of Heartbreak Hill. So this crazy guy, who seemed too stocky to be a real runner and too old to be doing what he was doing, pushed his son up that killer hill. The crowd was thicker there and the boy was still grinning and drooling and making noise and waving his arms like he's directing traffic. And this crazy man and that wild strange boy in that wheelchair were huffing and straining up the famous heartbreaking, gut-wrenching, dream-ending hill and they were freaking passing people. And the people they were passing were shouting out words of encouragement to them. And then you get it—you understand how they do it—one of them pushes—and somehow—don't ask me how—the other one pulls.

And then they crossed one of the most famous finish lines in the world—the finish line of the Boston Marathon on Boylston Street. The people there were just amazed and people were cheering and crying and hugging the Hoyts. This crazy man and that wild boy, that remarkable team of two, had just run 26.2 miles straight into the hearts of Boston sports fans. Their names were suddenly written large and forever in the storied history of one of the greatest annual sporting events in the world.

If they had never done anything else but that, I think they would still have to be considered pretty amazing.

I think that one of the reasons I felt so amazed was that I had seen first-hand what the alternative could have been like for Rick.

When I was in graduate school, I took a part-time job as an aide at a psychiatric hospital in Knoxville, Tennessee. It was a large 2,000-bed institution on sprawling tree-shaded grounds. A few of the facilities were modern, but some of the red brick buildings were a hundred years old.

Back then, in the days before "de-institutionalization," lots of people were essentially warehoused. Eastern State was the kind of warehouse where Ricky could have ended up. People who couldn't communicate with the outside world, people who couldn't care for themselves, people who were viewed as vegetables were simply stored there until they died. Each day they were fed, bathed, and medicated. The best most of them could hope for was to be wheeled in to the dreary day-room and left there all day while soap operas and game shows played loudly on the TV. If Judy and Dick and the extended family had not seen that light in Rick's eyes, if they had not seen that someone was in there—someone quite remarkable—if they had not realized somehow what his potential was, I hate to think about what Rick's lot in life could have been. And if Ricky, with his amazing heart and his wicked sense of humor and his willingness to work hard and work long and keep going—if Ricky had not fought his way out to the light from day one—this would be a very different book—a very different story. One that would break your heart, not lift it.

I would work with Dick and Ricky to do television stories about their milestones many more times along the way. When Ricky graduated from Boston University, when they tried the Hawaiian Iron Man Triathlon for the first time, when they ran across the country beginning at the Santa Monica Pier, I would see people come up to them—come up to Rick. But now, unlike that timid boy back in Albany all those years ago who didn't know what to make of Rick, people now had read about them, seen them on TV, or heard about them from another runner, another athlete. They often came up just to say thank you.

In Hawaii, when they were on a training run across the hot lava flats, getting ready for the Ironman Triathlon, a woman in a station wagon zoomed past, realized who they were, pulled over, and walked back a ways in the direction of the Hoyts. She waited for the Hoyts to run up to her because she wanted to say thank you. Thanks for opening her eyes. She had a handicapped son like Rick. And it was seeing what the Hoyts could do together that changed the course of her life with her son. They ran, too. And they too were out there changing the world, one encounter at a time.

The Hoyts do that to people. I met a lovely woman just last year at a party for TV people thrown by my former TV co-host, Robin Young. And the woman I met at Robin's party told me about seeing the Hoyts on TV—and how her son, movie-star handsome, was profoundly intellectually handicapped, but the Hoyts had shown what was possible. The dad and the son ran together—the way the Hoyts did. That father and son got out in the world and they met people and they had challenges and had triumphs and tasted joy. The boy died not long ago. He died far too young, and that just broke his parents' hearts. But by God, he had lived. He had lived large, thanks to his loving, giving parents—but also, in part, thanks to the Hoyts.

If you work in TV long enough, you tend to meet some pretty interesting people, from movie stars to murderers. I have had the chance to meet the likes of George Clooney and OJ Simpson, Paris Hilton and Hillary Clinton. But if you get really lucky, you will also meet a few truly unforgettable and extraordinary people along the way who will leave such a powerful and lasting impression on you that just knowing them makes you a better person than you might have been otherwise—in ways you can barely begin to understand. People like Dick and Ricky Hoyt.

Choosing to Be a Terrier

by Rick Hoyt with Todd Civin

> "Parents rarely let go of their children, so children let go of them. They move on. They move away. The moments that used to define them—a mother's approval, a father's nod—are covered by moments of their own accomplishments. It is not until much later, as the skin sags and the heart weakens, that children understand; their stories, and all their accomplishments, sit atop the stories of their mothers and fathers, stones upon stones, beneath the waters of their lives."
>
> —Mitch Albom

When I look back at all the amazing accomplishments that Dad and I have been fortunate enough to achieve, it is mind-boggling. To think that I was supposed to be nothing more than a vegetable, and yet have competed in thirty Boston Marathons and over 1100 athletic competitions, been named with my father to the Iron Man Hall of Fame, have run across the country, traveled the world and met hundreds of incredibly famous people, really makes me feel both blessed and amazed. But take all of those accomplishments and stack them up, one on top of the other, and they don't make me feel nearly as proud as the fact that I graduated college from Boston University with my degree in Special Education. Imagine a non-verbal, spastic quadriplegic with cerebral palsy studying at the same university as Geena Davis, Tipper Gore, and even Leonard Nimoy and Rosie O'Donnell. All attended BU, though I did tease Rosie a bit when we appeared on her show for being a drop-out.

Both Dad and Mom had their own ideas on where I should attend college. Dad wanted me to go to Westfield State because we lived close by and I would still be able to live at home. Mom wanted me to go to the University of Massachusetts in Amherst due to the fact that she received her master's degree at UMass and knew a lot of the professors.

I think that part of the reason life has been so incredible for me is that I was very fortunate to be a part of a really caring, committed, loving family, where coming together through love and understanding was the foundation. It's probably pretty obvious that it has been a group effort with a lot of give and take and understanding. I am so grateful to my mom and my dad for making the decisions they made to fight in every way for my inclusion. They encouraged me to succeed no matter how high the mountain. So when it came time to make the decision as to where to attend, I listened to my parent's advice, but then had to make the decision on my own. I wanted to become a Terrier, and I am proud to be a graduate of Boston University.

My mind was set on going to the big city of Boston. In reflecting back, it was from all of the trips to Children's Hospital Boston and to Tufts University that made Boston such a warm and inviting place for me to go. Having now run thirty Boston Marathons, I think I know every house, every neighborhood, every street, even every pothole and pebble that dots the pavement from Hopkinton to the finish line. I knew Boston was not that far from home. There was a huge road block, however, due to the fact that the Boston Center for Independent Living stated that I was too communication-limited to attend BU without accommodations being made. I had to begin in the spring semester, as the school had to make concessions and adaptations for me to have a PCA in attendance to help me get around the campus. They then created a program, similar to an IEP, to help me to succeed and not to fail. I had a lot of emotions entering my only choice for a college. My emotions ranged from elated to worried, constantly wondering if I could really do this.

I also spent many sleepless nights wondering if the guys in college would mind that almost all of my PCAs were females. What if they were getting hit on and left me by myself? Would I be able to handle the work? How the heck was I going to handle money? What if I failed? The overriding feeling that I didn't want to live in Holland with Dad and Mom for the rest of my life kept pushing me towards my goal. To earn an education and to be able to live independently while doing it was a driving force for me.

From the minute I moved into the dorm at BU, I knew I had to make some adjustments. I lived on the same floor as the men's hockey team, who was a rowdy bunch, to say the least. All the members on the floor had been in school for a full semester prior to my arrival, since I started in the spring. It was bad enough showing up as an incredibly handsome spastic quadriplegic without having to deal with the new kid on the block syndrome. However, all of my new floor-mates graciously overlooked my obvious advantages over them and accepted me onto the floor.

On the first night, once my parents dropped me off, I remember being a little homesick. As luck would have it, the guys in the room next door were having a party and they invited both me and my PCA. After a few drinks, I felt better, and don't think I was homesick again during any of my next nine years of college. That night as the evening ended, I told my PCA that I was ready to go to my room, and I knew that I had made a good life decision.

My room was an average size with a mattress on the floor. I had a large safety switch for nights, since I would be alone. The switch, when activated, called a hospital and the campus police. My dorm room was a pretty typical single with lots of posters of hot women hanging on the walls. Just like today, my PCA never slept over. I went to bed at a certain time and I would let the PCA know what time I would have to get up.

Even today I have a calendar to show what my plans are for the week, and my PCAs are aware of when they need to come in early, especially for a race.

I think I blended in with the students who attended BU, and though I was disabled, I was only one of many disabled people who attended. The fact that I am disabled and attended college is not as unusual as being a non-verbal communicator who attended and graduated. BU is a very large college—you are not able to know everyone on campus. While attending school, I think some people knew of me, but I wasn't known as a famous person or a big man on campus. The campus is so large and people are caught up in their own challenges and issues to even be aware that I was an interesting person. I don't even consider myself to be a famous person now, let alone in 1985. Dad and I were really just beginning our racing career, and though some people knew that we competed in the Boston Marathon, we certainly weren't as popular as we are today. Remember, this was in the day before YouTube, Facebook and other social media, so though our story was told by those who knew us, it certainly wasn't as widely known as it is today.

I attended BU from 1985 to 1993, and though I joke in my speeches that it was because I was a bit of a party animal, the truth is my nine-year journey was pretty much by design. I would try to take two classes per semester according to my Individualized Education Plan. Sometimes I would continue during the summer months, as well. My course load consisted of all the math and English requirements, along with other classes needed to get a Special Education degree. I did not take any foreign languages, as it is challenging enough for me to spell and converse in English without trying to communicate in a foreign language too.

College was not easy for me. I wrote all my own papers and I took my own tests and final exams. I was given time to complete them according to my IEP. I used my computer to do oral presentations and to type and print my papers or exams. I was administered tests orally if they were multiple choice questions. The professor would ask me the questions and then give me the multiple answers, and I would be able to say what letter the answer was. I had my own personal note takers during lecture halls, which were provided through Boston University.

I graduated in 1993 with my degree of Special Education. I partied a bit too regularly in the beginning and had to get back on track with my studies. Like any college freshman, there were temptations at being out on my own for the first time, and even though I began college at the age of twenty-three and didn't graduate until I was thirty one, I needed to find the balance between work and play. I saw partying with the guys on my floor as a way to fit in, but I soon learned that if I participated too much I would never achieve my goal. Rick Hoyt, college graduate, sounds way better than Rick Hoyt, college drop-out due to one too many late night binges.

Back in my college days, Rum and Coke was my drink of choice. Today it all depends on my mood. I enjoy Sex on the Beach, Cape Codders, and Screw Drivers. I would mostly party in the dorms with my friends and would occasionally go to a club called Crossroads Irish Pub with the guys from the floor. Crossroads was located in the Back Bay of Boston near Fenway Park and, let me tell you, the place got rowdy. I did not participate in recreational drugs, but had a feeling that some smoke may have seeped in under my dorm room door on occasion, as some nights I felt a bit better than others.

My graduation day was amazing. I remember being totally unable to sleep the night before. I never doubted that I could accomplish this, but when faced with the realization that I had, I really couldn't believe it. If I had the ability to pinch myself, I probably would have, to convince myself that I wasn't dreaming. I dressed for graduation, wearing my crimson robe and white tassel, and was wheeled onto the field where graduation was held. We were broken up into individual schools and I, of course, was seated with the School of Education. Dad says it was one of his proudest moments as a father, which in turn makes it one of my proudest moments as a son. There were several newspapers there to cover the graduation, and several of them printed stories about my graduation from BU.

The ceremony was a lot like my high school graduation, but even bigger and more incredible. As my name was announced, the whole crowd stood, even before they finished announcing my name, and clapped and screamed for what seemed like ten minutes. I waved my arms and smiled uncontrollably. I was proud of myself, and I know my family was very happy that I graduated college, too. My diploma, which hangs proudly on my wall to this day, reads Richard Eugene Hoyt, Jr., Boston University Class of 1993, School of Education.

My brother, Rob, was quoted as saying, "I think Rick—a non-speaking quadriplegic person—graduating from a major university—it still blows my mind."

Though I graduated several years ago, I still have aspirations of using my college degree. I would love to adapt my knowledge and life experiences to teach Special Ed and to educate others on how to use the computer to communicate. I think I would be able to educate parents to learn that there are options when considering communication methods. How I am able to communicate is just one of many ways I can educate.

It took me a while, but I did it, and that is all that really matters; another lesson in life. Stay true to your dreams, never give up, and remember that in some races, the winner isn't determined by the time showing on the clock. Crossing the finish line, no matter what place you finish, is better than never choosing to lace up.

My hope is that by seeing what I can do and learning about my achievements, that all people—especially young people—will realize that I am just like them.

A Matter of Trust

by Julia Song

Rick's PCA, Boston University 1988-1992

> "People with disabilities have abilities too and this is what this course is all about, making sure that those abilities blossom and shine so that all the dreams you have can come true."
>
> —Mary McAleese

I saw Rick for the first time during my freshman year at Boston University. He was eating lunch with a PCA named Neeta. We were in Sleeper Hall, one of the three dormitories that make up the West Campus of BU. Claflin, Sleeper, and Rich Halls, where many athletes lived, were located near the football field, steps away from the athletic center. As soon as I noticed Rick, I sensed that the entire dining room was tense from struggling to act normal around this very unusual man. Neeta was feeding Rick his lunch. Rick was seated in his one of a kind wheelchair with a hospital style bed liner tucked under his chin. He needed this industrial sized bib to catch all the food and drink that he involuntarily spit out of his mouth as a result of his reverse tongue. I tried not to stare but was unsuccessful in my attempt. Neeta placed a spoonful of food in his mouth. Sometimes he would chew and swallow, and other times he would spit the food out. Rick took gulps of juice while Neeta held a hand towel under his chin. But you wouldn't have noticed any of this unless you watched for a long time. The thing that you could not help but notice was that his arms flailed uncontrollably and sometimes he shrieked. I was intrigued.

Weeks later I saw a flyer in an elevator in one of the engineering buildings. The ad read something like "disabled, non-verbal, quadriplegic student looking for personal care attendants…" Looking back on this, I realize what a testament this is to youth and innocence. Think about this: disabled, non-verbal, quadriplegic. Yet, I was unfazed. I ripped off one of the tabs with the contact information and called later that day. This must be the student I saw eating in Sleeper. I couldn't articulate what compelled me to answer this ad; I felt that it was something I could handle. The ad sounded upbeat and I wanted to make myself useful.

I went to meet Rick in his dorm room at Shelton Hall. Two older students met me in his room. I can't remember their names, but they were cute, bright, and cheery. There was no interview. No questions like, "Why do want to work for a disabled person," or "What makes you qualified for this type of work?" They showed me the schedule where I could choose my hours and let me read a three ring binder with all of Rick's personal information. They taught me how to communicate with Rick. Rick had a little bit of control of his head and he could nod. They grouped the alphabet by vowels: A-E-I-O-U. When he nodded at a vowel, I was to stop at that vowel and go through the letters in that group. A? A the letter? No, then B, C, D? Yes, D is the first letter. Once you got to know Rick, it became easier to guess what he wanted. I? I, the word? Yes. Then W. Okay, I want, I will…?

I worked for Rick twice a week and occasionally on weekends when there was a special trip. Rick and his father, Dick, raced together, a concept I couldn't imagine. I didn't know much about marathons, triathlons, or road races. This was 1988, and running was popular but certainly not the craze it has become. One weekend that fall, I accompanied Rick to a speaking engagement somewhere in Massachusetts. Rick's mother Judy picked us up on a street corner on campus. We piled into her small hatchback Honda Civic: Judy, Rick, his oversized wheelchair that did not collapse, and me hunched over in the backseat. I had to take long slow breaths to keep from having a panic attack crouched in the fetal position in the back of that car. Once we arrived at the banquet hall, it seemed all very familiar for Rick. He lit up as friends hugged and kissed him, shook his hand affectionately, and told dirty jokes. Someone gave him a Sex on the Beach cocktail. After the cocktail hour, Rick's father, Dick, went to the podium to speak. He told the story of their lives and how they had come to run together. It was the most incredible story I had ever heard. I stood at the back of the room hanging on every word as tears streamed down my face. Dick is a wonderful storyteller. He has a very calm manner and a smooth, soulful voice that is enhanced by his New England accent. His piercing blue eyes seem on the verge of tears every time he tells the story, and I have come to hear the story many times.

I enjoyed working for Rick. It didn't feel much like work. It was more like helping out a fellow student on campus. I took him to classes, helped with meals, and picked him up from swimming. Rick loved to go swimming. He said that being in the water and racing with his father were the only times he didn't feel handicapped. However, it was a challenge for me to get him out of his wet suit. Rick has two metal poles in his back that limit his flexibility. At the time Rick weighed about 86 pounds. I am 5'4" and weighed 110 pounds. I never doubted that I could lift Rick in and out of the chair. The first time I went to pick Rick up from swimming, the PCA who swam with Rick handed him to me without any instructions and left. I grew up working in my family's Asian grocery store in Wisconsin. Every Wednesday, my father woke up at dawn to drive four hours to Chicago to buy goods for the store. He returned at night and my two brothers and I, along with my mother and grandmother, met him at the store to unload the van. I knew that I could lift 50 and 100 pounds bags of rice so I felt sure that I could lift Rick. I only dropped him once.

I also did a lot of laundry for Rick. I didn't do much of my own laundry, but I did loads and loads for Rick. I felt very content leaving his room with the lingering scent of detergent and fabric softener behind. This was usually during evening shifts. I would leave him in his bed with the lights out and door unlocked for the PCA in the morning. To my knowledge, nothing bad ever happened during the night involving theft, pranks, or other bad behavior among students.

The only time I did not want to go to work was the Saturday night that my friends were going to see *Wayne's World*. It was pouring rain outside. When I got to Rick's dorm room in Shelton Hall, I asked him if he would like to go to the movies with my friends and me. He said yes. I packed some Bacardi and Coke for Rick, his drink of choice on the weekends, covered him with garbage bags, and we walked the mile and a half back to my dorm at West Campus. We walked another few miles to the movie theater. Normally, we would have taken the T to get there, but no one minded walking since we couldn't get Rick on the train. Rick loved it. We all laughed like crazy through the entire movie. We were soaking wet but we had a great time.

Another memorable experience was taking Rick to a doctor's appointment at Children's Hospital. I had heard how renowned this hospital was and how much the doctors there had done for Rick. I felt very privileged to take him there. Rick needed x-rays, and he had to be moved from his wheelchair to the table. The two doctors and two nurses could not lift him out of the chair, so eventually I stepped in and did it. They all remarked that Rick always brought the prettiest PCAs to his appointments, and I felt proud to among that group.

Come to think of it, I never met a PCA that wasn't good looking. One night I crossed paths with a great looking upper classmen who was finishing his shift. We got to talking and he encouraged me to go home with Rick for Easter weekend to Rick's grandparents' house in Cape Cod. So I went. There I met Rick's two brothers and their wives. As the family joked around the dinner table, I heard the story of how Rick reacted to the first date his brother went on. As the story goes, Rick lay on the kitchen floor and cried as his brother and his date walked out the door. I wondered how he must have felt at that moment, years later with his brother and his brother's then very pregnant wife. Rick liked girls. This was no secret. He had Playboy centerfolds taped to a wall of his dorm room. Needless to say, it made me uncomfortable.

I enjoyed those special weekends with Rick's parents because Rick glowed after a race. His parents took far better care of him than any of us ever could. Rick's father would give him a bath, a shave, and a haircut. When he got out of the bath, he glistened, and I was happy to see him so refreshed. Rick generally preferred to be fed by his mother instead of by me. She didn't go through the painstaking process that was required of PCAs of asking which bite he would like to have next. She simply fed him everything and it all went down. And of course, he was never happier than when he was racing with his father.

It has been almost twenty years since I left Boston University and stopped working for Rick. I now have three children of my own that I hover over endlessly. Occasionally, I have to stop myself and think about Rick. During those quiet moments when I'm watching the children while they're asleep or when I'm looking out the window at my kitchen sink as they play outside, wanting nothing more than to protect them from the world, I sometimes think about Rick. He is the bravest, most trusting man I have ever met. He left his care in the hands of a group of young students who had no experience taking care of a person with special needs. I never saw fear or doubt in his eyes. He never expressed any frustration or voiced any complaints about the quality of his care. I'd heard from his brothers about a few PCAs who mistreated Rick, but it didn't seem to deter his faith in people.

During a long drive back from the Marine Corps Marathon in

Washington, DC, Rick's mother told me about how hard she fought to get Rick into public school. How she had testified before Congress as an advocate for equal rights for people with handicaps. From the very beginning when doctors told Judy and Dick to place Rick in an institution and forget about him, they were resolved in their belief that they had an intelligent child. And they worked tirelessly and endlessly to provide every opportunity for their son. This is not a perfect family and Judy and Dick were not the perfect couple, but when it came to their son, they were unstoppable. I wonder if I could ever meet such a challenge with the conviction and bravery they did.

Only slightly less daunting has been my goal to run the Boston Marathon. After ten marathons in sixteen years, I am still trying to win a spot in this prestigious race. Sometimes when I'm running I visualize imaginary situations for motivation: being a back-up singer for the Rolling Stones; having breakfast with Denzel Washington; curing childhood obesity; and running side by side with the Hoyts in Boston (impossible, I know). But it fills me with inspiration. So I'll keep at it and hope they don't quit before I get in!

Off the Deep End

by Jessica White Gracia
Rick's Former Swim Teacher

> *"Remember, a dead fish can float downstream, but it takes a live one to swim upstream."*
>
> —*Unknown*

"I used to swim at Springfield College" were the magic words that started the friendship between me and Rick Hoyt. All of a sudden Rick's eyes widened with excitement and eagerness to hear more. I told him, "If you ever want me to go with you I would love to." As we conversed in one of the rooms in the Boston Children's Hospital's Communication Enhancement Center, where I was completing my internship, Rick's personal care attendant (PCA) explained to me that he goes swimming at Boston University with one of his former PCAs. With a nod of his head he quickly recruited me to go swimming with him. We made plans to meet at the pool the following week.

One week later, I rushed home from Northeastern to my Brighton apartment, quickly changed, grabbed my swim bag and ran out the door. I proceeded down Commonwealth Avenue to BU. As I pulled up to the complex, I saw what I assumed was Rick's van parked out front. I quickly searched for a parking spot and proceeded to the Case Athletic Center. I opened the doors to the foyer and saw Rick, his PCA Naomie, and a tall slender woman with blond hair. "You must be Heather," I said. She greeted me with a smile and confirmed. "Nice to meet you, Jessica." We walked along the foyer through the double doors to a small rickety old elevator. Heather pushed the button and the doors opened. There was barely enough room for Rick's wheelchair, never mind trying to fit his PCA in the elevator with him. As the doors closed I was nervous they would not open on the other end. Heather and I took the small set of stairs to the next floor. We waited and waited. It felt like forever for the elevator to travel what was literally no more than seven feet vertically. This was the contraption that made the pool handicap accessible? Finally the doors opened and Rick and Naomie could escape its small confines.

We continued on to the pool area. Heather knocked on the door and one of the lifeguards let us in. The pool was a standard 25 yards with 6 lanes, but the pool area was rather small for such a large University. There were two diving boards and bleachers on both sides. We wheeled Rick to the shallow end where there was an old worn out lift to lower individuals into the pool.

Heather spent the first few minutes communicating with Rick about his swim agenda for that evening. She would use the same A-E-I-O-U method as I had seen my mentor at Boston Children's Hospital use with Rick. It was intimidating at how quickly both Heather and my mentor could retrieve the vowels then the consonants in order to provide Rick with a means to express his thoughts. I, myself, was still trying to learn Rick's A-E-I-O-U method, so I was relieved that Heather was there to bridge the communication between us all. Although Rick had his communication device mounted to his chair, he preferred to use this low-tech method.

Rick gave Heather and me a number of warm up laps to do, probably to see if I was as efficient a swimmer as I had claimed. After our warm up, Naomie carefully transferred Rick from his chair to the lift. Then, with an ungraceful jerk, the lift started and lowered Rick to the pool where Heather and I would release him. The pool was probably in the upper 80s, so it was a bit chilly for Rick, but he loved every second of being in that pool. I never asked him what his body felt like in the water, but I guess it must have felt rather freeing to be able to move with the subtle currents of the pool. Heather positioned Rick on his back and showed me how she used a typical rescue hold to tow Rick the length of the pool. She put her right arm over Rick's right shoulder, across his chest, and under his left armpit. I was familiar with this type of hold from the lifeguard training courses I took as a teenager. As she secured Rick with her right arm, she pulled with her left and pushed with her legs. She swam with Rick back and forth from one end of the pool to the other several times. Next, Heather showed me how Rick swims under water. While treading water behind him, she placed her hands under him on his back. Then, she flipped him to his stomach to let him swim underwater briefly, then flipped him to his back to breathe. Heather asked me if I would like to try swimming with Rick. I did not hesitate, as I was still a strong swimmer and was confident that I could safely swim the length of the pool with Rick. After several laps, Rick began to shiver and it was time for us to swim back to the lift. I survived my first training—or, better yet, Rick survived my first training.

As we exited the pool, Heather began to talk about her plans to move with her family to another state. I was surprised to hear that she would be around for only a few more weeks. I knew I could not fill the void of Heather's many years of friendship, but I could at least fill in as Rick's new weekly swim partner. As weeks turned into years, Rick and I would develop a friendship of our own with foundations built by the many experiences of our weekly swims.

The weeks progressed and I learned to communicate efficiently with Rick using the A-E-I-O-U method I never thought I could learn. I learned to drive his van, which was the largest vehicle I had ever driven. I also learned to work the lift. Over time, Rick got a wet suit so he able to stay in the water longer. He was also more buoyant and we were able to modify the original holds so Rick could swim more independently. Rather than using a rescue hold, I would now only hold the back of Rick's neck to tow him. This was much more energy efficient and we were able to swim more laps.

Rick and I always spent the first few minutes discussing our plans for the night. He was never short of creative ideas. On one occasion, Rick mentioned to me that he would like to touch the bottom of the pool. I said, "What? The deep end? It's twelve feet deep. How do you think we're going to get down there?" I was skeptical of being able to accomplish this aspiration, but I was up for the challenge. We swam to the other end of the pool, hung on the side and discussed how we would attempt to do this. The question arose, "Should I push him under water or pull him under water?" Not only did we have to get to the bottom, we also had to get there quickly enough that Rick wouldn't run out of air. Pulling Rick under water with me was probably impossible and was out of the question. So therefore our first attempt would be to push.

I put my right hand on Rick's back, then my left hand on his legs and turned his body vertical in a catapult-like fashion. I then dunk him under the water by pushing on his shoulders. We did not get very deep, as I could not seem to break myself away from floating on the surface. Again, we tried, and Rick's stiff body veered off towards the center of the pool. At this point, I was shocked the lifeguards allowed me to do this, as it blatantly looked like I was drowning him. For several weeks we would try different variations of the original plan. Finally, with Rick's determination and my persistence, we came up with a plan that would work. We continued as usual, one hand on Rick's back and one hand on his leg, only this time we would be in the corner of the pool. When I got Rick a few feet below the surface, I then stood on his shoulders and pushed on the sides of the pool to shimmy us down. I was nervous about his air supply, so I stopped just short of the bottom. Of course, with this new method I then had to swim to the bottom to pull Rick up from the depths of the pool. This was promising, so we tried it again. As I was bringing Rick to the surface on this second attempt, I was unsure of whether he actually touched bottom. As we surfaced, there was no longer any question of this as his excitement streamed through his body and the pure sense of accomplishment on his face.

While leaving the pool area one night Rick spotted a flyer for an intramural swim competition. Neither one of us were students at the school, but that was not enough to deter Rick from signing us up. With the competition only a few weeks away, Rick and I practiced by doing time trials. Previously, we swam laps of the pool at our leisure, never as fast as we could. We decided to start racing against the clock. We kept track of our times with one set being me towing Rick and the other set being Rick swimming on his own as I flipped him in the water. Each week we hoped to improve our times from the week before, but they remained rather steady.

On the night of the competition, we arrived at BU around seven as we usually did. This time there was a small crowd of college students at the side of the pool. We walked over and noticed that the students were signing up for their events. Eagerly, Rick and I decided to sign up for the 50 and 100 yard freestyle and backstroke events. As if this wasn't enough racing, I figured I would sign up for the 50 and 100 yard breast stroke events. Our first event was the 50-yard freestyle. Naomie and I lowered Rick into the pool as the other competitors approached the blocks. We heard, "Swimmers take your mark" and then the buzzer. We pushed off the side of the pool, and within seconds I couldn't see any of the other swimmers. We were not kidding ourselves. We knew that even swimming as fast as we could, we still would not keep up, but the competition was fun. I towed Rick and as we approached the other side of the pool, most of the other swimmers were done. I thought to myself, "Good thing the longest event we signed up for was only four laps." We completed all of our races that night, which was quite an accomplishment in itself.

As the weather began to get warmer, Rick asked if I would be interested in swimming at Walden Pond. I had never been to Walden Pond before, so I was curious about swimming there. As the conversation continued, I realized not only did Rick want to go swimming at the pond, but he wanted to swim across it. I was always used to swimming in pools or in open water where I could touch the bottom and I didn't think fish were swimming under me. Lucky for Rick, a few summers earlier I got over my fear of swimming in deep dark water when my Uncle Bill talked me into swimming across a glacier lake in Maine. So with that experience, I felt like I was prepared for this new challenge Rick set forth.

It was a hot summer night in July when I picked Rick up at his apartment. We drove out to Concord, Massachusetts, where the State Reservation is located. We parked the van and wheeled Rick over to the pond. It was beautiful there with the evergreen trees thickly lining the pond and the sun glistening on the water. Although the pond was busy with people, it was still a very peaceful place. There were several different parts of the pond roped off for designated swimming areas. However, it did not seem out of the norm to be swimming outside these areas, as I observed many people swimming the length of the pond. It looked like a spot where many triathletes must have trained. Rick and I prepared for our swim that would be several hundred yards to the other side. I eliminated any thoughts of fish and drowning, since there were really no lifeguards who would probably be able to see us or hear us if we went down. We began to swim across the pond. The water was warm with the summer's heat wave, soft and relaxing. It was invigorating to swim in a large body of water with no lane lines delineating our space from that of the person's next to us. We swam at our leisure, making it from one side of the pond to the other and back without any trouble. This would be our new summer time swimming hole. We would make frequent trips back to this spot over next few summers.

Rick and I had been swimming together for a few years when in

2005 BU opened the new Agganis Arena. We had anticipated its opening for months. This was a whole new experience. It was luxury right from the entrance of the arena. It was massive, bright and open. When we entered for the first time, we walked by a climbing wall on the right and large beautiful windows on the left, which displayed the Olympic size pool below. We no longer had to worry about the elevator's mechanisms breaking down. There were twelve lanes, a diving well, and a therapeutic pool with a hot tub. There was even a reliable lift to lower Rick into the pool. We no longer had those unexpected nuisances like we had at the old pool—or so we thought.

Rick and I swam at the new Agganis pool for many months, and for many months we practiced swimming under water. One night, Rick spelled to me, "I want to swim the entire length of the pool under water." Up until now, the most he swam under water was about eight yards, roughly a third of the length of the pool. Many times I was nervous and flipped him over for air after only a few yards. Again, I was skeptical and hesitant, but up for this new challenge. If this was something that Rick wanted, then I was not going to hold him back. We spent the next few months adding more and more yards to our underwater swims. I coached him on taking a deep breath, then letting it out little by little along the lap so he would stay relaxed and not become distressed. We made it about three quarters of the length of the pool when we decided it was time to go the whole way.

As Rick and I rested near the bulk head on one end of the lane, we spelled out our plan for swimming the length of the pool. I knew he was determined to do this and I was going to have to set aside my own fears in order for him to accomplish this. I just had to make sure I swam as fast as I could to the other side. I placed my hands on Rick's back and held him face up. Then, on the count of three, I flipped Rick face down as he took one last breath. I towed him as fast as I could to the other side. It usually took us about 40 seconds to swim one length of the pool. When we made it to the other side, I flipped Rick over and said, "We did it. We made it the whole way."

Then I realized that something was very wrong. I could hear Rick gasping for air. He was pale. His lips were blue and he was distressed. That was when I realized what I thought was a deep breath of air on the other side of the pool was actually a deep breath of water. He'd just swam under water for forty seconds without any air and choking on water. I talked to Rick and tried to calm him. After his breathing began to stabilize, I knew I had to get him out of the pool as I was afraid he was going to vomit. I waved Naomie over to help me. We didn't even bother with the lift that night. I pushed him up over the side of the pool and Naomie picked him up and put him in his chair. I told Naomie what had happened. Then I turned to Rick and asked, "Do you want to say something?" as I usually did when I caught his eyes.

Rick nodded his head and proceeded to spell out, "Call an ambulance." With tears in my eyes and a lump in my throat, I hurried over to the lifeguard station. As we waited for the paramedics, Rick spelled out, "I'm scared I'm having a heart attack." I thought to myself, "What have I done? How am I going to explain this one to Dick?"

The paramedics arrived within minutes. They put Rick on the stretcher and transported him to the hospital. Naomie escorted him in the ambulance and I took his chair in the van. The hospital admitted Rick, ran tests, and observed him over night. In the meantime, I had to call Dick to let him know what we had done and that Rick was in the hospital. He asked if Rick was okay, and when I said, "yes," he was no longer concerned. He just said, "What can I say? He thinks he's an Iron Man."

It was a long night, but we were thankful to find out that Rick was not having a heart attack. It was just a massive air bubble trapped in his stomach that was causing his pain.

I vowed that we would never do that again, but of course only a few weeks later Rick wrote me a note asking if we could attempt the underwater swim again. I never said no, but told him if we ever did it

Rick is understandably exuberant at Boston University
Graduation Ceremony in 1993. Rick is the first non-verbal
student to graduate from BU.

Ainsley's family in Virginia Beach moments before she ran her first half-marathon in September 2010.

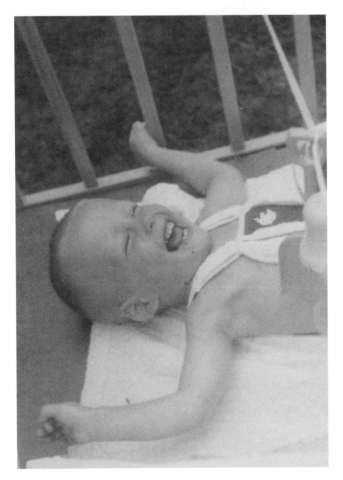

Always a smiling baby, Rick was happy in his playpen in 1965.

Dick carrying Rick from swim to bike transition at Ironman Germany 2000

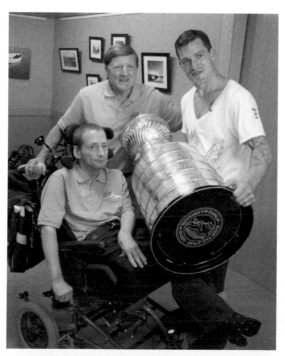

Dick, Rick, and Bruins defenseman Andrew Ference pose with the Stanley Cup at Spaulding Rehab Hospital in September 2011.

Dick, Rick, and Russell with Ronald Reagan, California 1990.

Fathers and sons at the Hoyt Race 2007 with Ted and Brandon Kucowski
from NJ in Waltham, MA.

Not only does it capture why we run but also the smile Rooster references in his chapter. Taken May 2010 at the Virginia Beach Oceanfront after Ainsley received her Young Life Capernaum 5K medal.

Rick and brothers Rob and Russell in 1971.

Rick and Dick crossing the finish line in Tokunoshima, Japan in 1994 during triathlon event.

Left: Rick and Dick dressed to the nines while receiving the 2008 Inspirational Freddie Award in Philadelphia from the MediMedia Foundation.

Below: Rick and Dick during their trek across the USA in the summer of 1992.

Rick and Dick enjoying the water at Cape Cod, summer 1964.

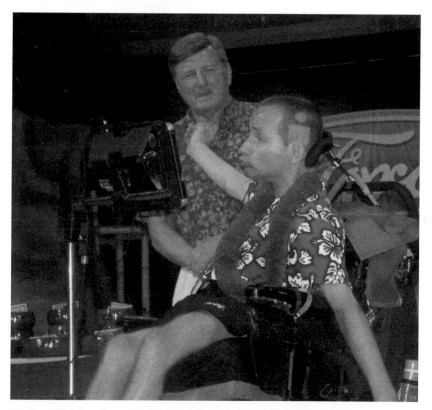

Rick and Dick take center stage in Kona, Hawaii in 2008 to be inducted into the Ironman Hall of Fame. Rick sports the Ironman logo shaved into each side of his head.

Rick and Dick with Team Hoyt VB in Virginia Beach - after the Rock 'n' Roll Half Marathon - September, 2008.

Rick frying up some fish in the backyard, summer 1966.

Rick cruising during the Half Ironman 70.3 World Championships - Clearwater, FL, 2007.

Rick with his dad and brothers Russell and Rob hanging loose in Hawaii, 2003.

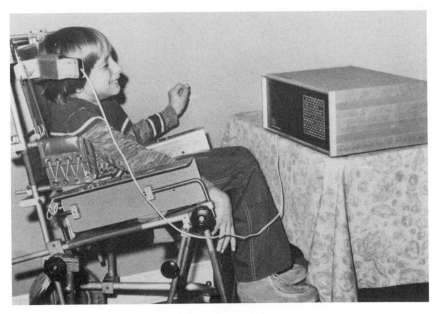

Rick with his first TIC (Tufts Interactive Communicator) in 1972.

Rick with his mom, dad, Rob, and Russell in New Orleans at the Million Dollar Round Table Event, 1991.

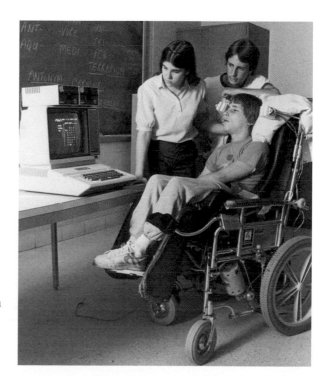

Rick with his TIC at school with brother Russell and classmate Wendy LaPlante Bicknell.

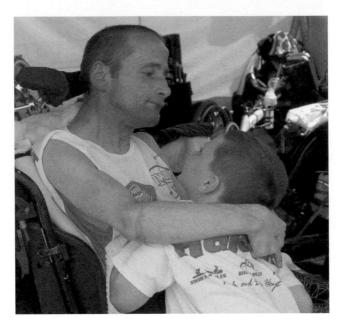

Rick with his nephew, Ryan, Hawaii 2006.

Rick with nephew, Troy, Hawaii 2006.

Dick and Rick near the finish line during the 2011 Boston Marathon flanked by Marathon Team runners Doug Gilliland (left) and Bryan Lyons (right).

Rick loving the Shamrock Classic 5K in Boston in 1992.

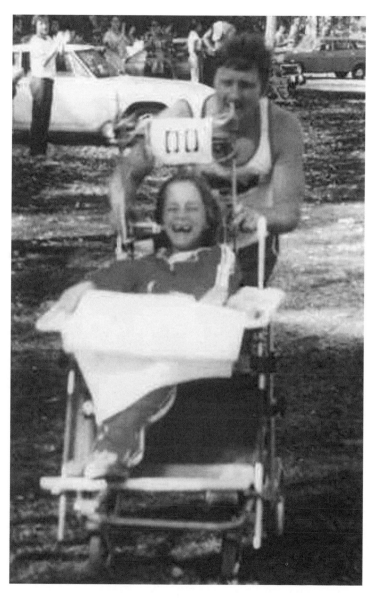

Rick and Dick wearing 00 in their first race in Westfield, MA, a 5 mile charity run for an injured lacrosse player.

Marine Corps Marathon- Washington DC, 1987, where Rick and Dick first qualified for Boston.

again, we needed a way to communicate while he was under water. We never quite built our way up to swimming an entire length of the pool again. I'm sure Rick was ready, but my underlying fear was too much to overcome. We continued our weekly swim trips to the Agganis Arena, but as time went on the beauty and the newness of the pool began to fade and I began to miss the charm of the old pool. The new pool was big and fancy, perfect for competition and athletes, but the old pool was quaint and inviting. Maybe I just preferred it because that was where I learned the most about Rick and where my earliest memories of our time together remain.

Later that year I moved to Quincy, but continued to make the short drive to Brighton to swim with Rick. Only a few months after my move, Rick told me he was moving to Sturbridge. It was then I knew that with me living south of Boston and Rick living west, it was nearly impossible to continue these weekly swim trips. However, I was hopeful that we would continue to weave in and out of each other's lives.

I am fortunate to have spent this time with Rick throughout four of my five years in Boston. He is an inspiration to everyone who has met him, and I've had the opportunity to experience this first hand. There was never a dull moment because Rick was always finding new challenges on which to embark. Nothing deterred him from accomplishing them, not nights when the lift at the pool was broken, nights when the elevator was out of order, or even nights when the lift on his van did not work properly. Rick always had a solution or a way around these predicaments, whether it entailed using a backboard to get him out of the pool or a custodian to help carry him down the stairs. I realized how much people take completing simple tasks for granted. It took time and patience for Rick to prepare for our swimming trips and to get from one place to another. He was never annoyed or upset with the mishaps that occurred. Although, I do not know that Rick saw them as mishaps. It was just life, and that's a good way to approach life. It's the way we all should approach life.

The Hardest Part of a Vegetable

by Heather Oman
Rick's PCA-Boston University-1996

> *"All the adversity I've had in my life, all my troubles and obstacles have strengthened me...You may not realize it when it happens, but a kick in the teeth may be the best thing in the world for you."*
>
> —Walt Disney

I met Rick my senior year at Boston University. I was about to graduate from a program in speech therapy, and I was looking for a job that would look good on a grad school application. I noticed the post for a Personal Care Attendant (PCA) on the BU job board. A young man with cerebral palsy needed part time help. Duties: bathing, dressing, feeding, light housekeeping. Competitive pay, flexible hours. Therapy majors preferred. Contact Rick Hoyt.

It sounded perfect. I called and set up an interview with the woman who answered the phone. I thought Rick just hadn't answered the phone because he was unavailable or something. It never occurred to me that Rick didn't answer his phone because he couldn't speak. Or actually pick up a phone, for that matter.

I was totally unprepared for what met me when I went to the

interview. The same woman I talked to on the phone answered the door; Rick sat in his wheelchair by the table. He was smiling at me in a goofy way, laughing with a sort of snort, and moving all of his limbs at once. I have since learned that's how he acts when he sees a woman that he thinks is cute. At the time, I only saw a spastic, nonverbal quadriplegic man making odd sounds. I felt like bolting for the door, right then and there.

But I didn't. I took a deep breath and I stayed, and learned what it means to take care of Rick. It means quite a lot, actually, and initially I felt overwhelmed, under qualified, and simply not strong enough. I felt that I wasn't emotionally strong enough to deal with Rick's disability on such close terms, and also not physically strong enough to lift him in and out of his wheelchair. He doesn't weigh much, but it took a while before it was easy for me to swing him around.

It took far longer for my arm and back muscles to get used to it than it did for my heart. I found out pretty quickly that Rick is easy to get along with and has a wicked sense of humor. That first day I worked, I was going over his feeding instructions. The list said that because of Rick's swallowing issues, he had a difficult time eating vegetables and almost never did. I looked up from the paper and said, "You can't eat vegetables?" He nodded, and then spelled, "What's the hardest part of a vegetable?" I was still stuck on his swallowing issues, and, wracking my brain, said, "I don't know, the stalk?" He grinned his trademark toothless grin and spelled, "His wheelchair." Another time, I remarked that the plant on his windowsill had died. He grinned again and spelled, "It committed suicide."

I worked for Rick for almost two years, so it was inevitable that I would accompany him to a few races. I even got to work the Boston Marathon. I got Rick up at five a.m. to prep him for the race, and was there in the morning when Rick and Dick took their place at the starting line. I've never heard such a roar from a crowd as I did that day when Dick strutted out there, pushing Rick, looking like they owned the place.

And in a way, they did. Rick has often said that the Boston Marathon is their race, his favorite one. And after seeing firsthand the reception they got, I can understand why. Boston loves the Hoyts just as much as the Hoyts love Boston.

But it wasn't at the finish line that I spent most of my time with Rick Hoyt. It was in the pool.

Rick loves to swim. And he can do it, sort of. His mother taught him and he told me that he loves the feeling of being in the water. Once a week, he and I would go to the pool at BU. While treading water next to him, I would flip him over to his stomach, let him flail all his limbs for five seconds, then flip him back over to let him breathe. I'd let him catch his breath, and then ask him if he was ready. He would flop his head to one side, his signal that it was time. Then we'd start the process all over again. When he got tired, I would tow him for a lap or two, one arm wrapped around his chest, the other arm swimming the side stroke. Rick would straighten out his arms, and I would feel his body release completely. I know that's why he loved it. He was weightless—not fighting his constant battle with gravity—his muscles finally at rest.

The lifeguards always looked worried. I would give them a little wave, as if to say, "I've got this, guys."

Getting Rick ready for swimming was no easy task. He had this wet suit that he liked to wear because it kept him warmer in the water. Wet suits are hard to get on in the best of circumstances, but putting it on Rick was a nightmare. I would lay him down on his bed, and start at his legs. Rick's legs are permanently bent slightly at the knee, so I had to use baby powder to make it easier to slide the rubber suit around his legs. Then I'd yank it up to his waist, and use more baby powder to maneuver it around his arms before I could zip the long zipper up his back. Rick's limbs are stiff and spastic, and he has no control over them, so the whole process of getting him dressed for swimming took easily a half an hour. Getting that suit off of him was even harder. When Rick is cold, his limbs get tighter, making it even more difficult to undress him. And since I couldn't exactly take him to the men's room at the pool, we had to use the lifeguard's office to get him changed. I would lay a towel in his chair, put him in the chair soaking wet, and push him into the office. Then I would lay Rick down on a workout mat I found in the office, and just start yanking that thing off of him. There was no other way to do it. I'm surprised I didn't dislocate one of Rick's hips, or something. Sometimes I would be so exhausted from the whole ordeal that I would just wrap Rick in his towel and rest next to him while he warmed up.

I hated that suit.

But logistics aside, Rick and I always had a great time in the pool. One year, Rick made a goal to swim across Walden Pond. So we spent the winter months training in the pool at BU, and when it got warm enough, I packed Rick up in his van and we headed out to the pond.

The first time we tried it, I thought we were both going to drown. Walden Pond is no Lake Superior, but it's not exactly a pond, either. The water was colder than we expected, and Rick started shivering uncontrollably. I was cold, too, and got exhausted well before we reached the other side of the pond. A lifeguard saw me drag him out of the pond, and came rushing over, thinking Rick was a drowning victim. I think I made a quip that he hadn't drowned yet, but I'm pretty sure Rick and I were both too tired to laugh.

We were both spent, and Rick was dangerously cold, too cold to go back in the water for the return trip to the original shore. I started to pick him up to carry him back around the shore of the pond, when that blessed lifeguard volunteered to do it for me. He carried Rick back to his chair, and, exhausted, I slowly pushed him back to his van. I was convinced that this would be the end of the whole affair.

But it would take a lot more than cold water and a tired PCA to make Rick Hoyt quit.

Every Friday for the rest of that summer, we returned to Walden Pond to work on our goal. And as the water got warmer, we both got stronger, until the time came when Rick finally swam across the pond, fueled mostly by his own steam.

I learned then why Rick's father does what he does. He does it because Rick asks him to, and because Rick pushes him to do it. And when Rick pushes you to do something, there's no way out but to do it. Rick will always ask you for everything you've got. After all, it's no less than what he asks of himself.

My time in Boston eventually came to an end, and, as planned, I left Rick to go to graduate school in Washington DC. My life moved on. I got married, graduated from school, started a career and a family. But when my husband got accepted to Harvard Law School, I once again found myself living in Boston. I called Rick to let him know that we were back in the city, and that I'd like to get together sometime.

"Meet me at the pool?" he asked.

Always, my friend. Always.

Life Lessons from the Hidden Curriculum

by Michele Kule-Korgood
Rick's Former PCA

> "I discovered early that the hardest thing to overcome is not a physical disability but the mental condition which it induces. The world, I found, has a way of taking a man pretty much at his own rating. If he permits his loss to make him embarrassed and apologetic, he will draw embarrassment from others. But if he gains his own respect, the respect of those around him comes easily."
>
> —Alexander de Seversky

As I signed up for my first teaching practicum at an elementary school in Concord, Massachusetts, it never occurred to me that I would learn so much more from one of my college classmates than I ever would from the teacher or the third grade children that I student-taught. As a college student at Boston University, I was bussed out to Alcott Elementary School in Concord—quite a distance from Boston—for the teaching practicum. One of my classmates in the teaching practicum had more than his scheduling to be concerned with. He had to figure out how to get on and off the bus. So simple for most—just step right on. We wouldn't even think twice about it. But my classmate, Rick, at age twenty-something, had already faced more adversity in his first two decades than most people will, even if they live a century.

Rick was born with cerebral palsy, affecting almost every major nerve and muscle in his body. Though no one would be able to prove it for a decade, Rick was born a brilliant child trapped in a body that wouldn't respond to him. By the time I met Rick at Boston University, he was a college classmate just trying to get someone trained to lift him on and off the bus to Concord. The year was 1985, and this was before lift busses were common. The lack of someone to lift him on and off would have precluded Rick's ability to participate in the teaching practicum. Though I weighed only about 110 pounds at the time, I volunteered to be trained. It just seemed like a good and helpful thing to do. I never imagined that Rick would give me more and affect my life more profoundly than I could ever hope to give to him.

Slowly, through the teaching practicum, I got to know Rick. The more I got to know him, the more I became intrigued by Rick and by his refusal to be defined by his disability. I was intrigued by his mischievous personality, that twinkle in his eye that said "I'm up to something," and by his courage and persistence in living his dream—to be an adult, independent of his parents.

After the practicum, I joined Rick's staff of PCAs. We were a group of young people who acted as Rick's arms and legs. The rules were simple—Rick was our boss and he was in control. He directed, and we acted. Over time, I came to understand the true power of Rick's achievements. Here was someone with almost no control over his muscles and limbs, but who was in greater control of his destiny than most of us will ever be.

When I think of my time working for Rick, a variety of memories flood my mind. There is the obvious—I remember watching Rick type out a paragraph for a class assignment. Using his head switch and his revolutionary Tufts University augmentative communication device (talking computer), it took Rick more time to type that paragraph than it would take me to construct pages and pages of typing. For each letter, Rick would wait while the computer scanned rows and then columns of letters on a green DOS screen (remember those?), and would then click his head switch when the computer highlighted the correct row or column. It was an exercise in stamina—but I would learn a lot about stamina from Rick. You had to wonder where that deep wellspring of persistence came from.

As I learned more about Rick and his family, I came to understand the remarkable environment in which he grew up. I spent a weekend in Holland, Massachusetts, with Rick at his family's home by the lake, and went to one of the early triathlons that he participated in as a team with his dad. And to look at Rick's dad, Dick—he is the very picture of persistence. Seeing Dick and Rick compete together (and truly be competitive) in marathon after marathon, the heritage of persistence in achieving goals was obvious. But in addition to the very public heritage of persistence demonstrated by Dick, I learned about a different kind of persistence from Rick's mom, Judy. Here was a woman who wouldn't take no for an answer. Rick was barred from school for approximately the first decade of his life. He'd been born at a time when children like him were denied entry into schools and either not educated at all or educated in highly restrictive, institutional settings. There were no laws to protect Rick and his right to schooling. But that didn't stop Judy. She advocated valiantly and relentlessly, and didn't stop until Rick was allowed to attend school and until Massachusetts passed the first law establishing the right to an education for children with disabilities, known as Massachusetts Law Chapter 766. Our nation followed her lead, and there is an entire generation of adults with disabilities who received an education due to the seeds sown by Judy's tireless advocacy. (Though I may quarrel with the districts that do not provide an appropriate education for the children I represent, I still recognize the leap forward our country has taken since Rick was born in requiring an education in the first place, due in large part to Judy and her advocacy). Later, I would learn that Rick's family had a history of "bucking the system" when the system put up roadblocks. I understand that when Rick was born, the doctors told his parents to put him away in an institution because "he would never be more than a vegetable." It must not have been easy to ignore the doctor's advice, and with no training and no guidance, to take Rick home and make the decision to raise him as they would raise any child. But what a message. From the time he was a baby, Rick was taught that courage and persistence bring results.

But there are also the not-so-obvious things I learned from Rick. I can still picture the bumper sticker on Rick's dorm room mirror at Shelton Hall "I can't be overdrawn; I still have checks left." I was always so serious, but Rick taught me humor. He took everything in stride. One of my responsibilities as Rick's PCA was to help him bathe. An awkward situation no matter how you slice it. I was only seventeen or eighteen, and Rick had to bathe in a non-accessible bathtub in the men's bathroom at Shelton Hall. So off we would trek, me in my bathing suit calling out to the men's bathroom to make sure it was empty before we would head in for Rick's bath. One day, the unthinkable happened. Like many people, I was stronger on one side than the other—I was able to lift more on my left. But the bathtub faucet was on the left, so I had to bear more of Rick's weight on my right side to lift him out of the tub. You can imagine that with soap and water, it was slippery. I went to lift Rick out, with his upper body on my right side, and my arm slipped and down went Rick, headfirst on to the bathroom tile. I was petrified and horrified that I could do such a stupid thing, and what if Rick was really badly hurt because of my actions? But there was Rick, laughing at me and my inept ability to handle the soap and the whole situation. Again, Rick taught me to take things in stride, and not to take everything so seriously.

Rick taught me patience, which is great because by nature, I'm not a particularly patient person. But imagine growing up as Rick—to go for so many years with so many thoughts and feelings without being able to express them. To have others make decisions for you because you didn't, or they wouldn't let you, have a voice. And yet, Rick never became bitter. If he did resent it, boy, did he hide it well! Instead, Rick saw the humor in everything (which is an especially wonderful lesson for me, as I take everything too seriously!). Rick played pranks, and made people focus on him. On whom he is—not on his disability. Anyone who spends any amount of time with Rick is captivated by his infectious enthusiasm, his amazing grin, and his incredible wit.

The more I got to know Rick, the more I understood that Rick's greatest gift is that he forces everyone to see beyond his disability and to see him. In addition to extraordinary courage and persistence—and a fabulous sense of humor—I came to learn that Rick had a very mischievous side too. Just like many other college students, Rick liked to frequent the bars in Boston. And he really liked Rum and Cokes. One day, I remember Rick asked me to take him to one of the bars near school. As with many bars in Boston, this was in a brownstone building and you had to walk up a pretty impressive flight of steps to get into the bar. No ramps for accessibility there. But that wasn't about to stop us—I simply carried Rick up the steps. (Mind you, I was a very young college student—only twenty when I graduated with my Bachelor's Degrees, but no one stopped to "card" me while I was carrying Rick up the steps to the bars).

Rick would order his Rum and Cokes, and I distinctly remember that his muscle tone (which was usually very hypertonic—tight muscles that he couldn't control) became much looser with each drink. When a pretty waitress would come by the table, Rick amazingly could direct his muscles in such a way as to end up touching the waitress. And such plausible deniability! Again, I learned that Rick would force us all to see past any limitations and to face the fact that he is just like all of us—a person with great qualities, a few vices, and strong likes and dislikes. Rick has so many gifts, but it seems to me that his truest gift is that by example, Rick teaches people to see beyond their differences to the similarities between us all, deep down inside. Rick exudes such a strong sense of self, refusing to be defined by his circumstances, but instead defined by his incredible personality.

I think that often when people see someone who appears different from themselves, they are both struck by and stuck on the differences. I imagine that when people first meet Rick, they don't know how to conduct themselves. They are afraid of what they don't understand; afraid because he communicates differently, gets around differently, eats with a little help from another. Yet the more time anyone spends with Rick, the more quickly they learn to see far beyond his disability to what makes him the person he is—to see his incredible sense of humor and his amazing fortitude and persistence. Spend a little more time and learn about Rick's history, and people eventually see someone who is so positive and so strong that he didn't become bitter by all the challenges life threw at him and by all the obstacles society threw in his path, but became empowered by them.

It's been so many years since I have seen Rick. I've corresponded with him a few times via email, and now my children, ages ten and fifteen, have read the book *Devoted* about Rick and his dad. But Rick, you should know that you inspired me. Not just for a moment or a month, but because of you, I have spent most of the last twenty-five years in a career trying to empower other people who happen to have a disability. If I have done any good for any of them, they have you to thank. And I have you to thank for giving me not only a great part-time job in college, but for giving me purpose and meaning.

A Great Life Experience

by John Passarini
Rick's College Classmate

"Being challenged in life is inevitable, being defeated is optional."

—Roger Crawford

Rick and I were in a graduate class together in the early 1990s at Boston University, which made a lasting impression on my life. Getting to know Rick has been a "Great Life Experience." We meet many people in our lives who make immediate and lasting impressions and teach us valuable life lessons. Rick Hoyt is one of those people in my life. When Rick was wheeled into our first class, he had a big smile on his face. The smile lasted all semester. We all learned very quickly that Rick was extremely smart and extraordinarily funny. When Rick wanted to contribute to class or answer a question, he would signal his personal care attendant and she would begin to say certain letters in a certain pattern of vowels and consonants, and Rick would move his head and hit a switch to spell words. His answers would take a little longer, but they were always intuitive and to the point. Rick's determination to contribute to the class was evident, and he quickly earned the respect of everyone. I would look forward to each and every class to learn Rick's thoughts and watch and listen to his answers.

When I met Rick, I was a veteran teacher of twenty years and the System Wide Adapted Physical Education Specialist in the Wayland Public Schools. Prior to coming to Wayland in 1988, I was a Physical Education and Health teacher for eighteen years in the Waltham Public Schools. However, working with individuals with disabling conditions was my main interest and focus, and it was in Wayland that I found my dream teaching position. The impact that meeting Rick has had on me and my interest in working with students with disabling conditions was first influenced by my father, Adolfo, who was born with cerebral palsy and taught me to have a "CAN" attitude at an early age. I learned many lessons from my father, and I see the same celebration of life personified so beautifully in the Rick and Dick Hoyt team. My father helped me bring my "CAN" attitude to my everyday life. Rick Hoyt confirmed my "CAN" attitude and helped me bring it to another level in my teaching and coaching. Every student and athlete I have taught for nearly the last twenty-five years has benefitted from my meeting Rick. My motto is "Nobody is disabled; we are all differently-abled." Rick Hoyt personifies this belief and inspires me to approach every student, athlete, and many challenges with an "I CAN" attitude.

Nearly ten years after my class with Rick, I was invited to a pre-marathon celebration for the Children's Hospital Marathon Team called "Katie's Team," named after Katie Lynch, one of my former students in Wayland. The names of guests would be announced as they entered. At the celebration, I learned Rick and Dick were present and hosting a book signing for their new book. I was excited to see Rick again. When I found them, I gave Rick a hug and introduced myself to Rick's personal care attendant. After telling her my name, she said, "Oh, you are the person that Rick got so excited about when he heard your name." I was so moved to learn that Rick remembered me after so many years of not communicating with each other. At that moment I realized that although I had not seen Rick for several years, he remembered me and his spirit grows inside of me every day.

I show my college classes the "CAN" video during the last class of every semester. I am renewed in mind and spirit every time I show the video, and tell my students about Rick and Dick and my experiences with Rick. Many of my students do not need to be introduced to the Rick and Dick Hoyt Team because most everyone knows their remarkable story. The video is so right when it describes how one does not need to go further than the Rick and Dick Hoyt story to learn what is truly important in life.

In the words of the legendary UCLA basketball coach John Wooden, "Success is peace of mind, which is a direct result of self-satisfaction in knowing you made the effort to do your best to become the best that you are capable of becoming." With these famous words in mind, we can see how Rick and Dick Hoyt have helped so many people around the world achieve this level of success in their lives because the first believed they "CAN."

My Patient, My Friend, My Brother

by John Costello

Director of the Augmentative Communication Program and Speech Language Pathologist at Children's Hospital, Boston

"John Costello is the Director of the Augmentative Communication Program and Speech Language Pathologist at Children's Hospital Boston where he has been for twenty-seven years. John did his undergraduate work at Boston College and received his graduate degree at University of Massachusetts Amherst. He has worked with Rick for many of those years and has grown to be more than simply Rick's speech pathologist, but perhaps one of Rick's closest and dearest friends. Rick the patient and John the clinician have a unique and mutual respect for each other that extends far beyond the typical client/clinician relationship. The relationship is filled with love and respect with a heavy splash of sarcastic and biting humor. Their relationship was never more evident than when I witnessed John roasting Rick in honor of his fiftieth birthday celebration, where the two exchanged barbs based on the long standing and good natured rivalry between Rick's college alma mater, Boston University, and John's alma mater, Boston College."

—Todd Civin

My relationship with Rick began back in the mid 80s. I met him initially when I was observing as a student. Later on, I had the good fortune of coming on staff and working with Howard Shane at Boston Children's Hospital. Rick had his back surgery at Children's. We hadn't really worked all that much together to that point, but when his mom, Judy, stopped by I asked her if I could go up and see Rick with her. I went up and Rick looked pretty sick. He was in obvious pain and he looked miserable. I saw Rick and said instinctively and sarcastically, "I don't think I ever saw Rick look so good. He should have surgery more often." Rick laughed and I laughed, and that is what started our long relationship—being sarcastic with each other and taking every opportunity to insult and joke with one another.

After he was discharged from the hospital, Rick started seeing me for treatment. Originally, it was difficult for him to travel, so I would go to his home in Holland and spend time with him there. I would also often go over to his dorm and we'd work on communication technology. Sometimes I would go to his apartment because he didn't have a ride to my office, and other times he couldn't make it in because he had a hangover. He was, after all, living the good college dorm life. We continued to work together throughout his college years with our focus being on trying to find ways for Rick to use technology more than dependently communicating and also working with tools and strategies that would give him increased efficiency. Because his limited motor skills affect his ability to consistently hit the switch, we worked on strategies that would allow Rick to be efficient.

When I began to see Rick regularly rather than having him work with Howard, it was simply because, given Howard's duties as director of the department, it made more sense for Rick to have a clinician who could work directly with him, had a more flexible schedule, and could go over to his dorm to work with him. At the time that it became clear to Rick that he was not going to have Howard as his regular therapist and that he and I were going to be working together, Rick, in his typical style, asked for me to call Howard in during one of our sessions. Howard entered the room. Rick presented him with a check from his personal checkbook. He started out by saying, "Before I present this to you, I would like to thank you, Howard, for everything you have done for me and thank you for our time together. As a show of my appreciation, I want to pay you for what I think our time together was worth." And at that point, Rick gave him a check for twenty-five cents. A prime example of Rick's incredible sense of humor.

During the early part of our relationship, there was a pivotal point in the way we worked together that helped to define what our goals were. Rick had just graduated from BU, and he was living on his own. He had a Personal Care Attendant who was with him all the time. The attendant lived there as well, so they were roommates. Rick would come in, and I would wait for him to put together a message rather than jump immediately into conversation. As we know, it takes a fair amount of time for him to put together a message. As Rick would near the end of creating his message to me, the PCA would jump in and make a comment regarding the very topic that Rick had just spent about six or seven minutes trying to write. I also noticed over time that the PCA would do things like put his foot on the edge of Rick's wheelchair and move it around while Rick was trying to write. Of course, any little movement imposed on his wheelchair would sabotage his capability to communicate and operate the switch.

At the time, I had a little Nerf basketball in my office and the PCA would bounce the basketball off the wall while his foot rested on the edge of Rick's chair. I was aware that all these things were sabotaging him, but I also knew that Rick was an adult and a college graduate and managed his own staff, so I didn't think it was right for me to call the PCA out. At one point, the PCA stepped out of the office and I voiced my concern to Rick. I said, "I know, you're an adult and you manage your own staff. I've tried not to say anything, but I can't let it go on any longer. I don't know how to say it so I'm just going to blurt it out. I'm shocked at the way you let people treat you. They don't respect you." I went through a whole litany of things I had noticed. I waited for Rick to tap out his response, and when he did, his response was shocking. Rick said, "I didn't think I had the right to say anything or do anything because I rely on him for everything."

That opened up a very long period where Rick and I worked together on issues such as recognizing rights and him recognizing and documenting what he thought his rights were as they related to his own personal disability. We talked a lot about the fact that just because he has a disability, he should not expect anything less of people in terms of respect. We ended up spending a very long time working on this. Rick wrote a paper that he and I presented together in Maastricht, Holland, at an international conference on developing patient/therapist relationships and what people who use technology for communication should expect from their communication partners.

It became the cornerstone of our interactions ever since and the cornerstone of what Rick expects from other people. He began to incorporate some of the tenets in his interaction with other people, as well as identifying what his PCAs need to do. Simple things, such as waiting for him to tap out his message or not speaking for him, not looking over his shoulder and interrupting when he is trying to communicate, and not sharing with others what he wanted to remain private. Rick recently did a radio interview for the hospital in which he said that one of the things he has learned is that he should expect to be treated with dignity and with the same rights as everyone else. Having a disability should not affect the way he is treated by others, and this respect should carry over not only to his rights as a communicator, but to all other aspects of his life as well.

One of the other ways Rick and I work together is in making sure that his speeches are in order. His speaking engagements come at him fast and furiously, and we often have to prepare one speech after another. I've always been very interested in making sure that Rick has the opportunity to present himself properly. Despite the fact that he has such notoriety and that many people see him lecture with his computer, and despite the fact that there is lots of discussion about his being a college graduate, many people cannot break out of their preconceived notions that due to his physical disability and the fact that they don't see Rick talk or they don't see him doing things completely independently, they presume he isn't intelligent. So one of Rick's goals, and therefore one of my goals, has always been to make sure that he is always recognized as the smart, witty, and sarcastic guy that he is.

We've also spent a lot of time focusing on and figuring out ways to try to help him, as quickly as possible, use his computer to speak. I am currently working with a couple of manufacturers with hardware and software. We've actually lined up an interview with the manufacturer of the hardware that Rick currently uses so that he can provide input to explain what he would like to see changed. Despite the fact that there is a lot of technology out there and that there are lots of access strategies, Rick is not able to use most of them. Eye tracking is one that many people often ask about. Rick's eyes are not currently a good match for the eye tracking technology. We are always trying to find ways for Rick to become more efficient on all levels of communication.

Because I know him so well and because I respect him so much and because I am personally injured by statements people still make like, "Does he understand?" or "Does he know what is going on?" I am always focused on how we make sure he is recognized as the competent man that he is.

Rick and Dick have both wanted to do something for my department in the hospital, knowing that we have a mission in our center to be able do much more but need funding. They have tried to allow the hospital to use their celebrity to raise funds. Though it may not have worked the way anyone would've liked it to work, they continue to try and they believe in our program. Both Dick and Rick have said they are forever grateful for the things we've been able to accomplish together and the time we've spent beyond just coming in for our weekly sessions that have helped impact Rick's success. And so I see him as a friend and as a person who wants to make a difference with the work we do at Children's.

Rick has continued to realize that he can be a strong role model for people with disabilities, as well as to be a spokesperson who will be heard by people without disabilities. He tries to take that role seriously, knowing that since he and his dad have some celebrity, that people pay attention, and what he says may have impact on listeners. That has been his goal all along, to teach people that just because you have a disability, it doesn't mean you aren't smart and can't accomplish things. Every chance he gets, he takes the opportunity to deliver that message. Over the years, he has evolved and refined this message with more of an insightful, personal touch. Like all of us, as we mature, we become more introspective; we become more observant of the people around us. We evolve in the way we speak and become more empathetic. I've seen Rick do that as he prepares and creates new lectures.

Personally, I feel enriched on so many levels by knowing Rick. Again, he's a friend, and through his eyes, I'm able to understand and have better insight into the considerations of everyone I work with. We've had time to talk and explore many topics and considerations about his disability and about augmentative communications. That has allowed me to provide better service to other people. Also, Rick is someone who I know is genuine and sincere, and I know that he respects me as not only a clinician, but as a friend. I do the same for him. I like Rick as a person and I care for him as a person. What I have gleaned from him on a professional level has allowed me to provide better insight and services to others.

Though Rick and I maintain a clinical relationship, I think our relationship has changed over the years. For one thing, we are very close in age—only months apart. We both share the same sense of humor. We don't like to let an opportunity go by where we aren't sarcastic or insulting. Rick has often said that the sense of humor we share is the cornerstone of our being able to work together. In one of his lectures, he said it can be a long, hard road trying to figure things out, and it can be frustrating at times, but it is through humor that he's able to keep his closeness with many people.

I consider Rick to be a friend, but maybe *brother* is an even better description. I hold our relationship on a higher level than just a patient/clinician relationship. As I said, I feel personally injured when Rick is not recognized for the person that he is. And I know that he recognizes the support that I give to him in return.

Rick Hoyt: Consultant, Test Pilot, Teacher

by Jim Gips
Boston College

> *"Technology is nothing. What's important is that you have a faith in people, that they're basically good and smart, and if you give them tools, they'll do wonderful things with them."*
>
> —*Steve Jobs*

Back in 1993, colleagues and I at Boston College invented a technology called EagleEyes. EagleEyes allows you to control the mouse pointer on a computer screen by moving your eyes. EagleEyes works through five electrodes placed on your face, around the eyes.

In 1993, I knew little about people with disabilities. I had never worked with anyone with disabilities. Truth be told, I felt uncomfortable around anyone in a wheelchair.

We didn't invent EagleEyes for any real purpose. I just thought it was cool to be able to control the computer strictly through electrodes on my face. I could play simple video games and spell out messages just by moving my eyes around and having the signals sensed through electrodes.

The technology was written about in the press, and we were up for a

Technology of the Year Award from *Discover Magazine*. A brief television piece was done on the technology. Along the way it became clear that EagleEyes might be more than a toy. It might actually be useful for people with severe disabilities. We began trying the technology with children and adults with severe disabilities. Parents and schools began requesting systems to use at home and in school.

I don't remember how I connected up with Rick, but he came over to try an early version of EagleEyes in our lab. EagleEyes wasn't really appropriate for Rick for full time use. He could use it, but he already had a communication system that worked for him, both a switch-based computerized system and a communication system he used with his aide. It began to dawn on me what a great contribution Rick could make to our project. Students were developing applications software to use with EagleEyes. We were trying to develop a portable EagleEyes system that would work well in homes and schools. But our primary users could barely communicate with us. Rick could become our expert user, a consultant on the project who could test the technology and advise us on what was working and what needed to be improved or added.

Rick and I met in my office with his aide to work out arrangements. First I was fascinated by the spelling system that Rick uses. I had been reading about spelling systems that might be used with EagleEyes. Rick's is a two-level system where the aide runs through groups of letters Group A, Group E, Group I, etc. Rick gives a slight shake of his head at the correct group. If it's "Group I," then the aide goes through the letters in the group: I, J, K, etc. Rick gives a slight shake of his head at the correct letter. At first it seemed like it took a long time for Rick to communicate. It does, but with one reliable motion that Rick is able to consistently repeat spelling things out is a tough problem. Rick's is perhaps the best system I've seen. Dividing the alphabet groups at the vowels is genius. It's really easy to remember. It works over the long haul. There is a whole academic literature on spelling systems. We have written a couple of programs based on Rick's method. One is on the web for free download at staggeredspeech.org. We have taught Rick's system to many people with disabilities and their caregivers.

Rick began coming in to our lab a couple of times a month to work with our students and advise on our projects.

Before I started working on EagleEyes and before I met Rick, I had assumed that people in wheelchairs are fragile. They are, in a sense. But Rick is one of the toughest guys I've ever met. If Rick weren't born with CP, I imagine he'd be a hockey player or a fighter pilot or a racecar driver. Whenever he came into the lab, he'd want to use EagleEyes to play flight simulator. EagleEyes just substitutes for a mouse, so it doesn't provide all the controls you need for flight simulator. Rick didn't care. He'd fly as long as he could, and then crash and laugh. It wasn't just in the virtual world. I know all those marathons and triathlons are tough for Dick, but they're tough for Rick also.

I recall once when Rick had a new aide. After his time with us at BC, she wheeled him out to the van. He was in his wheelchair as the lift at the back of the van was raised. Unfortunately, the aide had forgotten to lock the chair in the lift. The chair rolled slowly off the back of the lift and flipped with Rick falling face first into the parking lot. We ran over there and lifted Rick up. His face was all scraped, but he was laughing; just another adventure in the life of Rick Hoyt.

I was lucky to get to know Rick a bit. I went to his apartment in Brookline to see if we could rig up a system for his TV. We went out for a beer with some students at a bar in Newton Center and down to Faneuil Hall for a fundraiser at a comedy club.

I learned to listen. I try never to predict what Rick is spelling. I tell myself to let him finish his own thoughts. Don't cut him off. If I guess then he might just agree and I'll never know what he's really trying to say.

I remember meeting with Rick for an hour in my office. Joking around with him. Listening to his insightful suggestions for improving our technologies. Then when Rick left, I met with a former student who was about Rick's age. This former student was doing well in his high-tech career. He was married. Had children. A house in the suburbs. Money. And he was miserable.

How do I square this? What are the sources of human happiness? Rick seems to have nothing. He can't even move his arms or legs. Yet he's always laughing and genuinely seems to be happy and enjoy and embrace life and its challenges. My former student seemed to have everything, but he was miserable. Is happiness just an innate disposition? Are people born happy or unhappy? If it's dependent on the circumstances of one's life, what is it that determines whether one is happy? If I had to trade places with one of these people, with Rick or with this former student, which would I choose?

Rick seems to have a positive impact on everyone he comes into contact with. Certainly on my students. His positive outlook is infectious. Rick is one of the most interesting and vital people I have ever met.

A parent donated a power wheelchair to us. We had an experimental version of a portable EagleEyes system. A small group of students decided to design an interface between EagleEyes and the wheelchair that would allow a person in the wheelchair to control the chair just with his eyes—a great project for a group of undergraduates.

Here's the way the user controlled the wheelchair: look up and the wheelchair moves forwards. The higher you look, the faster it goes. Look down and the wheelchair stops. Look to the left and the wheelchair goes left. Look right and the wheelchair goes right.

When the students had a working system, I gave the eye-controlled wheelchair a try in the corridor. It was tough to control. We are not used to using our eyes to control where we go. The powered wheelchair could go really fast. If you look at an obstacle, that is where the chair goes. The best I could do was to look up for a bit and then look down. The wheelchair would go forward a little and then stop. I moved in brief chunks.

Of course, right at the beginning of the project, Rick started asking if he could drive the chair. He'd get that gleam in his eye.

Towards the end of the semester, I decided to let Rick give it a try. I emphasized to Rick the need for caution and told him just to raise his eyes a little and then drop them down. He smiled at me. We lifted him into the chair and then put the five electrodes on his face around his eyes. We connected the electrodes to the EagleEyes box and the EagleEyes box to the notebook computer and the notebook computer to the student interface box and the interface box to the wheelchair controller. We were in the fourth floor corridor of Fulton Hall outside my office. We pointed the wheelchair down the corridor.

OK, I told Rick. You're in control. Rick gave that screech of pure joy he does when he's really happy.

Immediately, Rick raised his eyes as much as he could and the wheelchair accelerated like crazy down the hallway. Now I realized a crucial design flaw. There was a "kill switch" on the wheelchair that would shut it down. But we didn't have a remote kill switch.

It all happened in a flash. A good-looking female student walked around the corner at the far end of the corridor. It's hard not to notice from our past meetings that Rick has an eye for the ladies. As soon as she turned the corner, Rick stared at her. Of course, wherever Rick looked was where the wheelchair went. I imagine Rick's plan. He was going to scoop up the young lady into his lap and take off down the corridor and worry later about what happened next.

I didn't know what to do. I could try to explain to the student that an experimental, eye-controlled wheelchair was barreling down the hallway at her. Unlikely, and there was very little time. But even if I did, what could she do? If she tried to move out of the way, Rick would just keep staring at her and the wheelchair would redirect toward her.

Luckily, one of the students had the presence of mind to race down the hallway and hit the kill switch, stopping the chair before it reached the student.

Rick got to drive a wheelchair with his eyes. The students and I learned some valuable lessons about system design. And we got a bonus lesson from Rick about living life at full tilt and seizing the day.

I Am Just a Father Who Loves His Son

by Bill Potts

Friend of the Hoyt's and VP of Global Licensing for World Triathlon Corporation, Ironman

> *"Along the way you might fall down...sometimes in life, you might fall down and can't find the strength to get back up... do you think you have hope? Because I tell you, I'm down here and I have no arms and no legs... It should be impossible for me to get up, but it's not"*
>
> —Nick Vujicic

I asked Dick recently, "I've known you and Rick since early 1999, when your story was not as well-known. You are now in high demand for public speaking engagements. You receive so many requests from people, you could fill your calendar with them. You have been featured countless times on national television. Many touching articles have been written about you and Rick in magazines like *Sports Illustrated*. I watched you receive standing ovations at Ironman Triathlon event banquets—including receiving the Ironman Hall of Fame Award. I have witnessed people clamoring to get their photo taken with you. However, you have not changed a bit since I first met you thirteen years ago. How have you stayed the same despite the fact that you are famous—and a hero to many?"

Dick replied, "Bill, I don't consider myself a hero. I am just a father who loves his son, and this is how we like to spend time together."

I was speechless. Dick had just provided me with another one of those Hoyt gems of wisdom that I will treasure. After that chat, I pensively reminisced about my many personal experiences with Dick and Rick in an effort to chronicle the many ways he has impacted me and my family.

As the VP of Marketing at FosterGrant, I had committed FosterGrant as a sponsor of Dick and Rick as they dialed up their training to compete in the 1999 Ironman World Championship in Kona, Hawaii, in October. Consisting of a 2.4 mile swim, 112 mile bike ride, and a 26.2 mile run, the Ironman is known as one of the most grueling endurance events in the world. The Hoyts were going to attempt to complete it together. They had completed their first Ironman together here in 1989, and now ten years later, they were trying for their second finish.

I was in Kona days before the race. I saw Dick and Rick together at the Kona Inn, eating dinner, and I got a glimpse into the depths of Dick's love for his son as he fed Rick, cutting his food, wiping his mouth, and chatting with him. They were together, away from other people, away from the cameras. The real Dick and Rick—a father caring for his son. Seemingly unconcerned about the monumental task awaiting them. I thought, *How will they be able to finish the race? How will they overcome the waves of the ocean in the swim, the howling wind of the bike and the scorching heat of the sun radiating from the Hawaiian lava fields during the marathon?*

At the sound of the cannon, at seven sharp, the Ironman World Championship started as the sun peeked out from behind a volcano, winking at the Hoyts as they started their journey. I watched as 1,500 athletes took off like a lightning bolt into the gorgeous blue of the Pacific Ocean, headed to a huge turnaround buoy over 1.2 miles away that was barely visible. At the back of the pack, I watched as Dick, with a rope tethered around his waist, pulled Rick in a dingy. Rick was visibly excited, waving his arms wildly. I was mesmerized by them—by the effort Dick was expending—and by the realization that it was not a given they could finish the swim in the allotted two hours and twenty minutes. If they could not finish the swim, their dream of completing the race was over.

Less than an hour later, a steady stream of athletes began finishing the swim. About an hour and forty-five minutes into the swim, the majority of the athletes had finished the swim course, gliding into Digme Beach to begin the transition to the 112 mile bike portion of the race. The crowd, growing larger by the minute, was now focused on the Hoyts. The Hoyts were now easily visible. Mike Reilly, the announcer, led the way as the crowd cheered wildly, encouraging Dick to give it his best effort. Others were too overcome with emotion to cheer—they watched, tears in their eyes, as Dick battled to get Rick to shore. To the delight of the crowd, at just under two hours, Dick pulled Rick to shore. They had completed the first step of their three-step journey.

The task ahead of them, though, was daunting. In the swim-to-bike transition area, Rick was lifted into a seat on the front of Dick's bike with help from the amazing volunteers. I did not see the Hoyts again until well after dark. After completing the bike portion of the race, Rick was placed in an adult wheelchair modified for running, and Dick pushed Rick throughout the marathon.

It was no secret to any of the thousands of spectators lining Ali'i Drive near the finish line that the Hoyts were about to finish. It was now close to eleven-fifteen p.m. Yes, Dick had been pulling, carrying and pushing Rick for over *sixteen* hours. No doubt energized by the noise, by the lights, by the TV cameras, and most importantly, by the sight of the magical finish line, Dick and Rick crossed through the finish line arch to complete the Ironman World Championship! There was not a dry eye anywhere.

With tears still in my eyes, I thought that if Dick and Rick Hoyt can finish an Ironman, surely, with hard work and dedication, I can overcome anything thrown my way. That was my first gem of wisdom learned from the Hoyts.

Fast forward to 2007. I was now working for Ironman, and I was at the Athlete Welcome Dinner for the Ironman World Championship 70.3 in Clearwater, Florida. This was the first opportunity I had to introduce my wife, Kim, my thirteen-year-old son, Nick, and my ten-year-old twin girls, Sarah and Anna, to Dick and Rick. Little did I know how that encounter would change them.

Dick and Rick graciously posed for a photo with my family. Then Dick and Rick engaged in some chit-chat with Nick. They traded email addresses, and the next thing I knew, Rick was encouraging Nick via email. In the blink of an eye, Nick decided to become a serious runner, then a triathlete. During high school, Nick and I raced many half marathons and triathlons together. Despite my strongest efforts, my best performance against him was a tie in his first half marathon. When he was fifteen Nick gave a speech to a high school class about how the Hoyts had inspired him to work hard to accomplish goals, to have a positive attitude, and to overcome obstacles. He got an A. And I understood—again—how a simple act of love by a father to his son had changed yet another Potts.

Was it any big surprise, then, when my daughter Anna wanted to compete in her first triathlon at the age of fourteen? The Hoyts do it again!

Little did I know that four months later, I would need to heed the Hoyt mantra of *"Yes, You Can."*

Having recently completed my first Ironman 70.3, I was in the best shape of my life. Seeing a lump below my right ear while shaving one morning took me by surprise. I had surgery to remove it, and after a week of testing, learned my diagnosis. I traveled to Houston, Texas, to MD Anderson Cancer Center to begin treatment to eradicate the cancer. My first chemotherapy treatment for my stage 3 lymphoma, a blood cancer that cropped up out of nowhere, was appropriately nicknamed "Shake and Bake." Day turned into night, and as I lay quietly in the hospital, the scope of my challenge hit me like a brick. I was not alone, though, as through the window of my room, I could see others going through their trials as well. Yes, I can. Yes, I can. Yes, I can stay positive. Yes, I can get healthy. Yes, I can get back into great physical shape. Yes, I can. A familiar Hoyt refrain.

Twelve weeks later, I was in remission. On May 21, 2011, I stood silently with my family near the swim start at the inaugural Memorial Hermann Ironman Texas. It was six a.m. at Lake Woodlands, outside Houston, Texas. I was wearing a triathlon suit—and Nick's favorite baseball cap. I had number 93 (my goal now is to live to 93) written on my arms and one leg. I had a timing chip around my left ankle and an athlete band on my wrist.

Three weeks earlier, after many months of late night swims, all day bike rides, and long, hot runs, I was at dinner with my family at our home in Tampa, Florida. I shared with them the reason I was competing in my first Ironman. I wanted to inspire them that no matter what obstacles came their way, that no matter what hurdles were put in front of them, that with hard work and sacrifice, they could accomplish anything; a lesson I had learned from the Hoyts.

The cannon sounded at seven, and I began my journey to become an Ironman.

I climbed out of the water after finishing the 2.4 mile swim and heard my name yelled by Sarah and Anna. "Go, Dad. You can do it!" Then, while exiting to begin the 112 mile bike ride, I saw Kim and Nick waving to me.

After a hot and windy bike ride, I was eight miles into the marathon when I saw my family again—this time with the surprise addition of my mom, my sister Martha, and a close friend known as Aunt Jane. As I passed by them again at mile sixteen of the run, my mom asked my wife, "Is he supposed to look like that?" "Yes," my wife told her, "He is fine." Well, I wasn't, and my wife knew it. Training cannot completely prepare you for the back-to-back-to-back swim, bike, run efforts of an Ironman.

The challenge is daunting, and at this point in the race, I was hurting in ways I had not anticipated. My feet felt like I was running on glass (thanks to a bout of plantar fasciitis), my left leg and knee were cramping, and despite all the water and ice poured on my body, I felt like I was baking. *Yes, You Can.* I told myself.

Thirteen hours and forty-one minutes after I began my journey, with my family watching, I became an Ironman, crossing the Ironman finish line in the dark, with the same Mike Reilly who had called Dick and Rick across the finish line in Kona in 1999, yelling to the crowd, "Bill Potts, you are an Ironman!"

Thanks to ironmanlive.com, many had been able to watch my finish, and the emails started flowing in. As I sat in my hotel room, too excited to sleep, I pondered my journey that now had inspired not only my kids, but others I did not even know.

A journey I had not expected to take. A journey started by Dick and Rick Hoyt in 1999 in Kona. When a father, who because of his love for his son, inspired me and millions of others to remember that no matter what, "Yes, You Can."

Dick and Rick, thank you. Thank you for your courage. Thank you for doing what you do. You changed me. You changed my family. You inspired millions. And it all started as a reason for a father to spend time with his son—perhaps the best Hoyt lesson of them all.

It Takes More Than a Little Rain to Stop an Ironman

by Kathy Sullivan-Boyer
Team Hoyt Office Manager

> "I definitely want to show how beautiful the marathon can be. I am the opponent of all those who find the marathon bad: the psychologists, the physiologists, the doubters. I make the marathon beautiful for myself and for others. That's why I'm here."
>
> —Uta Pippig

In June of 2008, Dick, Rick and I spent a few wonderfully eventful days in the city of Los Angeles, California. Dick and Rick were being honored at a gala event, and the event organizers had put us up for a few nights at the Beverly Hill's Hotel. Back in those days, Dick and Rick traveled without a care attendant, so Dick handled all of Rick's needs by himself, including Rick's bathing, dressing, toileting, shaving, meds, and meal feeding. By the time Dick got around to taking care of himself, there was little or no time for anything else. Amongst the daily chores that were overlooked, he rarely had time to return phone messages while he was traveling with Rick.

During that memorable trip to LA, Dick received several messages on his cell phone from Ben Fertic, the President of the World Triathlon

Corporation, the company that owned Ironman. Although Dick was intrigued as to why Ben would keep calling him, he just did not have a free moment to return Ben's call. When we returned home, we found several emails and messages on the home phone from Ben. We figured something was up, but we got in very late that night, so Dick put Rick to bed and we turned in as well, exhausted from the long flight from the West Coast back to Massachusetts.

We were still eating breakfast the next morning when Ben called yet again and asked to speak to Dick. After the phone conversation, Dick told us what Ben had said. He turned to Rick and asked, "Rick, how would you like to fly to Hawaii to be inducted into the Ironman Hall of Fame?" Of course, Rick grinned from ear to ear and moved his arms and legs with unbridled enthusiasm. You could tell in an instant that he was overjoyed about the prospect of being the first disabled athlete ever inducted into this prestigious group.

The bubble burst just as quickly as it inflated when I asked Dick the date of the Hall of Fame induction. It was to be held at the awards ceremony of the World Championship Ironman event in Kona, Hawaii, the day after the Ironman Triathlon, or on Sunday, October 12, 2008. The date was all too familiar to me, as I knew Dick was scheduled to speak at a fundraiser event for Tomorrow's Hope on the preceding Friday evening in Milwaukee, Wisconsin. Our attendance in Hawaii would require Dick to fly from Wisconsin to Boston to get Rick and me before turning around and making the long trip out to California and then to Hawaii all in one day. Dick and Rick had proved that they were Ironmen, but this journey was beyond even them.

That night, we looked at flights, and Dick agreed that it could not be done. For once, "Yes, You Can" became "No, we really can't," so Dick called Ben back. He thanked him for the honor bestowed upon Rick and him, and said that he was very sorry, but because of another commitment, they would not be able to make it to Hawaii in time for the award ceremony.

Ben was devastated and immediately asked Dick if he could cancel his appearance at the fundraising event in order to attend the Iron Man event. Dick emphatically said, "No." Anyone who knows anything about Dick understands that once he makes a commitment, he does not back out of it for any reason. It's what makes Dick and Rick who they are.

The phone conversation with Ben ended with Dick repeating how honored he and Rick were, but that they could not make the event. Dick suggested that perhaps they could get inducted into the Hall of Fame during the awards ceremony at the 70.3 World Championships in Clearwater, Florida, that November. Dick and Rick would be in Florida taking part in that event, which consisted of a 1.2 mile swim, a 56-mile bike ride, and a 13.1 mile run, or literally a half ironman.

So it was a long afternoon for Dick and Rick, who were bummed beyond description that they could not go to Hawaii. Dick spent the night wide awake, tossing and turning. I could not sleep either, so I got up and did what I usually do when I can't sleep—go to work on my computer in our home office. I figured I might as well catch up on some office work and emails from fans.

After answering several emails, I went online to Orbitz to check out some flights. I had an idea, and by the time Dick got up the next morning, I had things all worked out.

When Dick got up, I explained my plan to him, and he got very excited and thought it may just work. I would drive Rick and a PCA from Rick's home in Sturbridge, Massachusetts, to Boston on Friday night the tenth of October. We would board a plane the next morning to Denver. Dick would fly from Milwaukee to Denver to meet us there when we arrived. Dick's oldest sister, Arline, and her husband, Chuck, always dreamed of taking a vacation to Hawaii, so they figured they would plan it around our trip. They would be traveling out in Phoenix and Albuquerque, so they would rent a car and drive to the Denver airport and meet up with us as well. Then we would all hop a flight to Kona.

Our master plan worked to perfection, and we arrived at Kona late afternoon, while the Ironman Triathlon was still going on. A friend named Linda, who we had met in Hawaii in 2006, picked us up at the airport, but when we tried to get to our hotel, we couldn't get down the street. Our hotel was right near the bike-to-run transition and also near the finish line. Linda literally dropped us off on a street corner a few blocks from our hotel, and we had to push Rick's chair and wheel our luggage down the street to the hotel weaving between all the triathlon spectators. Of course, Dick and Rick were recognized quite often, so they had to stop for pictures and to chat along the way. As you can imagine, it took quite a while to get to the hotel.

We finally arrived at the hotel and took the luggage to our rooms. We were starving, so we went to eat at an outdoor restaurant and watched the finish line of the Ironman event. We went to bed around nine p.m. Hawaii time, which was three a.m. EST, so we were pretty beat after being up for twenty-three hours and flying around the globe. Even then, it was difficult to sleep, as our rooms were on the main road across from the finish line, and we could hear the announcer, Mike Reilly, acknowledging the finishers right up until midnight.

Dick said it felt very strange to be in Hawaii watching the Ironman event and not taking part in it, but Rick was extremely excited to be in Hawaii, watching the event and knowing he would be inducted into the Hall of Fame the next evening.

We awoke to a beautiful Hawaiian morning. Dick and Rick went down to the beach and chatted with many of the athletes that competed in the Ironman the day before. They spent most of the day enjoying the sun and the friendship of the athletes.

The award event was being held that evening. It was located behind our hotel in the parking lot, as there is no indoor venue in Kona that will hold the number of people who attend the award ceremony. The evening began with some wonderful Hawaiian dancers and singers for entertainment. As the evening continued, it began to sprinkle a bit. We were not concerned, as it often sprinkles at dusk and then stops, leading to a beautiful sunset.

When it was time to call Dick and Rick to the stage, they showed a video of their triathlon career, and then Dick spoke as the sprinkles continued to fall. By the time Rick started speaking with his voice activated computer, it was raining a little harder, so Mike Reilly, the emcee, held an umbrella over Rick's head so his computer wouldn't get wet. After Dick and Rick received their awards, Dick turned Rick's head to the side so that everyone in the audience could see the Ironman logo that Rick had had shaved into the side of his head. They showed it on the big screen, and the crowd went crazy. Rick grinned with excitement and his arms and legs thrashed wildly.

Boston Marathon Race Director Dave McGillivray was the person who'd nudged them into trying triathlons back in 1985. The Hoyts remain forever grateful to their long-time friend for his support over all these years. Nearly twenty-four years after competing in their first triathlon, here they were being inducted into the Hall of Fame. One can only wonder if Dave had envisioned that when he encouraged Dick to give triathlons a try more than two decades before.

At that time, Dick had been initially told he could compete in the Ironman, but Rick would have to watch from the sidelines, as there were no provisions to include disabled athletes. As he'd done when they'd begun competing in triathlons, Dick explained that was not how they do things. Fortunately, they were able to work things out so Rick could also take part in the Ironman. In 1989, when Dick and Rick completed their first World Championship Ironman triathlon in Kona, Rick became the first disabled person in the world to ever compete in and complete the Ironman in Hawaii. Due in part to his efforts, Ironman now has a physically challenged division.

Nearly twenty-four years later, Rick became the first disabled person to be inducted into the Ironman Hall of Fame.

After Rick and Dick were inducted, the top ten male and female finishers from the Ironman event the day before were called up and received their awards. During the men's award portion, it began pouring buckets out. Someone got trash bags to protect Rick and his computer—they had him all bundled up. There were puddles under our table, and people were standing in the nearby porta-potties with the doors open watching the ceremony. By the time the top male athlete, Craig Alexander, received his award, the power to the speaker system had gone off and we couldn't hear him. Everyone in the crowd was drenched as the rain continued to tumble down from the ominous Kona sky.

As soon as the athletes left the stage and Mike Reilly wrapped up the evening's events, everyone ran for cover in the hotel. Because our table was right near the stage, we had a long way to get through the parking lot. We ran back to the hotel with Dick pushing Rick and dodging puddles the best he could. We were all laughing and continued chatting with the athletes as we went. The guys were in high spirits because they had just been inducted into the Triathlon Hall of Fame. They had done race events in all kinds of weather over the last thirty years—hot, cold, sunny, rainy, even snowy—so this little storm during their induction ceremony was not going to rain on their parade.

KONA, HAWAII - IRONMAN HISTORY - TEAM HOYT

1988 – Dick made the mistake of drinking a lot of replacement fluids the day before the race. He thought he was fueling up his body to get it ready for the Ironman, but he was actually drinking something that people drink after the Ironman to replace fluids they lost in their body during the event. It began affecting him while he was out in the swim portion, and they were not able to complete the swim portion of the event.

1989 - Dick and Rick completed their first Ironman event in Hawaii.

1999 - Dick and Rick had trouble with their bike and had to wait over ninety minutes for a support truck to come help them fix their brakes. They missed the bike cutoff, but were allowed to continue because it took so long for the support truck to show up to help them.

They were told they could continue on with the run as long as they finished by midnight. They finished at 11:15 p.m., passing some runners who were at one point two hours ahead of them.

2003 - Dick and Rick had a bike crash 85 miles into the bike portion. That year was the only year they used a cart in which Rick sat behind the bike that Dick towed. They'd gotten it just before they flew to Hawaii, so they didn't have time to train with it. Near a water stop, the cart tipped, causing Dick's bike to tip over as well. Dick believes they may have driven over a water bottle. They ended up in the hospital for five hours. Rick suffered stitches on his face while Dick ended up with a lot of road rash on his body.

2004 - It was a very windy day on the bike course. At the halfway point of the bike portion in Havi, Dick calculated how many hours remained before the bike cutoff. They would not be able to bike the rest of the course and make the cutoff in time. Rick was hurting sitting in his seat on the bike, so they decided they wouldn't continue.

2006 - Dick and Rick missed the swim cutoff by about fifteen minutes, and their day was over. There had been an earthquake the week before the Ironman and the water was still churned up. Dick had a good swim out, but on the way back, the current was extremely strong. Dick thought he was moving well, but in essence he was going through the strokes but not moving forward very quickly. The man on the kayak beside him said he saw him swimming and swimming but not getting anywhere.

He Ain't Heavy…
He's My Father

by Rick Hoyt with Todd Civin

> *"The thing I'd most like is for my dad to sit in the chair for once and I push him."*
>
> —*Rick Hoyt*

If I had to describe my dad in one word, it would be "strong." Dad is strong both physically and mentally. People don't realize what it takes to do the type of competitive athletics that we do.

Let me put it into perspective for you. The average triathlete probably weighs about 150 pounds and their bike weighs about 17 pounds. This is a total of 167 pounds. Dad weighs about 180 pounds and our bike weighs about 70 pounds, because it needs to be heavier and stronger to hold both me and my seat. Dad isn't very pleased about this, but I now weigh about 100 pounds, thanks in part to a regular diet of ice cream and chocolate cake. This totals 350 pounds, or almost 200 pounds more than the average triathlete with his bike. The same math could be used to figure out how heavy a load Dad has to pull over a two-mile swim as well. To practice when I'm not available, Dad puts a 94-pound bag of cement in my running chair to simulate my weight. How many runners would be able to compete while carrying a 94-pound bag of cement in their arms?

Dad is not only very strong physically to be able to push, bicycle, and swim with me, but he also works tirelessly to stay in shape. Many people would get lazy after doing this for so many years, but Dad refuses to give up and is actually a bit critical of himself that his times have slowed over the years. He is extremely strong-willed, having continued running through illness, injury, and terrible weather conditions. A weaker man would've said that he can't, but can't is not a word that is in the Hoyt vocabulary.

In 2003, when we were competing in the Iron Man, Dad and I were almost to the end of the biking portion of the event. In those days, Dad towed me on the bike instead of me riding on the front as we do today. Something hit one of the tires and we tipped over, ending up in the hospital for more than six hours. I had every kind of X-ray possible performed on me. In 2006, we didn't make the cutoff time in the swim portion of the Hawaii Ironman triathlon because the current was extremely strong due to the earthquake that occurred the week before, and was keeping Dad from moving. Even though we missed the cutoff time, Dad asked me if I wanted to continue. I didn't have to think twice because I knew people were counting on us and we have made our name through our never quit mentality. We continued and made great time during the marathon portion of the Iron Man. We ended up finishing 45 minutes ahead of the qualifying time. That made me realize once again how incredibly strong my dad is both physically and mentally.

I also describe my dad as one of the most determined individuals I've ever met; not simply determined to help me in my life, but also to help others. He networks endlessly to find people wheelchairs or medical help or answers to their questions, while never giving a thought to getting anything in return. He is determined to make life easier for other people using the experience we have gained while blazing the trail and breaking down the barriers we've been able to conquer. Once he sets his mind to something, come hell or high water, Dad will find a way to achieve his goal.

Hopefully, as years pass, I will be able to continue my dad's legacy of finding funds to assist charities that are important to us, like the Easter Seals. That also means that if something ever happens to my dad, I need to trust someone enough to handle that aspect of my life and to continue our goals of giving. I wouldn't want to let him and others down.

When we make donations to established organizations through the Hoyt Foundation, I swell with pride at the realization that we are able to help other groups for the disabled. When I was young, there was very little in the way of charitable foundations, so I feel overjoyed when we are able to help out now. Over the years, we've been able to help out organizations like Children's Hospital, Easter Seals of Massachusetts, Rehab Resources, and summer camps that help the disabled like the Hockomock YMCA and several therapeutic horseback riding organizations. Growing up, you didn't see much help for children with disabilities. I know that what Dad, Mom and I have done is only a small part of the changes that have occurred regarding the acceptance of people with disabilities, but I like to think that our efforts have had at least some impact on their world.

Day One of the Hoyts' Trek Across America

by Judy Hoyt
Rick's Mother

> Though Rick's mom, Judy, passed away on September 5, 2010, she was and will always remain a huge part of Rick's story. During the Team's Trek Across America in the summer of 1992, Judy kept notes and put together a story capturing the highlights of the journey. These memoirs have never been published, so we felt it would be a fitting tribute to this amazing woman to publish the Recap and Day One of her story posthumously.

Dick says that the idea really took shape three years before when he sat down with Rick to discuss the idea he had about doing a triathlon across the USA. Dick started talking to others about the idea and was told that the swim would have to be done indoors in Y pools and the like. This did not sit well with him, as he loves the challenge of facing the elements. He decided that maybe a biathlon would work better. Dick felt that this trek would show the country that people with disabilities can do things. He knew that he and Rick would cover areas of America they would never travel to in an organized sports event. He knew they needed a sponsor to do it right and to be able to pay the crew and PR people. All of this fell through at the last minute, however, and Dick and Rick decided on the spot that this was still the time to do it with or without support. Dick knew that they would make it no matter what. He knew it because of what he felt inside of him. People told him that he couldn't get out there day after day without allowing his body time to recuperate, and yet he knew that he could and would. He believed he would get stronger each day he was on the road, and Rick felt the same. Plans were made and there was nothing that would stop the Hoyts.

For over three years, we looked for a sponsor to support getting us across America. In the spring of 1992, a sponsor was 99% in place—or so we thought. Our entire family was elated that finally the dream was to come true. Two weeks before the start of the Trek, the sponsor had to pull out. This didn't dampen our spirits. We didn't let this disappointment stop us. We remortgaged our home and put the pieces together, along with support from several companies, friends, and family. This was also the birth of the Hoyt Foundation as it is known today.

I gave up my work in the field of human services and secured an RV for the Trek. Dick secured a support van and a masseuse, and trained diligently. Rick gave up drinking Rum and Coke and began drinking lots of fruit juices to prepare his body for the Trek. Russ, our youngest son, left his job and got permission to delay the start of a new position so he could coordinate the Trek. Rob, our middle son, got involved in putting the safety pieces into place.

The Trek Across America, as it became known, was truly an epic journey that brought out the best and the worst in all members of the Hoyt family. Did we think our Hoyt Team could do this 37,000 mile journey without taking a day off? We sure did. We knew that once Rick and Dick put their minds to accomplishing any athletic feat, they focus on that feat and that alone and just do it.

The Trek began on Santa Monica Pier in Los Angeles and ended at Boston Harbor on the Marriott Long Wharf. For forty-seven days, Dick and Rick biked and ran without ever missing a single step along the way or taking a single day off. The pair traveled through eighteen states, including California (four days), Nevada (four days), Utah (four days), Colorado (six days), Nebraska (three days), Iowa (three days), Illinois (three days), Indiana (two days), Ohio (two days), West Virginia (two days), Virginia (two days), Washington, DC (one day), Maryland (one day), Pennsylvania (two days), and New Jersey, New York, Connecticut, and Massachusetts (one day each).

The most miles they traveled in a day was 120 miles, and the least we traveled was 24.6. The hottest day was 124 degrees Fahrenheit, and the coldest day was 30 degrees. The total mileage of 37,035 was conquered in only 47 days. We met the grass roots families across America. We learned that people do care about people in this country. We missed tornadoes and earthquakes, sometimes by only a few hours. Our Trek allowed us to spread the word that people with handicaps are important too.

Our journey began on June 8, 1992, as we flew across the United States by plane. Rick thought a lot on the plane. He continued thinking as we flew over Nevada and the California desert. He stared out the window of the plane, silent until he finally turned to me and said, "Are we really doing this?"

Everyone was up early in anticipation of beginning the Trek. In all of the hustle and bustle of getting ready to begin the run, Dick forgot to eat. The kids saw Dick and Rick off in a flurry of excitement. The staff of *Hard Copy* filmed the departure, as Barry Nolan, *Hard Copy* host and long-time friend, encouraged Dick and Rick in their greatest venture yet. The vastness of our great country became apparent very quickly as the Trek left behind the confusion of the city of Los Angeles and climbed along the highway into the mountains and the beginning of the desert. It did not take long in the city for the van to lose Dick and Rick. As the Hoyt team rode on, Dick unexpectedly passed out, and he and Rick fell on the side of the road. Three people gathered and stood over them, not quite sure what to do or how to communicate with Rick, who's eyes showed that he wanted someone to help him and his dad.

When Dick came to, the folks around him tried to take them to the hospital, but Dick said no, that all he needed was some food. Someone got him some ice cream, and they were on the road again, wondering where the van and the RV were.

At a V in the road, Dick stopped to ask which way to go. He learned there had been a rock slide, which now blocked the route he was supposed to take. He had to re-route. But luck was with us, as at this moment the van caught up with him and Rick. The RV was frantically searching for them and, at this point, was still on the path to the road block area. The walkie-talkies between the two vehicles were not making contact. A biker stopped to tell the RV that they would have to turn around because the road was blocked. Those of us in the RV became extremely concerned because we feared that Dick and Rick might have already passed through this area. The biker insisted there was no way they could've—until we explained who the Hoyt team was. Then he became concerned too, because he knew they were no ordinary tandem team.

The biker was super. He took the time to check things out ahead and to double back in his truck to see if he could find the van and Dick and Rick to let them know about the rock slide and to re-route them. He eventually found them, re-routed already, and informed them of where we were. We finally met up at dark, pulled the RV to the side of the road, and set up camp for the night. Our first night was in the log book. We fell asleep in the mountains overlooking LA. We could hear the coyotes calling to one another in the pitch darkness—an unusual sound for New Englanders.

Everything felt calm and comforting, and we were overtaken by a feeling of serenity.

Places to Go and People to See

by Rick Hoyt with Todd Civin

> *"You know the hardest thing about having cerebral palsy and being a woman? It's plucking your eyebrows. That's how I originally got pierced ears."*
>
> —Geri Jewel

Over the course of my life I have met some incredible people and visited some amazing and faraway places. I tend to think that if my life had started out differently or my parents had made different choices, I wouldn't have been afforded such incredible opportunities. I know that if my parents had taken the doctor's advice and put me in a home, I wouldn't have had the opportunity to meet people such as former President Ronald Reagan, Marathon Champions Uta Pippig, Bill Rodgers, or Joan Benoit Samuelson, or Boston Bruins stars Bobby Orr, Zdeno Chara, Cam Neely, Lyndon Byers, or Andrew Ference. I feel quite confident that if my umbilical cord had not been wrapped around my neck at birth, it is unlikely that I would have appeared on the *Rosie O'Donnell Show* or the *Oprah Winfrey Show*; spent time with Celtics great Dave Cowens; been blessed enough to meet Patriots' owner Robert Kraft, players Matt Light, and Joe Andruzzi; or shaken the hands of Senator Scott Brown or the late Senator Ted Kennedy. Had I grown up a school boy from North Reading, Massachusetts, and followed my dad's footsteps into the United States Air National Guard, I might not have had the chance to visit El Salvador or Japan or even pedal across the United States with my dad. And as amazing as that may all seem to the average person and as envious as some may become by reading all of this, I also understand that if I had been born without disabilities, I may not have been able to have a positive impact on the thousands of people whose names I don't even know, from places I have never been, or whose smiles I have never witnessed. That is the part of my life that I wouldn't trade for anything. If I had to choose between being interviewed by TV greats Barry Nolan, Mary Carillo, or Natalie Morales, and helping a person who is in distress or in personal trouble, I think it would be easy to predict which one I would choose.

With that being made clear, I am so blessed that I have been fortunate enough to meet and spend time with all of these amazingly famous people. In December 2000, Dad and I were asked to appear on the *Rosie O'Donnell Show*. This was an unforgettable time for several reasons. First, Dad and I were able to appear on national TV with a famous host like Rosie. Second, I was given a Words + Freedom 2000 Toughbook Computer with a Micro CommPac voice synthesizer as a special gift from Words + and Panasonic TM for appearing on the show. They also gave me two more of these to donate in my name, one which I gifted to Tony Bonfiglio, from Mansfield, Massachusetts, who also has cerebral palsy, and the other I donated to the Children's Hospital Boston Augmentative Communication Department. This made me feel extra special. I thought Rosie was very kind and thoughtful and treated me like I was not disabled.

Rosie asked several questions about me, the athlete, and how I feel when I am biking, running, and swimming with Dad. I responded by saying, "Rosie, my disability seems to disappear. By that I mean that I feel just like any other athlete who is in a race. During the swim, every now and then, a few kicks from other athletes splash me, which makes me feel like I am right there in the water with them. During the bike ride, athletes pass me and they say things like, 'Go for it' and 'Rick, help your Dad' or 'You can do it.' During the run, when we pass other athletes, they give very positive comments such as 'Go get them' or 'You are both my heroes!'"

She then gave me the opportunity to speak about what it is like to live life with a disability. I told people about my accomplishments and how people think about those of us who have disabilities. She gave me a chance to actually be an advocate for those with disabilities. This is one of the primary reasons that Dad and I not only run and compete, but spend time doing motivational speaking around the country. Telling our story helps other people understand that those with disabilities are people, too. As I told Rosie, there are so many misconceptions about people with disabilities. Probably the biggest misconception people have is that they cannot get to know an individual with disabilities as a person. Many people don't take the time to get to know them. For example, when a kid sees a person in a wheelchair, the parent often pulls the child back, preventing them from going up to the person to ask questions. The parent hides their child or shelters them from something they don't understand. I strongly feel the behavior of the parent is wrong, because I cannot think of a better way to learn that a person with a disability is just like them than to interact with the person.

Rosie was warm and genuine. I liked her because she treated me like a person. I am a person. Off camera, Rosie kept calling me Ricky in a joking way because she knew I hated it. She was just teasing me, though, and when the show actually taped, she called me Rick. That was an experience I will never forget, but in a different way than being on Oprah. Sometimes what you see isn't necessarily what you get.

Dad and I appeared on the *Oprah Winfrey Show* in 2005, but this was not as nice of a memory as being on air with Rosie. You would think this would have been an amazing highlight in my life. You would imagine that meeting Oprah would be right near the top of the list. But as I look back on it, the whole experience was surprisingly frustrating and a bit disappointing.

First of all, her production lady called my friend and speech therapist, John Costello the evening before the show, and kept on the phone forever because she wanted him to find a specific sentence from my computer for the show. They also allowed us only a certain amount of money for dinner and we went over. At seven in the morning, while we were trying to get a good night's sleep before the show, the housekeeping at the hotel knocked hard on the door and woke us up. She finally came in and had disturbed us only to check the mini-bar. Though none of this was Oprah's fault, it all added to the frustration of a forgettable appearance on her show.

All of this happened before we even got to the TV studio. Once we were there, we saw Oprah backstage. She walked right by us and didn't even say hello. We felt this was very unusual, considering Oprah appears to be very kind and thoughtful once the cameras are rolling. This wasn't the case that day, as when the cameras were on, Oprah acted like I was contagious. She didn't try to shake my hand or even touch me. Maybe she was having a bad day, but someone of her importance should treat everyone she comes in contact with, with kindness and respect. Otherwise she may get a bad review if they ever write a book.

As I said earlier, I also had the opportunity to meet Bobby Orr, who is one of my all-time idols. If I weren't disabled, I would've wanted to be a hockey player. In 1972, in Game Seven of the Stanley Cup Finals, Bobby Orr went flying in mid-air after scoring the winning goal. That same year, I said my first words on my computer, which were, "GO, BRUINS." As the story goes, Mom and Dad wanted my first words to be "Hi, Mom" or "Hi, Dad," but they didn't win the Stanley Cup.

I have also met Bruins former right wing and current team president,

Cam Neely. I have a picture of Cam Neely, Dave Cowens, my dad, and I at a fundraiser for the New England Museum of Sports. Former Bruins tough guy Lyndon Byers is now a radio host. Dad and I used to do a bike ride for Special Olympics, and Byers would interview us before the event.

Dad and I are also close friends with Zdeno Chara, current Bruins captain and star defenseman. In 2005, Chara let my family use his luxury box, and we got to meet him after the game. Z, as his friends call him, also wanted my father to be his personal trainer for triathlons. Dad would have loved to but couldn't take the time from his own training to train someone else. Z still calls occasionally to discuss triathlon tips and pointers.

After the Bruins' Stanley Cup victory in 2011, we received the following email as a result of our relationship with Chara.

Hi, guys. I asked Zdeno Chara for your contact info, but he is already back in Slovakia and tough to get a hold of. First off, I want to say thank you for a new perspective on digging deep and giving it all you got. Our team watched your video before our finals and it was a great lesson for all of us. As a thank you, I would like to invite you to spend the day with the Stanley Cup and me at Spaulding Rehab Hospital. Andrew Ference.

With my love of the Bruins and the historic impact that the Bruins have had on my life since my famous first words, it was incredible to learn that our video had a hand in bring the Bruins their first Stanley Cup in thirty-nine years. To think that our video motivated and inspired guys like Chara, Ference, Nathan Horton and Shawn Thornton to victory nearly four decades to the day after I uttered "Go, Bruins" through my computer makes me excited beyond description. To think that we had a hand in the Bruins victory is an indescribable feeling.

Following that email, Dad and I, along with my brothers, Russ and Rob; my PCA, Mike Adams; and Todd, joined Ference, who is also a star Bruins defenseman, at Spaulding Rehabilitation Hospital to start our day with the Stanley Cup. We visited injured patients at Spaulding and then spent the evening in the North End of Boston eating Italian food and toasting to the Bruins and the Cup. Ference also participated in a flash mob down in the North End with the Cup and thousands of Bruins fans who were in attendance.

I have also been fortunate to visit many other countries, with the country of El Salvador being one of them. When we were there, the country was in the middle of a civil war. We entered a McDonald's, and an armed guard opened the door for my PCA and me. We visited a rehab center, which was very moving for me. I have been disabled since birth, so I've had a lot of time to get used to things. Many of the people in the rehab center have lived much of their life without a disability and became disabled due to war. My heart was in pain because all of the adjustments are new to them. At the time, I was taking a lot of classes in rehabilitation services because I was thinking about possibly switching my major to rehab. Later I realized that I couldn't do the job due to my own limitations.

At the rehab center, I asked "Why don't they have rooms for the different type of therapies?" They answered, "Because we have to make do with what the government gives us." It once again made me realize how lucky I am to live in the United States.

Dad and I were in El Salvador to compete in an Olympic distance triathlon. When we were waiting to go to the awards ceremony, people kept on coming up to the van looking at me, pointing and screaming. They thought that I was a god and were trying to touch me.

I saw myself as an ambassador when Dad and I went to Amagi, an island in Japan. They didn't integrate people with disabilities into the public, although they treated people with disabilities very well. The mayor greeted us at the airport. They held a welcoming dinner in a special room where everyone sat on the floor. They spread old newspapers across the floor so that my wheelchair wouldn't get the floor dirty. We went to many schools and spoke to kids about what integration was. At one school, Dad almost got run over by kids as they came running at us as we were getting on the bus. Our presence helped set a tone for the government of the island to integrate disabled into society. Though it may be a long process, I think we helped alter their way of thinking.

During our stay in Japan, five of the biggest television stations in the country were there to cover Dad and me in the half ironman. The day of the event, Mother Nature poured like a monsoon all day. Dad had the runs from eating sushi the night before, and we had camera crews following us the whole time. At one point, Dad sat the bike up against a tree while the crew was filming us. Dad had to go to the bathroom, and it too was like a monsoon. The crew said, "No, no," but Dad said, "Yes, yes."

After the bike portion of the race, Dad told me he didn't think he could finish, but I encouraged him to find a way to continue. Fortunately, after he had a couple of bananas he felt better and we continued. All through the run, the people along the course screamed our last name. It was a quite a memorable story of one of our runs—in more ways than one.

Sometimes It Isn't Easy Being Me

by Rick Hoyt with Todd Civin

> "Trust yourself. Create the kind of self that you will be happy to live with all your life. Make the most of yourself by fanning the tiny, inner sparks of possibility into flames of achievement."
>
> —*Golda Meir*

I wouldn't be telling the truth if I painted a picture that life has been in any way easy for me. Along with the physical challenges of spending each day in a wheelchair, there is a lot of frustration and mental anguish that I deal with. I'm not sure at times which really hurts more. For the physical pain, I take lots of medicine every day and eventually get drowsy and fall asleep. But the mental challenges of being excluded were a lot for a little boy, and even a growing teen or young man to handle.

It was always extremely difficult and frustrating to be able to understand what everyone around me was saying, while being unable to respond back at the time. I felt like I never would have the opportunity to express my feelings. Even though people would play twenty questions to attempt to figure out my response, they still didn't know exactly what I was saying. This was before we had the Russell Method, so my way of communicating consisted mostly of head shakes and nods. It was as if I were in a fishbowl looking out. I was able to see the world, but had this barrier between me and outside that made it impossible to really be a part of it. Think of yourself as a picture on the wall with moving eyeballs like you sometimes see in movies. This is sort of how I felt at the time. I was in the room and could see and hear everything that was going on, but was unable to truly interact. At times the frustration became so unbearable I just balled my eyes out. My heart seemed as if it were going to explode.

I still feel sad sometimes because many people tend to ignore me without asking me a question. They are not getting a chance to get to know me at all. I can answer any of the questions that a verbal person can answer. It just takes more work on both my side and the side of the listener. I am more than willing to put in the extra work. It is slow, but it is in no way painful or frustrating. It is far more frustrating for me to have a person ask me a question and then refuse to invest the time required to listen to my answer. Think how it would feel to you as a speaking human being if someone asked you a question and then walked away before they received the answer. Sometimes I'll be asked a question, and then see by the expression on the asker's face that he realizes I can't speak back. He looks away from me and then asks the question to my dad or the PCA. I understand it, I guess, but I'm not a dog. I am a living, breathing, thinking human with feelings.

I cannot read cursive writing, and I think this is because I've never had the ability to write. It seems like it would be a very difficult skill to acquire if you've never held a pencil or pen in your hand. Kind of like asking an artist who has never held a paintbrush before to paint. When I read, I prefer large print, and I actually have trouble seeing small print. Part of this comes with being fifty, but when I was around five I wore glasses, and when I was around three, I actually wore trifocals.

Even though my vision isn't very good, I consulted for Boston College on a project called EagleEyes in the late '90s. It was a game where illegal aliens moved around a computer screen. I would kill them with my eye movements, but as they got smaller my score got worse. I can look at women just fine though. No trouble there.

I have never had emotional therapy, but I think it would help me to deal with the frustration that I experience. I think I would have dealt with it much better than I do at times. As a child I knew I couldn't do what other children could do. I did a lot of kicking and flailing my arms. I would try to yell, but very little would come through my mouth for sound. I would cry to try to get my point across. I didn't know how to tell people that I wanted to be included in what they were doing. As I got older, it was easier for me to get my point across and my brothers would include me and try to show me how to do things. I know I may have been a little complicated to figure out at times, and sometimes people would forget that I was even there. To remind people I was in the room, I would have a "spaz" attack.

When I wanted to be called on in school to say something, I knew teachers wouldn't call on me because it would take me a long time to answer the question. Eventually they would let me answer, but only yes and no questions.

In college, it was harder for me to try to hold the frustration in. Here I was a young man and I didn't want it to look like I was a child. I had to show the students, the professors, and even myself, that I belonged there. I would get mad at myself more than at other people, oftentimes about things that I really couldn't control. I don't know how to spell very well because my use of language is verbal rather than written. I go strictly by how words sound, since I have never written on paper. If you watch children in a spelling bee, they make believe they are writing the word on their hand because that is how they are used to spelling. Since I don't write, spelling comes very hard to me. So I became very frustrated with myself because I couldn't spell better at my age. It took me much longer to do school work because I wanted to do the work myself without help.

Some professors just thought I didn't understand the work, when I really did. Luckily, most of those classes were just fillers. When the classes were related to my degree, I would work extra hard. I would try to talk to the professors by computer to make them realize that I understood what they were teaching. I would sometimes have a spasm to try to get my point across if I couldn't get my thoughts through using my computer. I know this was immature, but it was the only weapon that I had left. Candice, one of my PCAs while I was in college, would help me get back on track and refocus so I could get through the class.

As an adult, I get frustrated when people address the person I am with and ignore me as if I'm not even in the room. Last time I checked, there had been no reported cases of anyone ever contracting cerebral palsy after having contact with someone who has it. Yet, sometimes people just don't look my way as, if I have a disease. They don't know me and they should try to get to know me.

Sometimes I think people treat me like I'm a clothing store mannequin, just sitting there looking pretty. I try to move my arms to let them know I am in the room and listening to what they have to say. Often times, the person I am with will make sure they look at me to answer any question that is asked.

I also get very agitated when people don't think I have a functioning brain. It frustrates me when people don't let me talk after they have taken the time to ask me a question. I know my method can be a little bit tedious, but think if someone speaks sign language and you asked them a question. It would be rude if, as they started to respond, you turned away and didn't wait for the answer.

Often when I am spelling out an answer, someone tries to finish my sentence for me by guessing what it is I am trying to spell. This is an okay method if they are good at it and guess the right answer, but it really slows things down when they interrupt and don't have a clue as to what I am trying to say.

I am fifty years old and I still get frustrated when people treat me as if I am a child. I wave my arms if I don't like something. I know it may look silly, but this is one way I am able to communicate. When something is wrong I wave my arms and kick my legs to try to let them know I didn't like something. If someone is talking and I don't agree with what they have to say, I keep shaking my head no. If they don't understand, I wave my arms. I know as a grown man I shouldn't be waving my arms like a wild man. However, to get someone's attention, I can't just say, "Hey, I want to talk." I have to get their attention by other means.

I also know I may show mixed signals, because when I am both happy or upset I wave my arms. But as I was told by one of my PCAs, she could tell if I was upset because of the look in my eyes. I am told I have very expressive eyes. They say that when one of our senses is lacking, another sense often gets stronger. Maybe this is why my eyes are so expressive. Since I'm not able to express myself in a conventional way, perhaps God gave me especially expressive eyes so I can show my emotions in another way. If someone looks at my eyes they can tell if I am upset or happy.

Trying to control frustration is hard for me. I can't talk, so when things build up inside me I tend to bubble over. As things build up inside, I need to get someone's attention so I "spasm." I know that may be childish, but getting my point across without my computer is difficult. I have worked on improving this, as I know it can be a little annoying. If I need to get someone's attention, I have learned to use one arm instead of two and hope this cuts my annoyingness in half. I also try to move my head to get people to look at me so that maybe they will ask me if I want to say something. But I guess if I think about it logically, frustration is hard for most people to control, so maybe I fit in just fine.

Perspective

by Todd Civin

> *"Fairy Tales always have a happy ending. That depends . . . on whether you are Rumpelstiltskin or the Queen."*
>
> — *Jane Yolen, Briar Rose*

Last March, my wife, Katie, and I asked Rick to join us for an evening of minor league hockey at the Worcester Sharks game. The Sharks play in the American Hockey League and are the minor league affiliate of the NHL's San Jose Sharks. It is well documented that Rick is a huge Bruins fan at heart, as evidenced by his first words ever "uttered" using his computer—"GO, BRUINS"—back in 1972. Rick thinks that had he been born able-bodied, he would've aspired to play professional hockey. Who are we to know otherwise? If Rick says that is what he was going to do, then that's how the story goes.

In the interest of saving myself a dollar or two, since a Sharks ticket costs about the same as a beer does at a Bruins game, I figured we'd take him to Worcester instead of taxing my wallet by going to Boston to take in a B's game.

Although we didn't plan this in advance, it just so happened to be Special Olympics Night at the Sharks game, so there was a large population of disabled fans and their families in attendance. It seemed to be a perfect coincidence as it allowed me to witness Rick vis-à-vis with other people with disabilities. Everything is relative, and this became evident as Rick and I conversed about some of our neighbors sitting in the handicapped seating next to us throughout the game.

Before the opening puck dropped, a teenage boy with Down syndrome had the honor of skating around the ice while carrying the Special Olympics torch, an honor very similar to the day that Dick and Rick ran through the streets of Boston carrying the 1996 Olympic torch as it made its way from Athens, Greece to Atlanta, Georgia.

Tonight, the ice belonged to this proud young man, who smiled from ear-to-ear as he skated slowly around the DCU Center ice much to the adulation of the cheering crowd. There wasn't a dry eye in the house as he took slow strides from one end of the rink to the other, while pumping his fist skyward, as his image was telecast on the large screen overhead. I looked over at Rick and saw that his eyes had glazed over a bit as he waved his arms wildly in approval as this hero took the final turn and exited the ice.

I can't really recall the final score of the game, but came away with several indelible memories from the sixty minutes of on-ice action. For one, Rick is very similar to many hockey fans in that he loves a hard check into the glass or the occasional dropping of the gloves as opponents perform a mid-ice wrestling match far more than he enjoys a rush down the ice or a spectacular save. Like me, I think Rick would enjoy attending a fight and having a hockey game break out far more than the opposite. Every time the adversaries engaged in the corner, I'd glance over at Rick's toothless smile and knew without a doubt that he was envisioning himself going toe-to-toe with one of Philadelphia's Broad Street Bullies, who were the Bruins' nemesis in the early 1970s. If

Rick could have dropped his imaginary gloves and charged onto the ice as the third man into the scrum, I know he would have done so.

During the second period of the game, I witnessed a larger than life gentleman with a huge smile and an equally huge voice making his way through the crowd of the rabid Sharks fans. He was dressed in the black and turquoise colors of the Sharks and was interviewing random fans in the audience to get their opinions on everything from the taste of Papa Gino's pizza to the between period t-shirt toss into the sold-out DCU Center crowd. I approached this mobile Master of Ceremonies, who I later learned was Adam Webster, the roving PR man of the Sharks and popular morning newsman on radio station WXLO in Worcester. I approached Webster and told him, "I'm here with Rick Hoyt. I think the crowd may enjoy seeing him up on the big screen." I was surprised when he asked me who Rick Hoyt was, as I am under the assumption that everyone from Pittsfield to Provincetown and Toledo to Tokyo knows the Hoyts. I politely explained to him that the Hoyts are the well-known father and son race team where the dad pushes his son during the Boston Marathon and that they'd be appearing in their twenty-ninth Boston Marathon later that month.

Again, I was shocked when he said, "Okay, so what is it that you want me to do?" I thought he was messing with me, as it seemed that seeing Rick's mug up on the screen would be far more interesting then catching some unsuspecting fan picking his nose to the delight of the easily amused crowd. I explained that I thought with the Boston Marathon being less than a month away that fans would recognize Rick and would appreciate the fact that Rick took time away from his training schedule to take in a game of the local six. Webster advised me that he would try to come over between the second and third stanzas, if he was able to break away from his previously orchestrated routine.

I assumed I'd never see him again unless a flying t-shirt happened to ricochet off one of the overhead rafters and magically tumble into Rick's unsuspecting lap. This is why I'm not a betting man, as with 10:02

left in the game, I was tapped on the shoulder by my new buddy, Adam, who came through as he promised. I later learned that Webster does some incredible work with many charities, so it should have been expected that he would take care of my boy, Rick. "Okay, now how many marathons has he run?" I shook my head in slight disbelief and told him again of Rick's heroics. The camera panned to Adam while Rick's image appeared on the overhead screen. Before he had nearly a chance to utter a word about Rick, the crowd spontaneously stood and gave Rick an ovation for well over a minute. I had chills running up the back of my neck and couldn't hold back my tears as Rick grinned and waved his arms uncontrollably. I sensed that the sellout crowd shared the overwhelming emotion. Webster waited for the crowd to become nearly silent before announcing to the crowd, "I guess you know who this is." A slight chuckle emanated from the crowd in unison. Adam patted me on the back and thanked me for introducing him to Rick, as the rest of the adoring crowd obviously already knew him.

Rick and I have since returned to see the Sharks play and were immediately recognized by Webster, who graciously repeated the introduction of Rick to the equally enthusiastic crowd of Sharks fans prior to his thirtieth Boston Marathon. Webster also invited Rick and me to appear on his morning radio show following the release of Rick's book.

One more everlasting memory came sometime earlier in the game when I caught Rick glancing over at some of the other inhabitants of the wheelchair accessible row that we sat in that afternoon. Rick cannot walk, talk, or control his muscles from the neck down. He has never fed himself, bathed without assistance, or even brought a glass to his lips without aid, yet Rick is what I would describe as far less disabled than the rest of the population that made up our row. Unfortunately, many of our adjoining neighbors seemed incapable of enjoying or even being aware that there was a hockey game in progress below.

A few days later, I asked Rick how he felt while sitting with the other disabled people at the game, and he said, "I feel very fortunate when I compare my life to theirs. I enjoy the life that I have. I am able to go running with my dad and I have friends that take me places.

"I have finished high school and graduated from college, and I spend quality time with my family, sharing laughs and joking around about things. I may not be able to use my legs or move like some people can. However, I can get around with someone pushing my wheelchair. I may not be able to use my own voice, but I am very fortunate to have the technology to use my computer as my voice."

I guess that is what you call perspective. Before you complain about your own life, take a walk in someone else's shoes, or take a ride in their wheelchair, as the case may be. Life is relative. It all depends on what you know and how you define the things that make you happy.

One Flavor at a Time

by Bryan Lyons

> *"I am only one, but still I am one. I cannot do everything, but still I can do something; and because I cannot do everything, I will not refuse to do something that I can do."*
>
> — *Helen Keller*

I ran my first marathon in February of 2000. Only one year later, I not only couldn't run, but thought I may never walk again. Or breathe or laugh. Or eat ice cream.

On the night of February 6, 2001, while driving home from work, I was struck by a drunk driver. It took me exactly eleven months to the day of the accident to run even one mile without having severe back pain. Prior to the accident, I could go out and run sixteen to eighteen miles on any given day. It took me almost five years to be able to run five miles again. In January 2006, I ran my first half marathon since the time of the accident. My finishing time was about a half hour slower than prior to the accident. Instead of being elated that I had completed the race, I was very discouraged with my performance. Upon discussing this with a childhood friend, he suggested that I try a triathlon as there was less emphasis on the running. So I did and I was hooked!

I joined Tri Fury, which is a local triathlon club. I was content with competing in triathlons, since I had never done one before the accident and therefore I couldn't compare my performance to previous triathlons. At the time, I knew that someday I would complete another marathon, but I was not ready mentally, physically or emotionally. In September 2008, a club member posted that Team Hoyt was looking for runners to join their 2009 Boston Marathon Charity Team. I grew up seeing the Hoyts in the news each year as they competed in the Boston Marathon and was always in awe and inspired by them. I was from New Hampshire, so we didn't celebrate "Marathon Monday" (Patriots' Day) as a holiday. It wasn't until I was a dental student at Tufts that I was able to observe them run. Much like Rick, or so I thought at the time, I was speechless.

The first time I met Dick and Rick was at the Ninth Annual Groton Road Race in April 2000. I was so overwhelmed with emotion that I could barely speak. I humbly informed them how inspirational they were to me. I knew I wasn't the first person to ever tell that to Dick, yet I could clearly tell that he was touched that he inspired me.

When the opportunity to run with and for Team Hoyt arose, I knew immediately that this was the only catalyst I would need to take on the challenge of another marathon. For that marathon to be the Boston Marathon, often referred to as the greatest marathon in the world, was an added bonus. Many people think that the Hoyts are to the Boston Marathon as Michael Jordon was to the Chicago Bulls.

The experience of training to run my first Boston Marathon with Team Hoyt was simply amazing. Three-time Boston Marathon Champion Uta Pippig graciously and generously offered her knowledge and skills as the Team Coach. Imagine the astonishing surprise of answering the phone for the first time to a sweet, soft-spoken woman with a German accent telling you, "It's Uta." Even better, imagine telling your girlfriend that you'll have to call her later because Uta is on the other line. I don't think there was a guy on the team that didn't get all giddy, like a little school boy experiencing his first crush, when Uta would call. There were numerous stories from teammates' wives similar to the following: "I can't get Randy off the couch to bring out the trash, but when Uta calls..." Or something like, "Doug, your girlfriend is on the phone."

Uta would send weekly directives and tailor them to individual needs. She would check in regularly to see how we were doing. First and foremost, she made sure we were healthy and well before proposing the next training objectives. I vividly recall discussing an upcoming half marathon that I would be using as a training run. She suggested that I run the first half at a fast comfortable pace and then *really* pick up the pace for the second half. I replied, "Uta, I only have one 'fast' and it ain't that fast!"

Needless to say, her efforts were not wasted; her encouragement and guidance promoted the Team Hoyt "Yes, You Can!" attitude. The mileage increased and the training runs became more grueling in the frigid Boston weather. Before I knew it, I was running with almost twenty other Team Hoyt members from all over the country—as well as the occasional Canadian that slipped across the border—all with the same goal in mind. We were raising money to educate society about the inclusion of people with disabilities and to help those who are physically disabled become active members of their community, school or workplace. It was magical! Right, Uta?

Since the Boston Marathon in 2009, I have met up with Dick and Rick at hundreds of road races and triathlons to compete with them and promote the cause. I'm not going to lie; Rick also has a tendency to attract the ladies. Early on I was intimidated to speak with Rick. One of my first and most memorable conversations with Rick was at the Fourth Annual Mission Possible Holliston Road Race in 2010. Holliston High School has a beautiful football /sports field. I mentioned to Rick that my high school field was not nearly as nice as that field. Through his PCA,

Linda, Rick replied that his high school field was all mud and dirt. It was at that moment that I realized Rick was no different than me. Now I speak with him as I would my own brother. I just don't expect an immediate answer. Actually, I guess that would be much like speaking with my brother.

What started as a chance opportunity for me has evolved into a cherished friendship. It seems Rick and I share an affinity for ice cream. I've notice that most of the races in which Rick chooses to compete have an ice cream shop conveniently located nearby. Coincidence? I think not! I always look forward to racing with Rick and undoing all of our hard work by devouring ice cream afterward. One race at a time; one flavor at a time; one letter at a time.

When I reflect back on the decision to join the illustrious Team Hoyt in September 2008, I realize that it was not Team Hoyt that needed me; it was I who needed them. What started as the inspiration to tackle another marathon has grown to become a way of life for me. Since joining Team Hoyt in 2008, I have completed eight additional marathons, almost 100 triathlons including Ironman Arizona (2.4 mile swim, 112 mile bike, 26.2 mile run) and over 150 road races. During every race, triathlon and cycling or swim event since the Boston Marathon in 2009, I have worn a small photo that I took a couple years earlier of Dick and Rick competing in the Massachusetts State Triathlon Championship. Even a quick glance at the photo is a great source of motivation and inspiration. Having Team Hoyt "with" me has helped get me through many difficult times not only in my athletic endeavors, but in my personal and professional life as well. Countless others have commented on the photo during races and have shared their personal feelings and connections to them. They have touched and enhanced so many lives and families; I am privileged to be a part of Team Hoyt and truly honored to call them my friends.

How Rick Inspired myTEAM TRIUMPH

by Ronald Robb
CEO of myTEAM TRIUMPH

> "I believe a strong society is an inclusive society. If we want to win big then we'd better include everybody because we need everybody."
>
> — Cyndi Lauper

Thirty years ago, after his first race, Rick typed into his computer the now famous words, "Dad, when we're racing it feels like my disability disappears." I wonder if he could've possibly known how this sentence would eventually change the lives of literally thousands of individuals with disabilities around the world.

It was the summer of 2007 when I went through a small mid-life crisis brought on by coronary issues generated from many years of poor life choices, including smoking and overeating, just to name a few. Although I had exchanged those choices for healthier ones—I was now running, biking and swimming six days a week—the damage had been done and I was paying the piper.

I had just received my second stent, which is a small, expandable, cylindrical device placed into the heart to keep a blocked artery open. These little gems are incredible. You can go from being at high risk of having a heart attack to being totally healthy in a matter of hours. In fact, when I received my first stent, I felt so good that I completed a sprint triathlon a week later. It's worth noting that this was not recommended by my cardiologist.

But not so the second time around. A week after the procedure, my chest still hurt, and it hurt badly. I was not able to continue my usual routine of running, biking and swimming, and I was questioning if in fact I was "damaged goods" and would never be able to do those things again.

This led to an emotional and existential crisis that I think could be categorized as a "mid-life" crisis. I eventually became sick and tired of lying around hoping for the pain to subside, so on a hot summer night I went for a long walk to commune with God.

And so with a mind full of doubt and a chest in full spasm I began to think, and think, and think. I thought about how I wished I could rewind my life and make different health choices. I thought about how my life would be forever changed if I could never run, bike or swim again. And I especially thought about what I could do with all the time I'd have if I weren't doing those things six days a week.

So I asked God for patience, but I also made it very clear that this wasn't working. If it was His will that I would never swim, bike or run again, then could I please get some guidance on what it was that He wanted me to do with my time?

I completed my walk, and on a whim decided to check my e-mail. And there, among the jokes and chain-letters and ads for Viagra, was a link to the now famous video of Team Hoyt doing the Hawaiian Ironman set to the song "I Can Only Imagine" by Mercy Me.

The YouTube video, named "CAN," had gone "viral," although I was seeing it for the very first time. A friend of mine had sent me the link ostensibly to "cheer me up," but instead the video would, in fact, change my life and the lives of so many others forever.

In the final scene of the video, Dick and Rick are racing towards the finish line, the music peaking, the crowd cheering, Rick waving his arms, and me crying. What a beautiful thing, I thought, that the exhilaration of crossing a finish line could be experienced by Rick along with the other athletes that had conquered Kona—and themselves— that day.

As I was getting ready to delete the e-mail, it hit me that while it was great that Rick had his father to team up with in these events, what about all the children, teens, adults and veterans who didn't have a father or other loved one who had the wherewithal to do this? What if an organization could be formed to match people with disabilities with able-bodied athletes, equipment and venues?

And just like that, myTEAM TRIUMPH was born, the unlikely but providential offspring of a middle-aged man going through a mid-life crisis and a video that captured the joy experienced by Rick Hoyt while racing. And as it turned out, Rick was working his inspirational magic on the hearts of others who would form the original board of myTEAM TRIUMPH.

The time and effort involved in pulling an organization like myTEAM TRIUMPH together would also solve the problem of what to do with the extra time I had been given by not being able to swim, bike and run anymore. But as it happens, this was not a problem. I found out that I was just fine. My chest pains were nothing more than the after-effect of some "cleaning" that was done by scraping the artery walls clean. There's a name for the procedure, but it sounded a lot like the coronary version of a Roto-Rooter to me.

I was not "damaged goods" after all. Yet, ironically, the experience of having pain in my physical heart led to a softening of my spiritual heart, which in turn is what provided the incubator for turning Rick's inspiration into what is now a national program serving hundreds of individuals with disabilities.

One thing that all of us at myTEAM TRIUMPH agree on is that if we had to come up with a single word to describe Rick, it would be "inspirational." He has and continues to inspire us on many different levels. Many people will let the slightest bump in the road slow them down or even cause them to quit. But not Rick. No amount of headwind can stop him or even slow him down.

One shudders to think of what might have been (or not have been) had Rick's parents placed him in an institution as they were advised by doctors shortly after his birth. It is hard to imagine how life would be different for so many people with disabilities who now enjoy racing with myTEAM TRIUMPH and other organizations.

After all, the video "CAN" wouldn't have been made, because Team Hoyt would not have existed. Their first race never would've been run thirty years ago, and Rick would not have typed the words, "Dad, when we're racing it feels like my disability disappears."

Rick is the reason there is a "Team" in "Team Hoyt." He is also the reason there is a "TEAM" in myTEAM TRIUMPH. We, and other similar organizations, owe our very existence to Rick's inspiration. His ten thousand watt smile has now been duplicated hundreds of times by myTEAM TRIUMPH "Captains," bringing to life the motto "Yes, You Can!"

I have had the honor of meeting and spending time with Rick, during which I learned that we have some things in common. For example, we both have bachelor's degrees from prestigious institutions. We both took longer than four years to get our respective degrees, although Rick was doing it one letter at a time. And we both occasionally enjoy a good party.

Rick has gone from nearly being institutionalized as a baby to "rock star" status as an adult, and in so doing has helped others with disabilities become Rock Stars in their own right. No longer are people with disabilities considered mysterious, even when their earth-suits are severely damaged.

This is an incredible legacy.

She Does Not Talk or Walk. She Does Not Play for Fun. But She Smiles, While Out for a Run.

by Major Kim "Rooster" Rossiter
USMC

> *"When you talk about inclusion, it says to me, 'Please include me.' We're not asking to be included; we want to participate and lead."*
>
> — *Sharon Shapiro-Lacks*

I do not know who first said, "Life is not measured by the number of breaths you take, but by the moments that take your breath away," but my family refers to it often. For you see, it is when a slight wind takes Ainsley Rossiter's breath away, that she smiles the brightest. As she approaches her ninth birthday, Ainsley's heart-capturing smiles are now few and far between, but represent those moments that take our breath away. Voluntarily or involuntarily, today's occasional smiles are the only way we think she may be communicating with us, and many of these smiles have come while she is out for a run.

AN ANGEL IS BORN

Born on Camp Lejeune, North Carolina, on December 10, 2003, Ainsley proceeded to meet all of her first year milestones. From pointing toward the garage door and saying, "Da Da," as my car pulled into the driveway to smiling while swiftly crawling toward my arms as I came through the door, Ainsley embarked on her second year just as most children do. I recall my excitement while writing the note left for her on the eve before deploying to Iraq in February 2005. "Ainsley, Daddy looks forward to seeing you run around the backyard with your sister when I get home!" A few months into this deployment, however, "mother's intuition" led my wife to voice concern to Ainsley's doctor about her inability to walk at fifteen months. These concerns yielded a twenty-four-month emotional roller coaster ride that included two MRIs, multiple blood tests, countless doctor visits, many emotional conversations, and a nerve biopsy. During a subsequent deployment in 2007, I received a message to phone home. As I dialed the long series of required numbers to reach my wife, who was halfway around the world raising our three children under the age of six, my mind raced. Soon she answered and proceeded to explain that the Oregon Health and Science University completed its study and clinically diagnosed our sweet Ainsley with an extremely rare progressive genetic nerve disorder called Infantile Neuroaxonal Dystrophy (INAD). Silence. Confusion. Anger. Uncertainty. Denial. Sadness. Life as we knew it changed forever, as there is no cure for INAD, and it affects the nervous system, globally. Because the dystrophy is progressive, it becomes worse over time and Ainsley will begin to lose skills that she previously had. At the end stages of the disease, generally between the ages of six to ten, children are usually blind, no longer have voluntary movements, and have lost all awareness. If you are looking for an example of the word devastated, look no further. Details of the following few months are blurry, but living up to the idea of always taking care of its own, Marine Corps leadership prevailed and I was eventually reunited stateside with my family. We received orders and relocated to Virginia Beach during January 2008.

AN ATHLETE IS BORN

We used our first six months in Virginia Beach to achieve stability and establish relations with the many professionals required to assist us with ensuring Ainsley received the best care possible. This included everything from introducing Abbey Bruckner, her preschool special-education teacher at Centerville Elementary School, to the various effective techniques used by Ainsley's previous preschool teacher in North Carolina, Michelle Smith, to ensuring the Individualized Education Program (IEP) captured the required goals and associated therapies. In fact, it was during one of these IEP-driven therapy sessions that our life as we knew it was once again changed forever, as Ainsley's physical therapist, Peggy Wolff, extended an invitation for our family to participate in a newly formed road-race running group inspired by Dick and Rick Hoyt. Team Hoyt Virginia Beach (THVB) is the only running team authorized by the Hoyts to use their name. The detailed story of how THVB was formed will perhaps become a chapter in my first book. Suffice it to say, when Dick and Rick visited Virginia Beach in 2006, they were joined at the starting line by Mike Mather and his son, Owen, who, like Rick, has cerebral palsy. The following year, another local father, Trey White, brought his child, Katie, who has Prader Willi Syndrome, to the starting line. The inspiration these two fathers received from Dick and Rick represents the spark that facilitated our life-changing experience on August 16, 2008, as Ainsley's first of many running-aided, wind-induced smiles took our family's collective breath away. Ainsley completed the Surfer's Healing 5K road race, received her finisher's medal, and became an official THVB athlete!

A THERAPY LIKE NO OTHER

In an instant, THVB provided our family with a therapeutic means to fight the devastation associated with learning your child has a terminal illness. The positive energy at the start line, the children smiling from ear-to-ear, the togetherness of every member preparing to run with the wind, the fearlessness of the athletes, the feeling of normalcy, and the love we all have for one another is a therapy like no other. Our teammate and critical element in the continued success of THVB, Ginny Cohen, captures the spirit of the experience in her blog: "Rick and Dick, you are right. It's a good life... And for all the rider athletes and their parents, thank you for letting me (us) be a part of it all. Your inspiration, strength and limitless love are such gifts."

A RENEWED SIBLING BOND

During Ainsley's first two years as a THVB Athlete, I pushed her in multiple road races and found myself becoming a runner for my daughter. She inspired me to run farther and our runs yielded unforgettable father-daughter moments, many priceless smiles, and experiences our family unit will never forget. Although Ainsley inspired me to accomplish goals previously unconsidered, it is perhaps her older sister, Briley, whom she has inspired the most. Separated by nearly two and a half years, Ainsley and Briley enjoyed everything from playing dress-up to hosting tea parties. Their mother enjoyed watching every moment her daughters shared during these sisterly moments, but these moments decreased as Ainsley's dystrophy progressed. After watching Ainsley complete her first half marathon in 2010, however, the idea of Briley joining Ainsley for a road race was born. A few months later a goal was established: the Rossiter Sisters would accompany THVB on its first "destination trip" to run with Dick and Rick in the Holland 5K during May 2011.

As winter turned to spring in early 2011, Briley, who was nine at the time, embraced the challenge associated with the Operation Smile Final Mile to train for her first road race with Ainsley. After completing 25.2 miles over a couple months, and the ceremonial final marathon mile, Briley turned her efforts to training with Ainsley. No amount of training, however, could have prepared my wife and me for the flood of joy we experienced as we watched our daughters complete their first 5K road race together on that sunny morning in hilly Holland, Massachusetts.

To see Briley and Ainsley accomplish this goal together is an experience we will remember forever.

THE CONVERSATION

Many more moments would continue to take our breath away over the twelve months following Ainsley and Briley's first 5K together. Serving as a trigger was a conversation I shared with Dick during our weekend in Holland. While Ainsley and Rick enjoyed lunch together—she actually spent the majority of the day by his side—Dick and I enjoyed small talk about our military careers. I mentioned to him that I was feeling guilty about not being able to run the 2011 Marine Corps Marathon (MCM) with Ainsley because my wife and I thought a five-hour race would be too much for her to sit through. Dick quickly turned his head, looked me in the eyes, and with his deep Boston accent said, "What do you mean you can't run the Marine Marathon without her? How long did she sit during the drive to Massachusetts from Virginia Beach?" He made his point, and his message was clear: "YES, YOU CAN" run the Marine Corps Marathon with your daughter! Of course, now we needed to gain permission from the MCM Race Director and perhaps more challenging, begin training. Seeking permission began with this e-mail to the MCM staff:

Mr. Dick Hoyt recommended that I contact your office on a matter very important to me and my family. I am an active-duty Marine Officer with seventeen years of service and am finally signed up to run the Marine Corps Marathon (my first, and possible last). I say this will possibly be my last because the only reason I began running in 5K, 10K, and half-marathon road races is because of my terminally-ill daughter, Ainsley. In 2007, Ainsley was diagnosed with a rare genetic disorder called Infantile Neuroaxonal Dystrophy (INAD). Shortly after this, the Corps sent my family from Camp Lejeune to Virginia Beach. In 2008, Ainsley's physical therapist convinced us to participate with Team Hoyt VB (www.teamhoytvb.com), and since then I have pushed Ainsley in nearly fifteen road races, including the VA Beach Rock 'n Roll half marathon last year.

Ainsley cannot walk, talk or move on her own, but when the wind blows in her face on the race track, she smiles the most wonderful smile—as if to say, "Daddy, go faster! This is fun!" Ainsley and I had the honor of visiting Dick and Rick Hoyt's home in Holland, Massachusetts, last weekend, and the MCM came up in conversation. I mentioned I was signed up to run it in October. But, like I told him, I am feeling guilty about running this race without Ainsley. She is the reason I run road races and to do one without her would not be right—just like being a career Marine and not running the MCM is not right! Ainsley will be eight years old in December (2011) and her illness is rapidly progressing. We understand that only seven cases of INAD are known in the United States and most children with this diagnosis pass on before reaching ten years of age.

This long email is to ask: Might "Team Ainsley" (of Team Hoyt VB) be able to run in the MCM? We understand the need to stay out of the way of other runners and promise to stay to the far right. To be clear, she would not be riding in a "stroller," but rather in a THVB "jogger chair," as Rick Hoyt often points out. If approved by MCM to push her, Ainsley's former physical therapist (who has completed the MCM) is willing to assist me with pushing, as well as to be with us for extra safety and adjusting reasons. I noticed the MCM wheelchair division starts at 0745. Our intent, if possible, would be to start with that group, but not to interfere with them. Trust me, we are a "no-maintenance" team and only require your permission. Team Hoyt's motto is "Yes, You Can" — and we hope you can say the same. Thank you for your time and Semper Fidelis!

To my amazement and perhaps as a tribute to Dick and Rick Hoyt, whose Boston Marathon qualifier was the 1981 MCM, my request was approved within twenty-five minutes! And with that, our sixteen-week marathon training plan began.

TRAINING, FUNDRAISING, LOVE

As the hot Virginia temperatures associated with the 2011 summer ensued, our training plan had to be creative. Of course, we leveraged and would not dream of missing the already scheduled THVB races to aid us in our marathon training. The Children's Hospital of the King's Daughters 8K road race came first. Although Ainsley had not required the services of this amazing facility thus far, the hospital has played an enormous role in the lives of many THVB athletes. As such, the event holds a special place in our annual race schedule. July and August included the final few races before THVB's annual fundraising race, the Virginia Beach Rock and Roll Half Marathon (RnR). During the previous year's fundraising efforts, Ainsley's supporters escalated her to attain the honor of THVB Top Fundraiser. So for 2011, we raised her goal and promised to finish the race with a faster time. Both were achieved, Ainsley was once again the top fundraiser, and our marathon training plan surpassed the halfway mark.

Fundraising accomplishments and marathon training goals aside, the most impressive part of the months leading up to the MCM was the overwhelmingly level of support provided by friends, family members, and teammates of Ainsley. Not a distance runner, but inspired by Ainsley to experience new distances, our friend and neighbor, Ronnie Petko, met with me at 0500 hours every weekend for our weekly "long run." As anyone that has trained for a marathon is aware, it is the multiple fourteen, fifteen, and eighteen-mile training runs that must be conducted before the summer sun rises that represent the difference on marathon day. So with the jogging chair appropriately weighed, we set out every weekend before sunrise. While it was too early to wake Ainsley for each of these runs, we made it a point to bring her on at least one of our five-mile runs during the weeks we did not have a scheduled race.

Ronnie's dedication and participation during this period goes beyond that of a typical neighborly friendship and I am forever grateful. While two Team Ainsley members from her first RnR (Andrew Juarez and Laura Pruett) had previously scheduled obligations, Ronnie agreed to join us this time. Team Ainsley veterans, her preschool teachers Abbey and Michelle, agreed to join us again for a second RnR. This time, however, these two ladies demonstrated a level of physical strength not witnessed the previous year. Together, the two of them pushed Ainsley for the first four miles before handing Ainsley and her chariot off to Ronnie and me.

The love and inspiration shared between Abbey, Michelle, and Ainsley was very evident to me that morning. As the next six miles ensued, Michelle suffered a foot injury requiring her to slow her pace in order to finish the race. Meanwhile, Abbey continued to run along Ainsley's side. At mile ten, Abbey turned toward me, and in an emotional moment, insisted Ronnie and I take Ainsley on the ride of her life. "Run with the Wind, Ainsley, for the last ten miles have been the time of my life. Now it is your turn!" With that, Ronnie and I, with tears in our eyes, increased the pace to a sub-eight-minute mile and provided Ainsley with many wind-induced opportunities to smile. What an emotional and awesome finish we had, as the entire team was soon reunited with our families and friends at the THVB post-race celebration.

AINSLEY'S ANGELS TAKING FLIGHT

Within a few days of completing her second half-marathon, Ainsley inspired once again. Touched by the outpour of support we received from friends and family around the world, Ainsley's godmother, Kristine Seaward, filed paperwork to establish a not-for-profit organization. Soon thereafter, Ainsley's Angels of America was born, and we hope to one day build it into a Foundation. Originally seeking to educate America's youth on the importance of accepting all children into "normal: society, to not be scared to say hello or to smile, and that there is no need to stare, its first mission was to aid in making Ainsley's MCM the experience of a lifetime.

Much was accomplished in the month that followed. Ainsley's deaf cousin, Blake, in Louisiana designed our logo; our THVB teammate, Jenny, made the T-shirts; a friend established a website; Ainsley's Angels signed up for a Facebook account; multiple businesses and friends contributed financial support; and our network of friends in Washington,

DC, was ready to receive us for the special weekend.

As we loaded the van for our trip to Washington, DC, concern loomed about the weather. An unexpected, unseasonable snowstorm was predicted to strike Northern Virginia. Nevertheless, on the Friday before the race, and with the windows on our van painted "Team Ainsley - MCM 2011," we headed north with enthusiasm.

From the moment we arrived in the nation's capital, Ainsley's Angels' support network of angels worked overtime. Our friends, James and Kristen, graciously opened their house to us to serve as "home base" for the weekend. Our son's godfather, Steve, and his wife Carolyn held a pre-race party at their home two blocks from the DC Armory (home to the MCM Expo). My college classmate, Jim, and his wife, Jen, offered to serve as our race morning navigators. Of course, our hundreds of supporters worldwide began to flood our Facebook page and e-mail inbox with words of encouragement and photos of them wearing their Ainsley's Angels T-shirts.

As I was walking to the MCM Expo on Saturday afternoon to pick up our race bibs, the snowstorm arrived. Although it eventually dropped an inch of snow on the race course, the temperatures could not cool our enthusiasm. In true Marine Corps fashion, we developed a weather contingency plan, and James secured a case of chemical hand warmers for us. We enjoyed the traditional carbohydrate dinner and headed to bed with a 0400 hours reveille. Before kissing Ainsley goodnight, we read her a few of the messages sent to us from family and friends around the world and made finalized decorations on her chariot. We were ready for race day!

RACE DAY

As alarm clocks sounded, reality struck—MCM 2011 had arrived. Happy that the snowstorm had moved out overnight and the temperatures were slowly increasing, I worked to keep my enthusiasm from inducing premature fatigue while we loaded the van. Ainsley was dressed in her Ainsley's Angels jersey, her hair was tightly secured in two long braids, and the first round of chemical hand warmers where strategically placed to keep her warm. With the race director's approval to begin with the Wheelchair/Handcycle Division at 0745 hours, we began our movement to the starting line. After following Jim to the Pentagon City Mall parking garage, we exited the van. As I positioned Ainsley into her chariot, I was confident she knew it was a race day, but neither of us truly realized just how big of a race day it would be. As we maneuvered toward the start, which is located between the Pentagon and Arlington National Cemetery—which serves to reinforce that this journey is about a shared sacrifice—the 30,000 runner crowd-size was overwhelming. Nevertheless, we linked-up with Ronnie and his family just as a division of Marine Corps Ospreys flew overhead. The pre-race ceremonies had begun, but it was going to take us at least fifteen minutes to make it to the start line. Just then, our teammate Laura called to let us know she was at our predetermined rally point. I told her we were on or way and told Ainsley, "We need to move or else we'll be late." A few minutes later, I heard the announcer counting down our division, and it was clear, we were going to miss the starting gun.

Just then, Abbey's familiar face emerged from the crowd. She quickly led us to the starting line. For, you see, Abbey had been training hard since we last saw her at mile ten of the RnR, and she'd made it her Ainsley-inspired goal to start and finish the MCM with her today. Five minutes after the Wheelchair/Handcycle Division launched, but with ten minutes to spare before the official start, we arrived at the starting line. Realizing we did not need to rush into a quick start, we stretched and gathered for a few photographs. Meanwhile, a motivated Marine gunnery sergeant cleared a path for us to receive our own individual start. After our families bestowed final kisses and wishes of encouragement, we were ready to go. I gave a thumbs-up and off we went on our 26.2 mile journey.

Ainsley's chariot, with its "Team Ainsley: Run with the Wind" posters and pretty pink feathers arrangements was hands-down the cutest jogger/armchair/wheelchair on the course. Of course, because it was a chilly morning, we were all wearing our Team Hoyt VB running jackets. Hundreds of runners and spectators patted me on the back, waved to Ainsley, or offered inspirational greetings such as, "Go, Team Hoyt" or "Yay, Ainsley!" as we jogged though the course. Meanwhile, Carolyn linked-up with our families to assist with ensuring they could cheer us on along the course.

As we approached mile fourteen, I received a text message from them indicating they awaited our arrival near mile sixteen. Upon sharing this news with Ainsley and the rest of the team, I felt our pace slightly increase at the chance to soon see our family. As we turned eastbound onto Independence, just south of the reflecting pool, I made eye-contact with my lovely bride. Energy and enthusiasm quickly returned to levels unseen since we began the race 2.5 hours earlier. I briefly stopped the jogger chair as she ran toward us, bent down, gave Ainsley a kiss on the cheek, and away we went with renewed resilience after witnessing this breath-taking mother–daughter moment.

As we approached an opportunity to see our families once again at mile twenty, Steve, his brother, and James figured out a way to join us for the final 10K of the race. Our team grew from five to eight, and so did the realism that we CAN and WILL soon complete 26.2 together. Shaking cowbells and yelling, "YES, YOU CAN" along the way, additional friends caught up to us for the final push. As the official clock neared five hours, we approached the final half mile and prepared for our 200-yard uphill jog to the finish line adjacent to the famous Iwo Jima Memorial. Filled with joy and proudly exclaiming, "YES, WE DID" upon crossing the finish line, I bent down to congratulate Ainsley with a kiss.

Our collective breath was taken away, as Ainsley was first to receive her finisher's medal from one of my fellow Marines. Following our progress on-line, and proudly wearing their Team Ainsley shirts, nearly forty of Ainsley's relatives in Louisiana celebrated her accomplishment.

Inspired by the many Facebook photos that captured our experiences, some went for a jog down the road, others mounted a treadmill, and a few even went for a mile run in tribute. She does not talk nor walk; she does not play for fun; but she smiles, while out for a run—and now she inspires from among the one percent of the world's population that can claim to be a "Marathoner!"

SIBLINGS PUSHING SIBLINGS: THE VISION

A little more than one week after our emotional MCM experience, our THVB teammate, Dennis (who would eventually qualify with long time THVB athlete Tim Brown to join the Hoyts in the 2012 Boston Marathon), sent me a link about two young brothers from Tennessee. Team Long Brothers, as they are known in the running/triathlon communities, were featured in an ESPN E:60 special. As I watched footage of their story, I was amazed to see another young sibling team sharing in the incredible experience of competing together. I quickly found their Facebook page and uploaded a photo of Briley and Ainsley crossing the finish line in the 2011Holland 5K. I added the caption, "Long Brothers, meet the Rossiter Sisters! Oh, how awesome it would be to see the four of you run a 5K together!" Within moments, Conner and Cayden's mother replied with her own level of amazement to see another young sibling team. Later that evening the vision was solidified, as Briley and Conner agreed to eventually join forces to push their siblings in a 5K together!

MORE THAN JUST A RUNNING CLUB

Ainsley's dystrophy makes her prone to upper-respiratory infections. As a precaution, we decided to not travel during the 2012 winter season. Despite our efforts, Ainsley suffered from pneumonia-induced upper-respiratory failure on February 22, 2012. It was very serious, and quite frankly, we made preparations for the worst. Ainsley's grandparents flew in immediately, my co-workers and teachers from Ainsley's elementary school began a dinner rotation plan, and our neighbors quickly provided a helping hand with Ainsley's siblings. After three weeks at the Children's

Hospital of the King's Daughters, many prayers, and much love, she defeated the illness and returned home to us. On the Sunday afternoon before she was released, over twenty visitors dressed in THVB colors arrived at the hospital to see Ainsley. For you see, THVB is much more than a "running club." It is a family, with a special bond generally unseen in the world today. Its growing number of members is too plentiful to list here, but trust we are forever grateful to be a part of such an amazing family. A family, inspired by the Hoyts' example, that gives its children the opportunity to feel the satisfaction associated with overcoming life's obstacles, while also seeking to always serve as one another's biggest supporters.

RUN WITH THE WIND

With Ainsley recently home from the hospital and only two months until THVB's second annual destination trip to Holland, we were unsure if we were going to make the journey. Nevertheless, Briley maintained optimism and continued to prepare physically to push Ainsley in their sixth 5K road race together. Furthermore, in an effort to share the emotion of running with her sister, Briley wrote a letter that appeared on the front page of her elementary school newsletter. Titled "Run with the Wind," Briley wrote:

"Imagine this: You're crossing the mile marker, marking the end of mile three. There is only 0.1 mile to go now! Your heart pounds harder when you hear the distant sound of excited people cheering on the finishers. Your legs feel like Jell-O. Can you make it to the end, or will you crumble to the ground? I need to stop. I can't do it! Wait, what am I saying? you ask yourself. You're doing great; don't stop now! Yes, you can! You pick up the pace, entering a new realm of speed and strength with every step.

Now imagine: An innocent eight-year-old girl with a dystrophy making it impossible for her to ever walk or run. She is sitting in a jogging chair, but you have been trusted to be her feet, so run like the wind!

Can you imagine this yet? Well, I certainly can, because I have done that before. You see, my younger sister, Ainsley, is that little girl, and I am her legs. Ainsley and I often go to local races and run together. So far I have pushed her in five races. My dad has done nearly twenty races with Ainsley, including the Marine Corps Marathon in Washington, DC. Even my little brother, Kamden, has found an interest in running. So with my mom cheering us on the whole way, it has really become a family hobby. Running is something special that I love doing with my sister, and the huge smile on her face tells me that she loves it too. I think that you should start running too, and who knows, maybe one day you will run with the wind like us!"

Upon reading this letter and receiving word Team Long Brothers were currently raising money to make the May 2012 trip to Holland, I knew we had to figure out a way to ensure Ainsley and Briley could "run with the wind"—and the Long Brothers—in Holland.

SIBLINGS PUSHING SIBLINGS: THE REALITY

Our THVB family sprang into action. Jenny secured a twenty-nine-foot RV for us to ensure Ainsley could be repositioned hourly, and Bretta, who frequently pushes her brother, Ben, in local races, secured the funding required. The vision of young siblings pushing siblings started to quickly become a reality. Ainsley's team of supporters (Peggy, Michelle, Amber) joined our family in one of two THVB RVs, while the rest of our THVB teammates departed via plane or car for Holland. Meanwhile, the Long family was on their way to Holland from Tennessee. Like the previous year, a Sunday morning race allowed for the Hoyts to host THVB at their house on Saturday. During our first trip, I found myself manning the grill. This year, however, Dick called me out on my promise to one day expose him to a Louisiana-style shrimp boil. As such, I boiled nearly sixty pounds of shrimp and all the fixings, while the adults socialized, the children rode on Dick's boat, and everyone enjoyed the beautiful weather.

If you recall, it was twelve months prior that a conversation between

Dick and I led to many breathtaking moments for our family. This year, however, the conversation was between Rick and me. For you see, the MCM ranks atop Rick's favorite events. As such, we discussed the possibility of Ainsley and I joining Rick and Dick in "one more" MCM experience in October 2012. While the jury is still out on a decision, this conversation might have caused enough of a spark (similar to the one Dick and I had twelve-months prior) for us all to be in for another great year.

Early the next morning, hundreds prepared for the starting horn. The promise made between Briley and Conner six months prior was about to hold true, as the Rossiter Sisters lined up next to the Long Brothers for a 5K race together. Making this moment even more special was the presence of yet another young sibling team, the Martinez Brothers, and of course, Dick and Rick. Anticipation filled the air, and after a few announcements and photographs, the horn sounded.

For the first half of the race, my concerns revolved around whether or not one of the sibling teams would be able to maintain the pace. This concern was quickly put to rest by Dick, as he insisted on ensuring the Longs, Rossiters, and Hoyts would all finish together. To see these two young sibling teams encourage each other throughout course's many hills was truly special. There isn't a word in the human vocabulary to express just how awesome it was to watch my girls partake in their sixth 5K together, on the same course where they experienced their first race together a year ago, with such great company. Stride for stride, various ages, different lives, different challenges, but all with one goal. In yet another emotional finish, they all completed the race together and, once again, took our breath away.

THE LEGACY: FROM RICK TO AINSLEY TO...

Watching Ainsley's continued progression has often threatened to crush our spirit. But we no longer question our God as to why, but rather, feel blessed that he trusts us with his Angel. In a few short years, this special little girl has inspired hundreds, maybe thousands, and I am overcome with emotion at the possibilities of just how far her reach will continue. During our recent Holland trip, I was introduced to Ron Robb, CEO of myTeam Triumph (mTT). Like many of us, Ron was inspired by the Hoyts' story and amazing accomplishments. As such, he created mTT with the aim to extend the same opportunities to others that Dick Hoyt has provided to Rick over the years. In four years, Ron managed to grow MTT to include over ten chapters around the United States. During the summer of 2012, and as a direct result of THVB's 2012 trip to Holland, three more mTT chapters were born. Ainsley's fellow THVB athlete, Jayden, seeks to one day transition from "Athlete" to "Pusher." As such, his family has founded a chapter in Cape Cod.

It gives me the greatest sense of pride to know that my daughter's legacy will live on long after she departs, as the other two new chapters are named in her honor! Near Ainsley's birthplace, her former teacher, Michelle, will serve as the president of Ainsley's Angels of Eastern Carolina. Meanwhile, in the region of the world where the majority of Ainsley's strongest support can be found, her godmother will serve as the president of Ainsley's Angels of Southwest Louisiana. The idea of seeing other families experience what the Hoyts have experienced over a thousand times and what the Rossiter's have experienced over twenty-five times (so far), is what has driven us to start these chapters. We aim to continue to make the Hoyts proud, while carrying Rick's legacy through Ainsley to as many people possible, giving them the opportunity to "run with the wind," while also living up to the philosophy of "Yes, You Can."

A CHAMPION

Throughout Ainsley's four years as an Athlete, our family has had our collective breath taken away on countless occasions. We watched THVB grow through love and passion from ten pushers, seven riders, and seven jogger chairs into a family of over one hundred fifty volunteer pushers, over eighty athlete riders, and with a fleet of seventy-five jogger chairs. Due in large part to yet another sibling team, Steve and Tim

Brown, our race schedule has gone from five races to over twenty opportunities annually. During this period, we have also watched Ainsley's dystrophy progress to the point of global paralysis, leaving her unable to communicate, but her beautiful, running-aided, breeze-induced smile continues to inspire.

Today, Ainsley continues to "Run with the Wind" and has compiled an impressive résumé. Ranging from 5K road races to the 26.2 mile Marine Corps Marathon, Ainsley has completed over twenty-five road races and has brought countless smiles to the faces of her many friends, family members, and supporters around the world.

Thank you to the original captain, Rick Hoyt, not only for all that you have done and continue to do, *One Letter at a Time*, but for the unselfish way that you have lived your inspirational life and the legacy you have passed to us all.

The Apple Doesn't Fall Far from the Tree

by Dick Hoyt

Rick's Father

> "When we got home from the race that night, Rick wrote on the computer, 'Dad, when I run it feels like my disability disappears.' As you can imagine, that was a very powerful message to me."
>
> — Dick Hoyt

A lot of people look at the Hoyt family and wonder how we've managed to succeed where others may not have even tried. It's because we never let events stand in the way of what we hope to achieve. We have learned through experience and through Rick that striving for excellence and for what we want is a continual process, one that has not been easy, but one that has brought with it countless rewards.

I was one of ten children. I was sixth—or right in the middle—and we all slept in two rooms. The girls slept in one room and the boys slept in another. We only had one toilet and had to eat in shifts because there wasn't enough room. We were known as the cleanest and healthiest kids that went to our school. It was amazing to me because there were never any arguments between anybody. It all just worked so smoothly. My father had his own garage. He was an automobile mechanic. He spent a lot of time at work. As far as I'm concerned, he and my mother treated everyone exactly equal. It's just that my dad had to work more hours and wasn't home as much. I think I was closer to my dad than all of the other kids because I did things with him. I went fishing with him and hunting with him and I used to box with him. He actually wanted me to become a boxer, but my mother didn't want any part of me being a boxer. My middle name is actually Eugene, because at the time there was a famous boxer named Eugene, so my father named me after him.

We just had a great family. We were all hard-working kids. I had my first job when I was nine-years-old. I used to go down to a farm and bring in the cows and had to shovel the stuff from behind the cows and milk the cows. I used to get paid ten cents a day and a little half a pint of milk. That's all we got. We had a coal furnace, so I used to go out in the woods and cut down the dead trees and get the fire started. At night I'd throw the coal in and keep the fire burning all night long.

I loved sports. We all loved sports. The boys and the girls all played sports together. We couldn't afford hockey sticks, so we used to cut branches off the trees and cut the branch so it was like a stick, then use little pieces of wood like a puck. We used to alternate using skates because we didn't have enough to go around. We were a very close family and we were very hard working.

After that I worked for fifty cents an hour on my hands and knees picking weeds out of gardens and stuff like that. I was also very active at school. I used to go in earlier than anyone to raise the American flag and take it down at the end of the day. There were times before I started playing sports I'd go to school and help the janitors after school. Go in and sweep and empty the wastepaper baskets and things like that.

I'd describe my parents as loving parents. We were a very close family and did a lot of things as a family, even as big as we were. They'd take us away to New Hampshire for the weekend. They had an old farmhouse and we'd go behind there where there were brooks. There was a big river where we could all go swimming and stuff, and we could go fishing with my dad. We were very close, and I just think that my mother and my father treated us all exactly the same. I can remember my mother chasing me around the house with a broom. I'd run away and jump under the bed and she'd try to get at me and stuff.

I had a couple of sisters that were very good athletes; very good softball players and basketball players. I think they could've gone on to college to play. But we had such a big family that none of us could go to college because we couldn't afford it. That is one of the biggest mistakes in my life, because I didn't prepare myself for college. I was a straight-A student up to sixth grade. I was a very shy kid, and the teacher used to ask questions. I wouldn't raise my hand to answer, even though I usually knew the answer. My face would get all red and I'd become very embarrassed.

Then I started playing sports in the sixth grade. I weighed only about ninety pounds, but I was playing football for the high school in North Reading. We only had eleven players because there were only fifty kids in our graduating class. Because there were only eleven players, we had to play offense and defense, with no one to substitute or come into the game due to injury.

We only had three sports, basketball, football and baseball, and I was fortunate enough to play all three. I was captain of both the baseball and football teams. When I played basketball they used to have me chase the ball; everyone else would drop off to defend the hoop. They used to call me "The Rock."

I actually tried out for the New York Yankees as a catcher. I loved catching, because you're a part of every ball that's thrown. I had a good arm and I could hit the ball, but my biggest problem—if you can believe it—is that I was too slow. It's funny, because I was eighteen years old and I was too slow. When I got into my fifties, I was twice as fast as I was when I was eighteen. How that happened, I'll never know.

I like to share a lot of these stories of my life growing up because it helped build me into the type of father I have become. It also explains much about the way Rick has adopted his "Yes, You Can" attitude that makes him so incredibly motivating and inspirational to me. As inspirational as Rick is to the world, he is what keeps me moving. There is something inside of me that Rick fuels. It is important for readers to remember that without Rick, there is no book. Team Hoyt wouldn't be possible if it weren't for Rick. He is the athlete. I just loan him my legs. It is his competitive spirit that gives me my strength and keeps me going.

Many people have told me over the years that I would've been a world-class marathon runner if I would've run without Rick. I know that's not possible because it is Rick who makes me run faster. That is why, when we first tried to enter the Boston Marathon, and when Dave McGillivray first tried to get me interested in triathlons, I said, "Only if I can do it with Rick."

After Rick was born and Judy and I were told there was something wrong with Rick, the doctor told us we should put him away; he would be nothing more than a vegetable. Rick and I joke now that we are still trying to figure out what vegetable he is. Judy and I disobeyed doctor's orders. We brought Rick home and decided to bring him up just like any other child. The doctors couldn't really tell us anything, so Judy and I decided we would just take it day by day as far as bringing him up. And that's what we did.

When we took Rick home, we paid a lot of attention to him. We'd watch him and hoped that we would see improvement in his behavior, but he wasn't progressing at all. He wasn't moving his hands, and we just knew something wasn't right. We'd put Rick to bed at night, and then we'd have to go into his room several times during the night and wake him to feed him because he wouldn't wake up on his own and he wouldn't cry. As he started to get a little older, he couldn't roll over and he just kept staring at us.

We would talk to him, and I just felt like he understood. Even though the doctors told us that he didn't understand, Judy and I knew after a while that he knew what was going on. He'd look right into my eye, and I knew even from a young age that there was a connection there.

It's Rick who keeps me going. For him, the easiest thing was to give up, because he can't talk, he can't use his arms, and he can't use his legs. He communicates by using a computer. But he didn't give up. We wanted Rick in a public school; we wanted him to get a good education; we wanted him to be like my two other boys—to go to school and go to college and be independent. We fought to get him into school. We taught Rick the alphabet and numbers and read to him. We could tell by looking in his eyes that he was paying attention and understood everything we talked about.

Everything that we did, we included Rick. Like when I had to go next door to get a gallon of milk or a newspaper and I'd take the other two boys, I'd take Rick too. He was in a wheelchair, so it took a little bit longer to run out and get the milk. It would've been easier to do without him, but that isn't how we did things. I think that really helped out with Rob and Russ, because everything we did, Rick was there.

We started going camping when they were all very young. We'd camp in a tent. We'd all go up to New Hampshire. It would be pouring rain and the rain would be coming into the tents and everything else, and we'd all be in there laughing and having a good time like any other family. He was always there with the other two boys. That's just the way we brought them up. So, all three of them did things together. When we would go camping where there was a swimming pool, we'd take Rick to the edge of the pool and throw him in. Everyone would look at us like we were crazy, but he would sink down and then come to the top. The boys or I would jump in and get him, and he'd be laughing. That is what made Rick love the water and enjoy swimming as much as he does.

I recall one funny story. When the boys were younger, we climbed Mount Monadnock in New Hampshire. I'd throw Rick up on my shoulders and climb up the mountain. Well, this one time, we were going up and I was ahead of Judy and the other boys were a little bit below me. I'd carry Rick over my shoulders, and sometimes he would drool a little bit on my shirt. Well, there was this couple coming down the mountain, and they had a couple kids with them. They saw Rick over my shoulder with the drool coming onto my shoulder. When they got down to Judy and the two boys, the family asked if they'd seen that guy up there who was climbing to the top of the mountain. "He's going up to sacrifice his son, because his kid is dead," exclaimed the youngest boy.

There was another time when we used to take him cross-country skiing. When you go cross-country skiing, there are a lot of hills. Well, one day I was skiing and there was a steep hill. I was towing Rick on a red sled behind me. Well, there was a couple below us and Rick got going too fast. He went in between my legs and knocked me onto the chair with him. The people down below us were laughing because they thought I was carrying lunches or something. They didn't know a person was on the sled. We had a lot of fun like that.

We also liked to play hockey. We'd take Rick onto the ice. He'd have his own special stick and we'd stand behind him and help him play hockey. He used to like to play ice hockey, so we would take a special sled with handles in back and get behind him and take a big piece of plywood and put it in front of the net so no one could score goals.

When Rick finally got into school, after all that work and effort, it was unbelievable. That was one of our goals—to get him into public school. When it finally happened, it was just awesome. Another one of our goals many years later, of course, was to see him go to college. When that happened, it was just amazing. Of all the highlights we've had, including getting into school, graduating college, getting accepted into the Boston Marathon, completing the Ironman and running thirty Boston Marathons, the single most gratifying thing is getting people to see who Rick was and accepting him as he is. When we first started, no one wanted anything to do with us. They didn't want anything to do with Rick, and now he is accepted everywhere he goes. That was a tough battle. After that, the next greatest highlight would be seeing Rick graduate from Boston University. For Rick to go away to college, a two-hour drive away from his family, and live by himself was amazing.

I remember one story when Rick was away at school that was a bit unnerving for a father. Rick lived on the fifth floor of a huge apartment complex on Washington Street in Brighton, Massachusetts—right across from the Whole Foods grocery store. He had care attendants that came in from ten a.m. until ten p.m., and then he was on his own until they came to get him out of bed the next morning.

Most of the neighbors did not speak English. They were much older and there was really no one around I could call if there was a problem or to make sure there was a care attendant there. If no one answered the phone, I had to assume the care attendants might be down doing laundry or that they took Rick somewhere in his van. It was very difficult living almost two hours away while worrying if Rick was all right at all times. But Rick wanted his independent lifestyle.

One night I got a call about four in the morning from St. Elizabeth Hospital saying that Rick was in the hospital. I got up and got dressed and made the long drive into Boston driving pretty fast. When I got to the hospital, they let me in to see Rick—and Rick, of course, was laughing his head off. Seems what happened is the fire department got a call from the apartment below Rick's that they had water coming through their ceiling, so they knew there was a water problem in Rick's apartment. No one was in the apartment management office in the middle of the night, so they called the fire department EMTs.

When the EMTs knocked on Rick's door, no one answered, so they broke the door down to get in, and found Rick in his bedroom in a pool of water. In those days, he slept on a waterbed, as it conformed to his body and was comfortable for him to sleep on. Because his body is spastic, his body is always moving, even in his sleep. They think his toe somehow got under the tab of the mattress and lifted it up, which caused the water to start seeping out. With his body pressure on the mattress, it made the water come out faster, and over time it accumulated and caused quite a puddle on his bedroom floor, which in turn leaked into the apartment below.

So when the EMTs saw a non-verbal man in the middle of the puddle, they didn't know what to do so they brought him to the hospital. When I got there, the doctors questioned me, as they thought it might be a child abuse case, but the nurses knew who Rick and I were and explained the situation to the doctors. Rick had a good laugh about it, and I brought Rick home, cleaned up his apartment, and went back to my home in Holland.

When Rick and I first started running, nobody wanted anything to do with us. They didn't even want us in races. We'd go there and people wouldn't talk to us or come near us, like we had a disease. Whenever we were told we couldn't do certain things, we would just go ahead and do them. As we've said, there is no can't in the Hoyt vocabulary. That goes back to the way we were brought up as I described earlier. It's how we were taught. When we first started running though, I used to get a lot of phone calls and letters from parents of disabled people. They were really upset and said, "What are you doing dragging your disabled son to all these races? Are you just looking for glory?" What they didn't realize is that he was the one dragging me to all of these races. After we started running for a while, people would come up to us and start talking to us. They could see that Rick had a personality and a sense of humor.

When we tried to do the Boston Marathon, they told us we couldn't because you have to qualify in your age group. We actually ran one year without an official number. We've run a three-hour-and-eighteen minute marathon and beat eighty-five percent of all the other runners, and they still wouldn't accept us. That was back in 1981. We ran again, the next two years, and we ran under three hours, and yet they still wouldn't accept us as an official entrant. So in 1983, I talked to the executive director and asked him why we couldn't be official entrants, and he said they didn't have any qualifying criteria.

At the time, Rick was in his twenties and I was in my forties, and they were using Rick's age for us to qualify, which meant we had to run under two hours and fifty minutes. That was just an excuse to get rid of us, because they thought there was no way a forty-year-old guy could push his twenty-year-old son in a wheelchair under two hours and fifty minutes. We went down to Washington, DC, for the Marine Corps Marathon, which is known as the People's Marathon because anybody can run in this marathon. Rick and I ran in that marathon in two hours, forty-five minutes, and twenty-three seconds, so that qualified both Rick and I for the Boston Marathon. So we took our official certificate and submitted it. At the hundredth running of the race in 1996, Rick and I were recognized as Centennial Heroes, so we've come a long way and we've been able to break down barriers along the way.

Before we started running, I didn't know what I was going to do for the rest of my life. I had been in the military for thirty-five years when we started running. I could've been a couch potato. It was all Rick who got us going, to do what we're doing. It's amazing how we're affecting the whole world. I just don't have the desire to be running out there by myself. There is something that goes from his body to my body that makes us go faster. He inspires me and he motivates me. He is actually the athlete. He is very competitive. It's Rick that wants to win.

Now, we're invited all over the world. We've been over to Japan twice. We've been to Germany. We've been up to Canada and down to El Salvador. We've visited a lot of different countries and competed in a lot of races. And now there are actually seventeen chapters in the United States that are doing what Rick and I are doing in a chair.

Now that Rick is fifty and I am seventy-two, my family wants me to quit and hang it up. I had a heart attack back in 2003. We were getting ready for the Boston Marathon and it was four weeks before the race. I had three stents put in. My doctor was going to let me run in the marathon, since I was in such good shape. He also told me that if I wasn't in such good shape, I would have died fifteen years earlier, so you can say that Rick really saved my life. I didn't do the marathon that year, but we did go out to Hawaii in October for the Ironman. My heart's still ticking now. Rick is going to keep going as long as he can. He enjoys it so much and the crowds are unbelievable. People come up to us and tell us, "You guys are the Boston Marathon." Rick has always said if we could only do one race, it would be the Boston Marathon, because he just loves it so much.

When we decide to hang it up, and that is Rick's decision, I'd like to see Rick live independently for the rest of his life. I think he is living a good life now. We have a lot of challenges because he wants to live independently, but that's what he has been doing all his life. I worry about that as I get older. He loves people, so I would just love to see him stay involved and do things to get more involved. It takes a little more involvement on Rick's part and on the part of his PCAs, but that is what I would like to see him do. I also think Rick could go around and do motivational speaking like I do, but on a smaller scale. He could go around and tell his story, show a video of what it is that we do and give a short presentation using his computer. So even after Rick and I stop racing and even after I'm gone, there is a lot that Rick can do to keep the Team Hoyt story alive.

Not bad for a vegetable.

A View of Life from Where I Sit

by Rick Hoyt with Todd Civin

> *"Just when you think it can't get any worse, it can. And just when you think it can't get any better, it can."*
>
> — *Nicholas Sparks - At First Sight*

One of the more frequently-asked questions when I conduct an interview is whether or not I'm angry about the way life began for me by being born a spastic quadriplegic. If you think about it, that would be a pretty horrible way to go through life— with anger and regret. Think of how much I would've missed out on if I spent my days worrying about things that don't go according to plan. Life doesn't always go as we expect it to. No one's does. Wouldn't life be sort of boring if everything happened as we expected it to? If we knew what was waiting for us around every bend? I have no anger in me. It's not in my nature to be vindictive. It would really be horrible to go through fifty years of my life being angry or wondering what if. This is my life and I honestly wouldn't change a thing.

Even though I need help with everything, I don't let my disability get in my way. I have fought long and hard to gain and maintain my independence and I wouldn't exchange that for anything. Being able to live on my own and graduate from college proves to me that I don't let my disability limit who I am inside. I sit in a wheelchair, but I am not controlled by my wheelchair. My definition of independence is being capable of making my own decisions. I once said in a TV interview that if I couldn't control my life I would rather be dead. I mean that. I feel for those who are not as fortunate as I am and are forced to live at the mercy of others and need others to not only feed them, bathe them and shave them, but also to make their choices for them. For some, it is a necessity, but I am so grateful that if given nothing else, I was granted enough to be independent. Without that, I'd rather be dead.

I have done a lot in my life that many people haven't, and I've done more than I would've if things had started out differently. I am amazingly happy when I look back and see what I've accomplished through hard work and effort. I think you become seasoned and grow stronger through facing adversity, much like the tree in the following story I read several years ago.

The young tree faced many storms through its young life. The powerful winds, torrential rains, famine, ice, and snow would lie across its branches.

At times the young tree questioned its maker asking, "Why have you let so many storms come into my life?"

His maker whispered, "You will understand one day, stand firm, you will make it through the storms of life." "The challenges will pass, keep this in mind."

The tree questioned his master, "If I go through one more winter the snow will surely break my branches, if I face any more powerful wind I will surely be uprooted and moved away."

His maker whispered, "Stand strong, dig your roots deep into the soil, you will understand someday."

Somehow the young tree kept the positive thoughts in his mind and managed to survive and make it through even the toughest of storms.

Somehow, even in the toughest of times, when the things it went through should have broken it down, it found a way to stand firm even through the worst of storms.

As the young tree grew taller, stronger, and matured the tree realized the storms of life had made it stronger. ~Unknown

I believe God had everything to do with the way my birth came out. The Bible says God planned our life even before we are born. When my umbilical cord wrapped around my neck, I believe it was part of God's plan. No one knew his plan; however, I think his plan is working out pretty well for me. Sometimes I do not like being this way, but then again, there are people who are in far worse shape than me. None of us ever know what God's plan is. We can only guess.

Maybe it is to blaze a trail so the people who follow behind me don't need to struggle the way I have at times. But that's not unique to me. That answers the question for all of us as to what God's plan may be. My purpose may seem to be a more spectacular purpose than some, and perhaps I've had the good fortune of touching more people than the average person, but who knows? I don't think anyone is keeping score.

The doctors said I would be nothing but a vegetable. They were obviously wrong, and I'm thankful Mom and Dad didn't take their advice, forget about me, and put me in an institution. But when I was born, the doctors didn't have the knowledge they do today. I don't know who the doctor was that said that, but maybe he followed me through the early successes of my life and realized that with hope and a "Yes, You Can" attitude, no one should be written off.

Sometimes I actually take advantage of my limitations by doing things like getting extra rides at amusement parks. I also let one of my professors believe that I couldn't understand the material of his class at BU. It was a class about micro-viruses, but I needed to fill my required credits, so he felt bad and gave me a free pass.

I see myself as ambassador for those people who don't believe they can set a goal and meet it. Not just disabled people, but anyone who is facing a challenge in life and questions whether or not they have the strength to continue; the strength to succeed. Dad and I receive hundreds of emails from people facing challenges of all kinds. We provide inspiration to people who are dealing with alcohol and drug addictions or mental health situations. We hear from mothers and fathers who may think they are failing at parenting, yet by learning about the strength and perseverance that my parents exhibited, they too gain strength. We also provide positive encouragement through our story to parents of disabled children, who may become frustrated and discouraged getting through each day. When they hear about how my life has progressed and the challenges that my family faced and ultimately overcame, maybe it makes their path a little more easily explained and understood.

I am also an ambassador to people who don't think that a person with my physical limitations can accomplish anything. Look at all that I have and will accomplish in my lifetime. I am not saying that everything has come easy. I have worked through really tough circumstances in my life. If life was too easy, would it be worth living? My answer is no; the tough times are what makes life worth living.

Robert Frost wrote a poem called "The Road Not Taken," and though I am no poet, I do understand this poem and see it as a good representation of my view on life. For those of you who don't know the poem, it goes as follows.

> *Two roads diverged in a yellow wood,*
>
> *And sorry I could not travel both*
>
> *And be one traveler, long I stood*
>
> *And looked down one as far as I could*
>
> *To where it bent in the undergrowth;*

Then took the other, as just as fair,

And having perhaps the better claim

Because it was grassy and wanted wear,

Though as for that the passing there

Had worn them really about the same,

And both that morning equally lay

In leaves no step had trodden black.

Oh, I marked the first for another day!

Yet knowing how way leads on to way

I doubted if I should ever come back.

I shall be telling this with a sigh

Somewhere ages and ages hence:

Two roads diverged in a wood, and I,

I took the one less traveled by,

And that has made all the difference.

Before you think I have the poem memorized, I don't. I had to look it up to share it with you. Having never had the need to recite a poem out loud, I don't have many memorized. My life is kind of like the road not taken, though. I think Robert Frost meant that the road not taken may contain many surprises along the way; both good and bad. In my life I have had many good surprises and some bad surprises, but I wouldn't trade either kind in exchange for a life without adventure. I tend to enjoy the good ones more and I try to lighten the bad by making jokes about my circumstances.

In life and in running, winning is great. Losing isn't nearly as great, but quitting or not trying isn't acceptable. That's why Dad and I believe that no matter what, We Can. Real failure is about never getting off the bench and playing the game. I was lucky that when I asked Dad to enter that first race, he wasn't the type of person who would be preoccupied with something that seemed more important or the type of person who didn't think enough of himself to even try. It's amazing what you may discover traveling without a map. So many times people are unable to experience success because they are afraid to take that road not taken.

It's sort of funny if I look back on all the things I've been lucky enough to do in my life, and in many ways it's because I am disabled. Not all disabled people are lucky enough to have experienced the same things I have. For that matter, there are many able-bodied people who would consider trading seats with me to experience some of the things and to have met some of the people I have met. How many can say they were able to ride across the country with their father, spending every waking moment breathing in this country of ours? Who can open up their own personal scrapbook and say they have spent time with Ronald Reagan and with Rosie and Zdeno Chara and had Bobby Orr come to their birthday party? I've spent the day with Lord Stanley's Cup and the Bruins' Andrew Ference. How many people have run thirty Boston Marathons and are not only members of the Iron Man Hall of Fame in Kona, but were inducted in alongside their father? I like to think if I was able-bodied, maybe some of that still would have happened, but I find it a bit hard to believe that all of this would have taken place.

As I look back at my life, I would not trade anything. I like my life. My family made sure that I was included in everything they did. They treated me as a person without a disability, so this is my regular life. It's all I've ever known. When people ask me if it frustrates me that I don't speak verbally, my answer is, "No, this is all I've ever known." To me, their way can be frustrating. Plus, I never get laryngitis.

At BU, they treated me like one of the guys. This is all I know. This is my "regular" life. My PCA, Jessica, and I once discussed that everyone has their own regular life no matter what situation you were born into.

Nobody is "normal." In fact, we don't even use the word normal or abnormal to describe my situation versus someone else's situation. To each, their life is "normal."

These days we hear a lot about bullying. I think this has always gone on, but I think we just thought of it as teasing. No child goes through school without being picked on, but in my case many students had never gone to school with someone who was disabled. When Mom fought to have Chapter 766 passed in Massachusetts, this enabled the disabled to go to public school for the first time. When something is new to someone, it creates a certain amount of fear and curiosity, and when this happens teasing can occur. I would get very frustrated when kids would stare at me or make fun of me. I wanted to get them back or I wished I would be able to tease them back. I'd be very frustrated because they didn't even know me or know what I was thinking. Sometimes my brothers got into fights at school because they'd stick up for me if someone treated me poorly. I remember when Rob went to school, he asked why there were no kids in wheelchairs. To him, being around me was the norm, and not having a family member in a wheelchair was abnormal.

When people tease me in a fun way, though, I see it as a form of comedy and actually think it's healthy. When they joke with me and tease me in fun, it makes me laugh and feel accepted. That makes me happy. They would get me with a joke and eventually get to know who I am.

My family has been wonderful to me, as well as the many people around the world who I consider to be my friends. I think I have only missed out on having a wife and children. My life feels fulfilled even without these things and I don't spend a moment wondering, *what if things were different?*

It makes me so proud when people overlook my physical limitations and see me as a hero. Me? A hero? A guy who has never taken one solid step on the earth below my feet and never uttered one word through my own vocal chords is considered a hero? Though maybe together our story can be considered a heroic one, by ourselves I don't think that Dad nor I can be considered heroes. Dad tells stories during his speeches of drug addicts who have turned their lives around after hearing our story. So, if we have been able to save lives or change lives for the better, than I guess we are heroes. Somehow, I think of heroes as people putting themselves in danger to save the life of another, kind of like Superman. It seems funny that a hundred-pound guy with arms the size of toothpicks can be mentioned in that class.

I spend each day with a sense of joy when people see me as a real person with an identity rather than just as some guy. I am loved by others and it shows. My body may be small, but my heart is overflowing, knowing that I am loved by my family, my friends, and my fans. I'm amazed to think that I am a role model to some when I look back and realize what Dad and I have achieved.

People frequently ask me if there are things I wish I could do, but can't due to my disability. I think I am probably like most people who wish they had a talent other than the ones they already have. Many people wish they could play the piano or the drums, but don't put in the effort required to learn. My wishes are different in that no matter how much I practice, I'm not going to be able to play the drums. Actually, I could, but it wouldn't sound very good. But if I were able to change something, I would like to be able to at least use my hands. I would like to be able to feed myself, maybe help a little more in bathing myself and going to the bathroom. Some people who are born with cerebral palsy are able to use their hands. They have a milder case than I do. I envy them because they are able to do many things that I'm not able to. It would be nice to able to brush my own teeth or hug someone without needing help. Think of how frustrating it can be to have a fly walking on your forehead and having no way to shoo him away. When that happens, I try to move my head a little bit and hope that he just flies away. I have thought about this, and though it would be nice to walk, using my hands would be better.

Sometimes people wonder if I would prefer to be able to talk. Of course I would love to be able to speak, but at least I can talk using my computer. I would love to talk by using my own vocal chords instead of using my computer or talking through family and friends. I would like to use my own voice to speak or to even know what my voice would sound like. Recently, my PCA, Linda, recorded me saying a sound that sounded like the word "Mama." We played it over and over again and laughed. It was just a sound that came out though, and since it isn't anything I can duplicate, it isn't really speaking. Plus it was in a high pitch, and I wouldn't want my voice to sound like that if I was able to speak.

I have thought about this, and as much as people may think I would want to be able to do everything they can, in some ways, I do. I just do things differently. I am able to go out and experience life, I can taste and do things. I am able to have fun and am able to use my computer to communicate. I am able to feel the wind in my hair as my Dad runs, and I am running with him in spirit even though I am not using my own feet. Some people, though breathing and technically alive, are not able to experience even that. Those are the people I feel really bad for. And to think, I did it...one letter at a time.

Letters to Team Hoyt

An Email to Dick and Rick Hoyt from Stephen Stoll
Subject: You Saved My Life

Dear Dick and Rick,

I wanted to take the time and personally thank both of you, from the bottom of my heart, for being the heroes that you are. I first learned of your story briefly in high school, during a devotion given by my football coach. At the time I was young, my priorities were not what they should have been and perhaps the story didn't have the effect it did until recently. I broke my back in two places in a bad motorcycle accident about two years ago. I was hit from behind by a drunk driver. At the time, I was 21 years old and ready to start a career in the Navy and training to become a SEAL. The doctors not only told me that my dream of serving my country was all but over, but that I would also be lucky if I were ever able to walk on my own again. Honestly, I began to feel sorry for myself, I got down and my focus was on all of the things that I could no longer do. I dropped out of college just one semester shy of graduating because I was embarrassed to have to try and get around a crowded campus in a wheelchair.

After my girlfriend left me and a few other things happened, it seemed as though the walls were closing in on me. Embarrassingly enough, suicide didn't seem like that bad of an option. I began to plan my last days out to the last detail. I was all alone and had no one who cared about me (or so I thought).

Just a few hours before I planned to end my own life, I was trying to search for a video on YouTube and accidentally ran across your video feature on Today's Real Heroes while searching for a song. I can honestly say it changed my life forever.

Not only did you two save my life that night, you gave me hope that I thought I would never have. You showed me strength that I thought wasn't possible. I cried for the rest of the night, knowing that it was no "accident" that I ran across your video. You showed me that ANYTHING is possible if you put your mind to it.

I decided to change my life, then and there. I decided to not go through with killing myself and started my "new" life then and there. All over a ten minute YouTube video. I just recently went back and watched the video again for the first time. You two created a burning desire in me to better myself and to do whatever I could to help others. I am proud to say that after two years of hard work, I am back to being myself again. I began walking on my own just four months after my accident and now am stronger than I was before. I can lift weights, run, swim, and bike all without any pain or limitations. So, from the bottom of my heart, THANK YOU. You literally saved my life, restored hope, and gave me renewed strength and drive. Both of you inspired me to better myself so that I could help others.

Rick, you have accomplished more in your lifetime than most people could accomplish in ten lifetimes. I am so proud of you. It would have been very easy for you to feel sorry for yourself, but you did the opposite of that.

Your response to the question, "What would you do if you could run?" by saying "I would sit my dad down in the wheelchair and push him for once" still brings tears to my eyes every time I hear it. You have changed so many lives and touched so many people. I cannot say thank you enough for being the hero that you are.

Dick, you also are a true unsung hero. I know all too well what it feels like to hear from a "medical professional" that there is no hope and that you would be better off giving up and moving on. Sure, the "easy" thing to do would have been to go along with the doctor's opinion, but you dug your heels in, went against the grain and changed the whole world. Thank you for not going along with that. Your drive and inspiration has not only saved my life, but I'm sure many, many others.

I just wanted to take the time to tell both of you thank you and that I will be forever grateful to you two. I'm sure you hear from people every day thanking you for your story, but I just wanted you to know that your story saved my life. If I told you thank you every day for the rest of my life, it wouldn't be sufficient for me. I am here on this earth today because of the unconditional love you have for each other.

Now that I am fully recovered both physically and mentally, I want to give back. I have done some research, with no success, trying to see if there is anyone or any program that helps handicapped people find volunteers to help, push, pull, or carry them across the finish line in races. I'm located in Lexington, Kentucky. Do you know of any programs that help do that?

Thank you both again, from the bottom of my heart. You saved my life and completely changed my whole outlook on this world. I wouldn't be here today without you. This world needs more good people like you two. Please let me know if there is ever anything that I can do to perhaps say thank you for everything.

May God bless both of you. Take Care, Stephen Stoll Lexington, Kentucky.

An Email to Rick Hoyt from Cherie Gagnon
From: Cherie Gagnon
Subject: Thanks for the Inspiration

Hello, Team Hoyt,

I am writing this letter to tell you how much I appreciate what you have done and continue to do. Joshua was born in December 2000 with a rare neurological condition called "Schizencephaly." This means he is unable to walk, talk or eat by mouth. He wasn't expected to live past his first birthday, but he's now eleven years old. His life is an inspiration. He's bright, uses a computer for speech and drives a power wheelchair.

Four years ago my husband started running just to get into better shape. As he became more involved with the sport, he stumbled across a YouTube video of Dick and Rick. We both cried. Rick reminded us so much of our son. We understood that Dick was only helping Rick participate in races. Rick was the runner, the swimmer and cyclist. The bond between father and son touched us to the core.

This inspired Grant to start looking into a running jogger he could use with Joshua. We acquired that three years ago. Joshua was a little uncertain and cried when he first sat in it. Grant started the process just by walking around the driveway. It didn't seem Joshua was too interested in going farther. Then one day, out of the blue, Joshua asked with his computer if he could go for a run. Grant dropped everything, put on his running shoes, and off they went. They ran four km. Joshua loved it!

Over the last few years, they have participated in a number of 5-8 km *races and raised money for local children's charities or organizations supporting people with disabilities. They have been responsible for raising nearly $10,000. Nathan, our other son, and I love to cheer them on from the sidelines.*

Joshua has severe breathing issues, so races have been on the shorter side, but we are hopeful that over time he could tolerate a longer distance (and I will try not to freak out). Team Gagnon hopes one day to run with Team Hoyt. This would make the circle of inspiration complete!

Regards, Team Gagnon ~ Grant, Cherie, Joshua and Nathan Gagnon

An Email to Rick Hoyt from Jamie Walker
From: Jamie Walker
Sent: Wednesday, July 11, 2007 10:12 PM
Subject: Thank You

Gentlemen,

I realize that you must have an enormous volume of e-mails and letters to sift through, and I am sure that this one may not get read, but it does not keep me from sending it. I have to tell you how your story has touched my life. Our pastor played your "Redeemer" video in church on Father's Day. It moved me to tears, and I knew it would have the same effect on my husband. He is serving in Iraq currently, and I have been trying desperately to somehow get the video to him.

See, without pointing fingers, it is safe to say he had a less than shining example of a father growing up. He still does not have much contact with him. From the day we got married, he has always been terrified of his parenting skills and if he will be able to be a good father to our future children. He is so afraid of repeating the cycle. I have always told him, all you need to be able to do to be a good father is love unconditionally and the rest will fall into place.

After watching your video, he called me, sobbing, and said "You were right." Maybe when he returns this time, we will be ready to start a family! Thank you for setting an example for the world by just doing what you do. If we just had more fathers like you.

And Rick, you are so far from disabled. You may be "physically challenged," but your mind and your soul are so beautiful. They are almost overdeveloped. You see more of this world in a year than most people see in a lifetime. I am so glad that you have your computer so the entire world can hear what you have to say.

You two are truly beautiful people and I am thankful that I was blessed to know of you. Not that you have, but if either of you has ever asked why God allowed this to happen, please know there is an entire world of inspired people ready to answer that question. Never forget us, for we will never forget you.

Jamie Walker

From: Jamie Walker
Sent: Tuesday, January 24, 2012 4:43 PM
Subject: RE: Thank You

Kathy,

We would be honored to have our letter included in your book. I also should include a few updates. My husband returned from Iraq in November of 2007 and finished his service with the military. I also graduated nursing school that same month. On January 7, 2008, we were surprised with a positive pregnancy test! In September of 2008, we became parents to Ofelia Walker, and in March of 2010, we brought Noble Walker into the world.

When Noble was born, he wasn't breathing initially, and while the assistants were preparing to resuscitate him, Johnny scooped him up in his arms and told him to breathe. Noble let out a cry you could hear for miles, and there was no need for oxygen! Johnny has found that everything he needed to be a father was inside him the whole time. Whatever we can do to support Team Hoyt, we will! You all are such a blessing.

Jamie and John Walker
Marion, IN 46953

I hope God blesses you all as much as you have blessed us!

An Email to Rick Hoyt from Terence Traut
From: Terence Traut
To: Team Hoyt

Thanks, Kathy. I received the books today.

The reason I ordered them was, once again, someone sent me a link to the video of Rick and Dick. This time it came from one of my cousins in Minnesota who simply saw a touching story. She sent it out to as many relatives and friends as she had emails (and I come from a large family with 101 first cousins, so you know the message got out there!) with only the statement, "Watch this. It's AMAZING."

I replied, saying that I not only had seen Dick and Rick in a couple of races, but had the pleasure of being a teacher's assistant in Rick's Intro to Education class at Boston University.

Over the semester, I, and everyone else, was amazed at the insight and humor Rick displayed. It was pretty cool. I think the coolest part was that Rick saw no limits where most people saw no hope. I wondered where someone could get such spirit.

I found out a couple years later when I happened to be in a triathlon with Rick and Dick. When I saw the dad, I knew the cloth the son was cut from. I was overcome with a sense of mutual devotion and admiration that father saw in son and son in father. One can't help but be moved in a very fundamental and deep level.

So, my CLAIM TO FAME is that I know Rick Hoyt, and that I've raced with him and his dad. My connection with Rick was brief and a long time ago, but the impact of that connection (and the subsequent elbow-rubbing) is life-changing. Rick's can-do attitude—supported most publicly by his father—cannot help but leave an impact. As a father, I use Rick's dad as an example of what I might be. I hope that my legacy leave children one-tenth the person Rick is.

Thanks! Terry

Terence Traut Entelechy, Inc. "unlocking potential"
Merrimack, NH 03054 www.unlockit.com

Team Hoyt by the Numbers

248	Triathlons (6 Ironman distances, 7 Half Ironman)
22	Duathlons
70	Marathons (30 Boston Marathons)
8	18.6 Milers
94	Half Marathons
1	20K
37	10 Milers
33	Falmouth 7.1 Milers (1 Falmouth in the Fall)
8	15K's
216	10K's
157	5 Milers
4	8K's

18	4 Milers
152	5K's
8	20 Milers
2	11K's
1	7K
1	20 Mile Bike for Best Buddies

Total Athletic Competitions through June 11, 2012: 1080

Best End Times

2:40:47	Marathon
56:21	15K
1:21:12	Half Marathon
40:27	7.1 Miler
13:43:37	Ironman Triathlon
35:48	10K
2:01:54	18.6 Miler
27:17	5 Miler
59:01	10 Miler
17:40	5K
2:10:45	20 Miler

- Biked and ran across the USA in 1992: 3,735 miles in 45 consecutive days.
- Biked the states of Connecticut, Rhode Island and Massachusetts with "Axa World Ride '95."

Personal Biographies of the Authors

Rick Hoyt resides independently in Sturbridge, Massachusetts. He is a graduate of Boston University, Class of 1993, with a degree in Special Education. He is half of the renowned father/son running team known as Team Hoyt. Together with his father, Dick, the tandem has competed in over 1000 athletic competitions including thirty Boston Marathons. Rick was inducted as the twenty-sixth member of the Iron Man Hall of Fame in Kona, Hawaii. Rick can be reached at his personal email address at rick.hoyt@yahoo.com or on the Team Hoyt website at www.teamhoyt.com. He can be followed on Facebook at https://www.facebook.com/rick.hoyt.353 or by liking The Official Team Hoyt Page.

Todd Civin is a 1983 graduate of the SI Newhouse School of Public Communications at Syracuse University, where he earned his degree in

Advertising Copywriting. Todd was born and raised in Spencer, Massachusetts, and currently resides in the town of Winchendon, Massachusetts. He is married to his wife of six years, Katie, and loves his "pride and joys": Corey, 26; Erika, 23; Julia, 21; Kate, 18; and Dakota 14; as well as one granddaughter, Addison, 2. He recently embarked on the next phase of his career when he launched Civin Media Relations; where he is working on several additional projects of this type. He spends his spare time writing sports and as Team Hoyt's Social Media Director. He can be reached at toddcivin1@aol.com.

Annie Mason is wife to Doug and mom to a beautiful young lady who is pursuing her degree in TV film production. Annie has been an art educator in the Westfield, Massachusetts' school system, and in Farmington, Maine's School Administrative District #9. She has also worked at the Yale Center for British Art in New Haven, Connecticut. Born in Westfield, she first met Rick as a fourth grader at Fort Meadow Elementary. Annie and her husband now live in Spotsylvania and have been married for twenty-three years.

Barry Nolan is a multi-Emmy Award-winning broadcast journalist with more than three decades of reporting experience. For CN-8, he has served as host and executive producer of *Backstage with Barry Nolan*. He also hosted and produced *Nitebeat*, a talk show for smart people that featured everything from politics to physics. He won Emmys for both Hosting and Commentary. Nolan served as senior correspondent for *Extra*, one of the nation's highest-rated nationally syndicated newsmagazine shows, served as co-anchor for the long-running newsmagazine *Hard Copy*, and hosted *Over the Edge* for ABC. For the past sixteen years, he has fielded a bewildering array of questions as a panelist for the National Public Radio show *Says You*. But New England audiences may know him best for his role as co-host of *Evening Magazine*. For his work on the show, he won three Emmy Awards, as well as Gabriel and Iris Awards. In 2009, Nolan moved from TV to politics, serving on Capitol Hill as the Communications Director for the Congressional Joint Economic Committee. He and his wife, Garland Waller, recently produced the award-winning documentary *No Way Out But One*. He is currently a contributor to *Boston Magazine* and a communications consultant. Prior to embarking on his broadcasting career, Nolan worked as a psychiatric social worker. A native of Alexandria, Virginia, he holds a bachelor's degree in psychology from the University of Tennessee, and studied neurophysiology and theater history as a postgraduate.

Bill Potts currently resides in Tampa, Florida, with his wife Kim, three teenage children, and their dog, Abby. He is the Vice President of Global Licensing for the World Triathlon Corporation. He met the Hoyts when he was the Vice President of Marketing for FosterGrant, based in Smithfield, Rhode Island. He graduated with an MBA from Tulane University and a BBA from the University of Texas in Austin. Not surprisingly, he enjoys swimming, biking and running—and became an Ironman in May 2011. He is on the Board of Advisors for the Halo House Foundation at www.Halohousefoundation.org. He and his family are honored to know the Hoyts, who have inspired them in many ways.

Bryan P. Lyons, DMD, grew up in Nashua, New Hampshire, and has two brothers and a sister with whom he is still very close. He matriculated from UNH and Tufts University School of Dental Medicine. He is an avid triathlete and runner. His proudest athletic achievements include crossing the finish line of the 2011 and 2012 Boston Marathons with Dick and Rick Hoyt, swimming from Alcatraz across San Francisco Bay to the mainland, and completing Ironman Arizona in 12:12:05. Dr. Lyons maintains a private practice in Billerica, Massachusetts, and is a former Associate Clinical Professor at Tufts University School of Dental Medicine.

Dick Hoyt is a retired lieutenant colonel, having served in the Army and Air National Guard for thirty-five years. When he is not training, running with Rick, or traveling the country doing corporate speaking events, he enjoys spending time with Rick, Rob, and Russ, as well as with his four grandsons.

Heather Oman lives with her husband and her two children in Virginia. She is a certified speech language pathologist, but spends most of her time these days making sure her own children say please and thank you. She likes growing tomatoes the size of softballs, running, and going on walks with her fat dog.

Jessica Gauthier was brought up in Southbridge, Massachusetts, and graduated in 1994. She served in the United States Navy, and graduated with a Bachelor's in Business Management in 2007 with a minor in psychology at Bay Path College. She has six beautiful children, and recently bought a house where she currently lives in Warren, Massachusetts.

Jessica White Gracia currently resides in Dorchester, Massachusetts, with her husband, Chris, and their boxer, Teemu. She works as a Speech and Language Pathologist at the South Shore Educational Collaborative in Hingham, Massachusetts. Jessica was raised in the small town of Longmeadow in Western Massachusetts. She graduated from Longmeadow High School in 1997, then attended Springfield College for four years. At Springfield College, she swam competitively for the varsity team and studied Rehabilitation with a concentration in Communication Disorders. During her college years, she developed an interest in Augmentative and Alternative Communication (AAC), a specialized concentration within the field of Speech and Language Pathology. After graduating from Springfield College in 2001, Jessica continued on with graduate studies in Speech and Language Pathology at Northeastern University in Boston, Massachusetts. During her graduate studies, she pursued an internship at Boston Children's Hospital in the Communication Enhancement Center. It was there she had the privilege of meeting Rick Hoyt.

Jim Gips is the Egan Professor of Computer Science at Boston College. With colleagues, he developed two technologies that help people with severe physical disabilities: EagleEyes (eagleeyes.org) and Camera Mouse (cameramouse.org). He and his wife, Barbara, live in Medfield, Massachusetts.

John Costello is a Speech-Language Pathologist and Director of the Augmentative Communication Program at Boston Children's Hospital where he has worked for 27 years. He first met the Hoyt's as an intern at Children's and has continued to work with Rick on augmentative communication strategies since that time. Rick and Dick have been dedicated supporters of the mission of the Augmentative Communication Program, recognizing that a key foundation to the message "Yes, You Can" is one's ability to communicate.

John R. Passarini, Ed.D., resides in Lexington, Massachusetts, with his wife Gloria. They have been married for thirty-eight years and have three grown sons, John M., Tom, and Mike. Tom and his wife, Jen, have a new son, Jacoby. John has taught for forty-one years—thirty-four years in public schools, including Waltham and Wayland, and seven years between Salem State University and Boston University. He is a Certified Adapted Physical Educator ("CAPE") and earned his doctorate degree in Special Education at BU in 2004. John was named the National Adapted Physical Education Teacher of the Year in 2000 and the Disney Most Outstanding Teacher of the Year in 2003. John is the director of the Purple Shoes Challenge (www.katiesraces.com), an athletic program for athletes with physical disabilities, which benefits the Katie Lynch Foundation. The Katie Lynch Foundation is a non-profit organization that is organized and run by volunteers. John was elected to the Massachusetts Wrestling Coaches Hall of Fame in 1986, and is also a proud member of both the Waltham High School Athletic Hall of Fame for coaching and the Newton South High School Athletic Hall of Fame as an athlete.

Julie Song lives in West Orange, New Jersey, with her husband and three children. She is a graduate of Boston University, where she worked as a PCA for Rick Hoyt for four years.

Kathy Sullivan Boyer was born and raised in Springfield, Massachusetts. She then moved to Belchertown, Massachusetts, where she raised her own family before moving to Holland, Massachusetts, in 2002, which is where she met Dick and Rick. She has been the Team Hoyt Office Manager since 2005.

Major Kim "Rooster" Rossiter is an active-duty United States Marine. He attended Marine Corps boot camp upon completion of high school, and is currently in his eighteenth year of service. He and Lori, his wife of fourteen years, hail from Lake Charles, Louisiana. Parents to Briley, Ainsley, and Kamden, they currently reside in Virginia Beach, Virginia, and have been active members of Team Hoyt Virginia Beach since 2008.

Margot (Boucher) Kawecki resides in Connecticut with her husband, Paul. They have been married for twenty-six years and have two adult children, Kimberley, 25, who lives in Boston and works in the non-profit arena, and Phillip, 23, who works in finance in NYC. Margot has been teaching since she graduated from Westfield State College in 1977, primarily in private schools. She specializes in early childhood education (Kindergarten and Pre-Kindergarten.) In her free time, she enjoys golfing, yoga, meditation, spending time at Cape Cod with her husband's family, and visiting her family all along the East Coast.

Michele Kule-Korgood, Esq. is managing attorney of Kule-Korgood, Roff and Associates, PLLC, a private practice with an office located in Forest Hills, New York. The practice focuses almost exclusively on representing parents of children with disabilities in obtaining appropriate special education services. Ms. Kule-Korgood has more than seventeen years of experience in special education law, representing families who challenged school district recommendations in more than two thousand matters. Her experience as a former special education teacher gives her unique insight into the complex issues surrounding these issues. She is admitted in the U.S. Supreme Court, the Second Circuit Court of Appeals, as well as the Southern and Eastern District

Courts of New York, where she has argued and presented dispositive motions and matters of first impression. Ms. Kule-Korgood serves on the board of the Council of Parent Attorneys and Advocates, and is a frequent speaker at conferences held by the Practicing Law Institute, Lehigh University Special Education Law Symposium, National Business Institute, Lorman, the New York Bar Association, and the Council of Parent Attorneys and Advocates. She is a member of the New York State Bar Association's Committee on Issues Affecting People with Disabilities, as well as other special education-related community organizations. She also lectures at various agencies that provide special education and/or advocacy services. Ms. Kule-Korgood earned her doctorate from Hofstra University School of Law. Prior to that, she obtained a Bachelor of Science Degree in Special Education and a Bachelor of Arts Degree in Psychology from Boston University.

Nancy Stackhouse is Ricky's Auntie and Judy's sister. She lives in Evergreen, Colorado, with her husband, David. Both of her children, Amy and Keith, also live in the Denver area.

Robert Hoyt is one of Rick's two younger brothers and the father of two young men aged seventeen and twenty-two. He is currently employed at Tri-County Contractors Supply in West Springfield, Massachusetts, as a parts specialist and rental consultant in the construction industry. Born in Winchester, Massachusetts, Robert was raised mostly in Massachusetts, and now resides in Holyoke, Massachusetts, with a wonderful woman, Zaida Cutler. Zaida's daughter Cassandra resides in Easthampton, Massachusetts. Zaida and Rob continue to support Team Hoyt's message and efforts any way they can.

Ronald Robb is the CEO of myTEAM TRIUMPH, a national nonprofit organization that provides an athlete ride-along program for children, teens, adults and veterans who are disabled. Mr. Robb is also an author, speaker, standup comedian (for charity), and a former executive in private industry. Mr. Robb has appeared on *NBC Nightly News, Sports Illustrated*, and numerous local media outlets around the country. The organization he founded was featured by *Runner's World Magazine* in their 2011 "Heroes of Running" edition. Mr. Robb will be releasing his latest book, *Chicken Goo for the Triathlete's Soul* in 2012. As the name implies, this is a light-hearted look at the world of triathlon, goals, and faith, and a not-so-subtle commentary on his own journey from obesity ("I could kick-start a 747") to running a marathon ("They timed me with a calendar, but I finished"). For booking information, please contact his office at 616-745-2200 or email info@myteamtriumph. org

Russ Hoyt is a husband to Lisa Hoyt, father to Troy and Ryan Hoyt, and a leader in the field of education. Mr. Hoyt, as he is known to the children at the Florence Roche Elementary School where he is the principal, or Mr. Russ, as he is known to the children as the Early Childhood Director of Boutwell Early Childhood Center for Groton-Dunstable Regional School District, he has a long history working in early childhood settings, including as Preschool Teacher, Early Intervention Director and as the statewide Autism Specialist for the Department of Education. In addition to his professional career, Mr. Hoyt has a personal connection to Special Education. Russ has two brothers, Rick and Rob. Rick, was born with cerebral palsy and cannot walk, talk, feed or care for himself without assistance. However, Rick has run the Boston Marathon thirty times, completed the Ironman Triathlon five times as a team with his father, and graduated from Boston University with his bachelor's degree in education. Russ is also involved in athletics, as he is a softball player, a former wrestler, and coach for his sons' basketball and baseball teams.

Susan Grillo is Rick's aunt and his mother's youngest sister. She lives in Newbury, Massachusetts, on Plum Island with her husband Rich. Susan's two daughters, Cara Frangipane and Aimee Frangipane, and Rich's three children, Alex, and twin daughters, Lauren and Liza, visit often. Susan is a realtor in the Greater Newburyport area. She married Rich Grillo in 2006. Rich is a runner and knew of Rick from his running experiences; now he's glad to be part of Rick's extended family.